BATTLEFIELD
ANGELS

• • • • • • • • • • • •

Saving Lives Under Enemy Fire
from Valley Forge to Afghanistan

SCOTT McGAUGH

First published in Great Britain in 2011 by Osprey Publishing,
Midland House, West Way, Botley, Oxford, OX2 0PH, UK
44-02 23rd Street, Suite 219, Long Island City, NY 11101, USA
E-mail: info@ospreypublishing.com

A CIP catalogue record for this book is available from the British Library

ISBN 978 1 84908 515 1

Jacket design and page layout by Brainchild Studios/NYC
Index by Alan Thatcher
Typeset in Janson Text
Originated by United Graphics Pte, Singapore
Printed in China through Worldprint Ltd.

11 12 13 14 15   10 9 8 7 6 5 4 3 2 1

Osprey Publishing is supporting the Woodland Trust, the UK's leading
woodland conservation charity, by funding the dedication of trees.

www.ospreypublishing.com

Front Cover: During World War II, a corpsman helps stabilize a casualty on
Peleliu while awaiting transport to a nearby aid station. (*U.S. Marine Corps*)

BATTLEFIELD
ANGELS

• • • • • • • • • • • •

Saving Lives Under Enemy Fire
from Valley Forge to Afghanistan

For Marjorie.

Your enduring courage, compassion,
and resolve arm me with strength and
perspective every day.

Contents

• • • • • • •

Foreword

• • • • • • •

By Vice Admiral Harold M. Koenig, M.D.
United States Navy, Retired
32nd Navy Surgeon General

Since the founding of our nation, more than 40 million Americans have served in our armed forces in times of crisis and conflict. They have left their families, their homes, and all they cherish to face a dangerous and uncertain future. Our nation has sent them to the Middle East, Asia, Europe, Africa, the Caribbean, and hundreds of remote locations throughout the world.

These brave Americans served with the belief that America is just and its vision noble, and that it would recognize and support their sacrifice and devotion to duty. When they joined the armed forces, few understood that their fate might well rest in the hands of a young man or woman who was a total stranger to them until they met on the battlefield.

A relatively small cadre of largely unsung heroes has made possible the eventual return home of countless soldiers. For more than two hundred years, corpsmen, medics, nurses, doctors, surgeons, medical technicians, and specialists have comprised a community within our armed forces that has been nothing short of inspirational. These extraordinary men and women have willingly confronted the horrors of war and faced conditions few can imagine. They have come to the aid of more than 1.4 million Americans who have been wounded in battle. They have been the link between trauma and treatment that ultimately enabled those injured soldiers to survive their wounds, or brought final moments of solace to many of those who did not. They have been a source of inspiration and motivation to their warrior comrades who were able to be more confident, resolute, and effective when they knew a corpsman or medic was willing to risk his or her life to reach and treat them on the battlefield. Their legacy is all the more remarkable because of the relative youth of these courageous individuals.

Battlefield Angels traces the odyssey of these American heroes from the hills of Pennsylvania in 1775 to the mountains of Afghanistan more than two centuries later. Their recognition is as worthy as it is necessary. These profiles of duty, devotion, and daring illustrate the strength of character inherent in every American generation, a strength that is never more evident or valuable than it is on the battlefield when life hangs in the balance. A stirring testament to the human spirit, *Battlefield Angels* also reveals how the accomplishments of these medical pioneers have resulted in numerous advances and improvements to civilian health care that have saved or enhanced the lives of countless people.

Today, more than 23 million veterans walk among us. Nearly 3 million receive disability compensation, and many more owe their very lives to an anonymous corpsman or medic. Millions of Americans and their families are profoundly grateful.

Future generations can take heart in knowing that there will always be battlefield angels alongside their sons, daughters, brothers, sisters, spouses, and sweethearts in uniform. They can take comfort in the courage, compassion, and skill of our nation's exemplary military medical corps.

—Vice Admiral Harold M. Koenig, M.D.
Medical Corps, United States Navy, Retired
32nd Navy Surgeon General

Preface

· · · · · · ·

Wars are won by killing. Death, destruction, disability, and disease have defined the battlefield for millennia as millions of warriors have waged war. Whether with catapults or cannon, arrows or artillery, the more permanent harm an army can inflict upon another, the greater the odds of victory. Yet within every war, within every battle and firefight, a handful of those in uniform have fought to save lives, including those of the enemy. The military medical corps has always faced a paradox: Its mission is to rescue the wounded and save lives even as those around them are intent on killing each other.

The history of military medicine reflects the evolution of both war and medical science. As weaponry has become more lethal from one war to the next, military medicine has been confronted with increasingly complicated conditions posed by torn bodies, horrific burns, radiation poisoning, and contagious disease. Industrialization has enabled world wars to kill as many as 35 million people. The spear has mutated into the nuclear bomb that produced more than one hundred thousand burn and radiation victims in a single flash over Hiroshima.

At the same time, the military medical corps has pioneered and field tested medical science advances in its war against the broken, infected, and diseased. Medical science and military medicine have become increasingly sophisticated as the destructiveness of weapons has grown. The practices of bloodletting, encouraging gangrenous pus, and applying blood transfusions directly from the arm of one soldier into another have been replaced by preventive medicine, antibiotics, plasma, and cutting-edge surgical care. Two hundred years ago, unfit soldiers were assigned as surgeon's assistants. Today's frontline medical personnel are highly trained emergency medical technicians equipped with the latest digital equipment.

A common denominator among all wars has been the young men—and more recently, women—who have made survival possible. Doctors, surgeons, nurses, and frontline corpsmen and medics have always faced enemy fire when others took cover. Their courage and compassion have enabled them to ignore their own mortality when confronted with even a remote possibility of saving another's life. Many have endured unimaginable conditions on the battlefield. Thousands have volunteered to jump into a bomb crater or climb down inside a burning ship to treat a sliced-open belly, legless stumps, or a filleted face.

Many came from humble, nondescript towns, farms, and cities. Caspar Wistar was a pacifist Quaker who volunteered as a frontline nurse in George Washington's army. Weedon Osborne, a dentist, became a hero as a medic in the trenches of World War I. Joe Marquez, the son of a Nevada miner, joined the Navy in World War II to escape a small-town destiny. Japanese-American James Okubo signed up for the Army from behind the barbed wire of a World War II American internment camp. Joe Keenan, an elevator repairman's son, boarded a troop transport bound for Korea, leaving a row-house Boston neighborhood in his wake. Monica Brown graduated early from a Texas high school to enlist in the Army and become a medic in Afghanistan.

These few represent the thousands of Americans who have joined the military and become battlefield corpsmen and medics. They are our neighbors, our children's friends, our sons, and, more recently, our daughters. As both war and medical science have driven innovations in military medicine, each successive generation of corpsmen and medics has personified the medical corps' devotion to saving lives with increasingly sophisticated care in the midst of war's greater lethality.

They have been the link between catastrophe and treatment after shrapnel has cut through a soldier, sailor, or Marine. Corpsmen and medics instinctively applied a few months' medical training to make instant diagnoses when they first pressed their hands against a man's sucking chest wound as foamy blood oozed through their fingers. Doctors and surgeons amputated, excised, stitched, and vaccinated within range of enemy fire. Nurses, technicians, and support personnel worked by their side, caring for and comforting the wounded. Their personal stories, spanning two centuries of America's wars, illustrate how ignorance, social taboos, and myths have been overcome by the diligence and daring of medical professionals in the laboratory, alongside the operating table, and at the frontline aid station.

Battlefield Angels is about the people who practiced battlefield medicine as it evolved from one war to the next: military medical personnel from Lexington to the Shenandoah Valley, from Vietnamese rice paddies to Middle Eastern deserts. It recounts the shattering effects of low-velocity Minié balls and the battlefield care limitations that produced thousands of one-armed and one-legged Civil War veterans, and it reveals the sophisticated battlefield treatments our modern warriors receive for wounds inflicted by snipers and remote-controlled land mines.

This book illustrates how survivability in war has improved dramatically in the face of increasingly lethal weaponry. During the Revolutionary War, more than 40 percent of soldiers wounded by the enemy died from their injuries. By the Vietnam War, that percentage had dropped to 25 percent. Today in the Middle East, it is about 10 percent. Beginning with the Revolutionary War, the total number of wounded who have survived their injuries is the equivalent of every resident in San Diego, California.

The genesis of *Battlefield Angels* lies in another book I wrote, *Midway Magic*, which is about the unprecedented forty-seven-year odyssey of the now retired USS *Midway* aircraft carrier. More than 200,000 sailors (their average age was nineteen) deployed on the longest-serving U.S. Navy aircraft carrier of the twentieth century (1945–92). On several occasions, horrific flight-op accidents left dozens of men broken, burned, and bleeding on the flight deck. Young corpsmen new to the ship sprinted toward billowing infernos and one-thousand-pound bombs lying in pools of jet fuel. Their bravery and devotion humbled as much as it inspired, though recognition often was sparse and fleeting. It led to another book, *USS Midway: America's Shield*, in 2011, written specifically for high school students and young adults.

I soon discovered dozens of other instances in which young men only a few years out of high school had been equally selfless, heroes who masqueraded later in life as insurance salesmen, hospital administrators, and dentists. The path of discovery led to the operating room as well as the laboratory, where assumptions about gangrene, malaria, third-degree burns, and amputation were challenged. *Battlefield Angels* reflects their collective legacy in military medical science. It also provides a deeply personal context to the war experience of more than 40 million Americans who have served on the battlefield.

The core of the book is based on interviews with some of the frontline corpsmen and medics who survived, with the men they saved, and with those who served alongside them in foxholes, submarine compartments, prison cells, and Humvees. The conversations with these heroes in places like Oceanside, California, and Boone, Iowa, often stretched into the night as they relived ingrained nightmares they had previously shared only in lowered voices at reunions with their buddies. Genuine humility occasionally prevented some from sharing their personal stories directly with the author.

Many times the interviews became especially difficult for the spouses, who often sat quietly off to the side. Some cried. Others grew angry upon discovering that nightmares had long haunted their husbands, who spoke of them for the first time to a stranger sitting on their couch. "It was just my job," a man often shrugged as he avoided eye contact with his shocked wife.

Many interviews with World War II soldiers and corpsmen as well as active-duty military personnel today provided remarkably precise detail. I discovered that in battle, many soldiers, corpsmen, and medics experienced a heightened awareness that allowed them to remember a particular sunrise, weather conditions, and even what they were thinking at specific points in time. Decades later in some cases, they were able to recall those details as clearly as if they had experienced them just the day before.

In some cases involving active-duty personnel serving in remote locations, direct interviews were not possible. Some politely declined out of modesty. Yet their stories are included based on extensive documentation and eyewitness accounts.

I also relied on recorded and written firsthand accounts from every war fought by Americans. The U.S. Navy's Bureau of Medicine and Surgery's collection of transcribed oral histories from hundreds of twentieth-century medical personnel was invaluable. Medical professionals such as Revolutionary War doctor William Buchan and Civil War surgeon William Williams Keen published reports and memoirs filled with detail. The diaries kept by doctors who were prisoners of war during World War II, official military records including after-action battle reports, medical training manuals, and other material in the collections of the U.S. Marine Corps, National Library of Medicine, Naval Historical Center, and the National Archives proved extremely useful. Empirical analyses and reports published by the federal government and medical journal articles provided a wealth of statistical data.

I have utilized information from all these sources—the most important of which are included in the selected bibliography—as accurately as possible. Where dates or statistics inevitably varied by source or estimation, I selected the most commonly used figures. The word choice and narrative are my own. I welcome any suggested corrections and clarifications.

Although the medical ranks on the front lines have been called different names dating back to the Revolutionary War, for the sake of clarity and consistency, I refer to them as surgeon's mates in America's early history and then as corpsmen in the U.S. Navy and Marine Corps and medics in the U.S. Army. Similarly, I frequently use "soldier" to refer to all those serving on the battlefield.

Many of the individuals profiled in *Battlefield Angels* received the Medal of Honor, America's highest award for bravery in war; the Navy Cross or its Army equivalent, the Distinguished Service Cross; the third highest honor, the Silver Star; or the Purple Heart, awarded to those wounded or killed in combat. Sometimes a pat on the back or a nod from a chief petty officer or sergeant had to suffice. In the end, judging valor and courage in battle has always been subjective, given the era, politics, the propensity to award medals, and the standards of military medical care.

Regardless of official recognition, the real story of military medicine begins with those who breathe life into others alongside a road, deep within a jungle, or at the bottom of a foxhole. That's where readers will find the most important insights of *Battlefield Angels*, the revelations of character defined by courage, duty, optimism, focus, and ingenuity. With these revelations comes the hope that each of us carries seeds of heroism buried deep within, that we all somehow have the capacity for greater courage and compassion than we dare imagine.

To the millions of fighting men and women who owe their lives to these heroes, they will always be battlefield angels.

Chapter 1

Perils of Independence

• • • • • • •

Revolutionary War

The night air chilled Caspar Wistar as he walked alongside a wagon filled with medical supplies, part of an eleven-thousand-man army creeping toward a small Pennsylvania hamlet. He wondered if General George Washington's medical corps would again run short of wound dressings when battle met the sunrise.

Washington had divided his army into four columns for a coordinated attack against nine thousand British soldiers bivouacked at the southern end of Germantown, about five miles north of Philadelphia. With luck, Washington's army would be in position by 0400 hours, rest two hours, then attack. More than twenty thousand soldiers would occupy a two-square-mile village, firing muskets and artillery practically at point-blank range. Nurse Caspar Wistar and a handful of surgeons, surgeon's mates, and other volunteers soon would be confronted by hundreds of wounded and dying men on October 4, 1777.

Two weeks earlier, on September 26, Lord Charles Cornwallis had led British troops into undefended Philadelphia and taken control of the colonies' capital. Losses by the Continental Army at the Battle of Brandywine and the Battle of Paoli had left Philadelphia susceptible to the British invasion. The British repeatedly defeated a Continental Army that was malnourished, poorly trained, and so ill equipped that some men fought barefoot. One year after declaring independence, the colonists had now lost their capital, usually a death knell in war. Once the British had secured Philadelphia, they left a force of three thousand men there to defend it and moved nine thousand soldiers north to Germantown.

General Washington saw an opportunity in the divided British army. If he could defeat the British at Germantown before the onset of winter, the Continental Army would be in a stronger position to retake Philadelphia the following spring. Equally important, a victory at Germantown would end the series of defeats the colonists had suffered on the battlefield and begin to restore the army's plummeting morale. Washington believed his troops were sufficiently trained and experienced enough to launch a complicated, four-pronged attack against the British.

Shortly after sunset on October 3, thousands of Americans on foot and some in wagons advanced through the misty, forested hills toward the British encampment. One was Isaiah Strawn, a Quaker from nearby Bucks County. Another was John Hoskins Stone, a colonel in the 1st Maryland Regiment. Just as the sun lightened the thickening fog at dawn, the woods around Strawn and Stone exploded with British musket fire and the cries of wounded Americans. Washington's attack had been detected by a British outpost. Men fell, bleeding onto a forest floor blanketed by fallen leaves. Whitish-blue smoke from muskets and cannon joined with the fog to reduce visibility even further. The Continental Army had lost the element of surprise.

The battle for Germantown quickly unraveled. One column of Washington's army somehow got lost on its way to the staging area. A second, advancing on British defensive positions, veered off toward another American column. Although the attackers had been told to wear a piece of identifying white paper in their hats, visibility had deteriorated so much that Americans began firing at each other. Casualties mounted as the sun rose.

Isaiah Strawn fell wounded after he rushed to pick up the musket of a friend who had been shot dead. Strawn was three weeks short of his nineteenth birthday and had enlisted only a few weeks earlier. Not far away, John Hoskins Stone dropped to the ground in agony and clutched a bloodied leg. A relatively old man in the army at twenty-seven, he had been fighting the British for two years. He was the son of a prominent Maryland plantation owner. An older brother had signed the Declaration of Independence.

Both Strawn and Stone had been wounded in the leg by lead buckshot, a common battle wound during the Revolutionary War.

Nearly two hundred years earlier, gunpowder had transformed the battlefield. For centuries, warfare had resulted mostly in cuts to the head, legs, and arms, as well as fractures and concussions. Punctures in the torso from arrows and javelins were less common. Gunpowder, however, caused unprecedented trauma to the human body. The shattering effects of bullets and artillery shells were so profound that military doctors believed the projectiles were poisoned by the gunpowder: for decades they treated gunshot wounds as poison cases.

By the outset of the Revolutionary War, some types of artillery could fire explosive hollow shells filled with gunpowder and shrapnel more than eight hundred yards. They were utilized at the beginning of many battles. As the opposing forces converged to within fifty yards of each other, soldiers opened fire with smooth bore muskets of limited range and accuracy. Large, round musket balls hit bodies hard, sometimes burrowing deep and shattering bone. The slice of the blade in hand-to-hand combat had been replaced by the concussive thunder of cannon and muskets from behind hills and in open fields. General Washington's troops walked into a storm of flying lead and iron.

After about three hours of battle, it became clear that the American assault on Germantown had failed. The four American columns retreated, carrying as many injured with them as possible. Some members of Washington's medical corps remained on the battlefield to treat the wounded while the remainder withdrew nearly ten miles to Pennypacker's Mill before the British gave up the chase.

The Continental Army was plagued by a paucity of qualified medical personnel, a dearth of medical supplies, and an understanding of battlefield medicine that in some ways was less informed than that which had been practiced by the ancient Greeks and Romans.

In 1700 B.C., treatment practices were first recorded on Egyptian papyri. One document listed forty-eight specific battlefield injuries and prescribed treatment for each. A skull fracture, for example, was treated with fresh meat the first day, and the patient was kept on a full diet. Grease, honey, and lint were applied daily thereafter.

The ancient Greeks also took care to prevent disease. They instinctively demarcated dining areas from bathroom facilities. That reduced the likelihood of epidemics that left weakened soldiers more susceptible to their battle wounds. More than one thousand years later, around 400 B.C., Hippocrates wrote seventy-two medical books that reflected the state of Greek military medicine. In addition to codifying medical ethics for the first time, he documented the use of wine to moisten and disinfect a wound, chest tubes for drainage, and traction for fractures. Regrettably, he advocated facilitating the development of pus in a wound as a means to reduce inflammation. Greek army doctors were pleased if, by the third or fourth day, the lips of a grizzly gash on a thigh turned white and the exposed flesh warmed to the touch and glowed pinkish red. They considered it a necessary part of the healing process, failing to recognize it as the onset of a frequently lethal gangrenous infection.

More than six hundred years later, Roman military doctors were the most accomplished of any in the ancient world. Galen, a physician to gladiators, wrote more than four hundred wide-ranging treatises that included diverse topics such as nasal polyps, plastic surgery, and the treatment of cleft lip. A Roman military doctor's kit included forceps, scalpels, arrow extractors, and catheters. Doctors recorded each case for medical schools back in Rome, boiled their instruments, and prescribed opium poppies as painkillers. Roman soldiers were trained in basic first aid.

Although Galen reinforced the concept that infected wounds retarded more dangerous inflammation, Roman military medicine achieved several milestones. Roman military physicians created the hospital system, wrote the first medical manuals, developed ligation techniques to control bleeding, and refined amputation procedures. But when the Roman Empire collapsed in the fifth century, its military medicine advances were buried in the debris.

In 1775, Congress created the Army's Hospital Department. Surgeons received $1.66 per day, while nurses earned $2 per month. But the Hospital Department created confusion on the battlefield, where Continental Army physicians treated the wounded alongside the doctors attached to the regiments each colony sent to war. Sometimes one regiment's doctor refused to treat the wounded from another regiment. Turf battles could hardly be afforded in the face of a shortage of medical personnel so acute that in some cases, one doctor and five assistants were assigned to as many as five thousand soldiers.

To make matters worse, Strawn and Stone might have been treated either by a trained surgeon or by a charlatan at Germantown. During the Revolutionary War, only about 3,500 doctors practiced medicine in the colonies, and only 10 percent of these had gone to medical school. Most had been trained as apprentices. None had to prove his qualifications in an era when doctors were not licensed. Almost anyone could claim to be a doctor, surgeon, or apothecary. Wounded soldiers had to take them at their word.

Volunteers such as Caspar Wistar often had no medical training whatsoever. Wistar came from a factory family that operated one of the largest and most prosperous glass factories in the colonies. The factory had been established by his grandfather in 1738. Wistar was one of many pacifist Quakers who either raised money for the war or who volunteered to help with the wounded. Only sixteen years old when he joined the Army, Wistar had developed an early interest in medicine and botany.

The day after the Germantown defeat, Washington's medical corps, such as it was, faced dozens of surgeries. Most military doctors had little experience treating the mangled limbs and pulverized bodies caused by gunshots. The explosive power of the bullet typically blasted dirt and bits of clothing into the wound. If the bullet struck bone, a compound fracture usually resulted. Although some doctors had probes to trace the path of entry of a musket ball, most inserted their dirty fingers and poked around. If they could not easily retrieve the musket ball, they left it in the soldier's body. Some Revolutionary War veterans lucky enough to survive carried the enemy's ammo inside their bodies to their deathbeds decades later.

Much of the limb surgery after a battle centered on amputation. A practiced surgeon could amputate a leg in less than two minutes. An officer was given rum or brandy, if it was available, before his leg was cut off. Enlisted men typically had to bite down on a stick as Wistar and other assistants tightly cinched a leather tourniquet four fingers above the amputation line. Once the leg or arm had been cut off, the surgeon typically used a crooked needle to snag severed arteries and blood vessels, pull them taut beyond the bloody stump, and suture them closed. Amputation was so traumatic that those who had lived through battle only to lose an arm or leg to the army surgeon stood just a one-in-three chance of surviving shock and near-certain infection.

Military doctors also faced massive numbers of bleeding soldiers. Among the few techniques available for slowing the loss of blood was a screw tourniquet. If the bleeding stemmed from lesser blood vessels, medical personnel burned them shut through cauterization. Effective anesthesia was unknown.

Wounds to the head were altogether different. Revolutionary War surgeons learned to drill holes in soldiers' skulls to relieve the swelling caused by a fracture or concussion. A Germantown casualty with a head wound had to sit upright in a chair and was steadied by several assistants. A surgeon cut the scalp away from the fracture, then used a trephine to drill a hole through the skull. Next he took a scalpel to probe the subdural matter to ensure it was free of excess fluid. Once the wound was drained, the surgeon's mates packed it with dry lint and held it in place with a handkerchief.

In the aftermath of Germantown's half-day battle, field hospitals were established in large houses, nearby settlements, and in clearings filled with tents. But recovery in Revolutionary War military hospitals proved more dangerous than facing the enemy in battle. Nine years after the war, surgeon Pierre Francois Percy described some of the challenges:

> *"In retreat before the enemy there is no more frightful a spectacle than the evacuation of mutilated soldiers on big wagons, each jolt bring[ing] the most piercing cries. They have to suffer from rain, from suffocating heat or freezing cold, and often do not have aid or*

food of any sort. Death would be a favor and we have often heard them begging it as a gift from heaven."[1]

Sometimes days passed before a soldier reached a military hospital. At that point, doctors often found caked blood covering serious wounds and field dressings contaminated with maggots.

Filthy, unsanitary hospital conditions increased Strawn's and Stone's 2 percent chance of dying on the battlefield to a 25 percent likelihood they would die in a field hospital. Hospitals were so poorly equipped that soldiers were expected to carry an empty sack that could be filled with straw as a makeshift hospital bed. Each was expected to provide his own blanket as well.

Medical supplies were a rare commodity throughout the Revolutionary War. Wistar and the surgeons with whom he served had little more than ingenuity and grit with which to treat patients. Some sold the fat and bones left from patients' meals to buy supplies. Sometimes they operated with razors instead of scalpels. In the days leading up to the Battle of Long Island in 1776, the 9,000-man army had been supplied with only 500 bandages, 12 fracture boxes, and 2 scalpels. More than 1,400 men had been wounded or captured or were missing.

If their patients survived surgery, Wistar and the doctors frequently took as much as a quart of blood from injured soldiers whose wounds almost invariably became infected. The prevailing school of thought held that a wound infection was the result of an imbalance in the blood. Bloodletting drained "impure" blood from the patient to allow nature to restore this balance. A wounded or ill soldier's hand was immersed in a bowl of hot water to swell the veins. Once a tourniquet was applied just above the wrist, a vein was sliced open at the heel of the hand. The soldier's hand was once again submerged in the hot water to facilitate bleeding until the doctor saw the soldier's face grow gray and his eyes flutter. Doctors put thousands of Revolutionary War soldiers into shock with this method.

Some men lying near Strawn and Stone likely had been burned in battle. If it was a minor burn, it was treated with wine or a superficial scalding of hog's lard. More serious burns required bloodletting. Once the burns became inflamed, doctors resorted to a bread-and-milk poultice that was softened with butter or oil and changed twice a day. Wine and opium were the drugs of choice for pain, for burn and trauma victims alike.

Doctors were equally reliant on herbal ingredients as medicines, though they were constantly in short supply. Hellebore root served as a diuretic. American wintergreen was administered for urinary problems. Even the poisonous nightshade was used as an antispasmodic.

Whether it was herbal enemas, bloodletting, or packing a burn site with bread and milk, Revolutionary War doctors practiced a decidedly holistic brand of medicine. An inventory of a permanent army hospital's medical supplies typically included powdered Peruvian bark (quinine), opium, camphor, calomel, jalap, powdered rhubarb, prepared chalk, castor and olive oils, barley, powdered Colombo, ipecuanto, tartar emetic, gambage, chocolate, tapioca, beeswax, wine, brandy or rum, vinegar, coffee, hyson tea, rice, sugar, and sago.

"It is nature alone that cures wounds; all that art can do is remove the obstacles, and to put the parts in such a condition as is the most favourable to nature's efforts," wrote Revolutionary War doctor William Buchan.

If Strawn and Stone somehow survived their wounds, their weakened condition made them more susceptible to disease. The disease mortality rate in the Continental Army was far greater than that inflicted by British gunfire. In February 1776, one in seven Continental Army soldiers was too sick to fight. Soldiers weakened by malnutrition and sickness were ill equipped to overcome their battle wounds. Most were rural boys who had not developed immunity to communicable childhood diseases. Many had relied on their mothers as the doctor in the family, who used herbal remedies she grew in her garden. But these homegrown approaches often were insufficient to treat the diseases that plagued the army. These young soldiers were as vulnerable to dysentery and malaria as they were to enemy fire.

Diseases in the 1700s often were poorly understood and misdiagnosed. No one knew that bacteria and viruses caused disease. Many doctors, including the military medical corps, believed all illnesses stemmed from nervous tension. A standard course of treatment included a reduced diet, aggressive digestive purges with enemas and diuretics, and frequent bloodletting to the point that patients passed out. Large doses of mercury were used to treat malaria, pneumonia, dysentery, typhus, yellow fever, tuberculosis, and other diseases. Doctors believed mercury cleansed the digestive and cardiovascular systems.

Isaiah Strawn and John Hoskins Stone were among the more than 500 soldiers who had been wounded at Germantown. More than 150 had been killed in battle. The British suffered more than 500 casualties as well. Though Germantown was another defeat, the Continental Army had fought so ferociously that the British retreated to reinforce Philadelphia.

General Washington regrouped and focused his attention on another British emplacement at Valley Forge. In the months following the Battle of Germantown, Washington ordered the construction of several new military hospitals, including one at Valley Forge. By December 1777, the Valley Forge facility listed 2,898 sick and unfit patients, a number that grew to 3,989 only two months later. It would be another six years of mounting casualties before America's first war ended.

Strawn and Stone both survived the Battle of Germantown. Strawn refused to allow surgeons to remove the buckshot from the hollow, or, arch, of his foot. He carried it for more than sixty years as he and his wife, Rachel, raised six children who in turn produced fifty-four grandchildren. When he died in 1843 at the age of eighty-four, he was among the oldest surviving Revolutionary War soldiers.

John Hoskins Stone's leg injury hobbled him for the rest of his life. His military career ended in 1779, when he was wounded a second time. Stone served as governor of Maryland from 1794 to 1797. He died in 1804 at the age of fifty-four.

The volunteer nurse, Caspar Wistar, never picked up a weapon during the Revolutionary War. He became a doctor in 1786 after attending the University of Edinburgh in Scotland. A noted physician, Wistar wrote *A System of Anatomy* in 1811, the first American medical text on anatomy. He was an advocate of vaccinating against disease, served as the chairman of the anatomy department at the University of Pennsylvania School of Medicine, and taught until his death in 1818. His scientific interests in paleontology and botany became so well recognized that botanist Thomas Nuttall named the plant genus *Wisteria* in his honor.

America's military medical corps was created as a result of war and literally learned on the job. Medical books about inoculation, military hospital pharmacology, soldier health, and hospital administration were written by a handful of leading military doctors during the Revolutionary War. The experience of medical incompetence early in the war prompted states to establish doctor-licensing criteria that ultimately improved civilian healthcare.

The most notable advance was effective inoculation against smallpox. The death rate for smallpox dropped from 160 to 3 per 1,000 in late 1783, when General Washington ordered his army to be inoculated— the first time in history an army had been vaccinated against disease. Regardless, an estimated 17,000 soldiers died of disease in the war, compared with about 8,000 who were killed in combat. Strawn and Stone were among the 25,000 who survived their wounds, though many historians believe Revolutionary War statistics are conservative for lack of detailed recordkeeping.

Shortly after the war's end, Congress disbanded the Continental Army to a force of fewer than one thousand men. Nearly eighty years would pass before America mobilized again for combat and looked to its medical community to save lives on the battlefield. It remained to be seen whether the lessons of America's first war had been lost in the passage of nearly three generations.

Chapter 2

Battlefield Evacuation

• • • • • • •

Civil War

Suffocating humidity thickened the uniforms of thousands of Union soldiers as they milled about, nearly shoulder to shoulder, in a park in Washington, D.C., (then known as "Washington City") on July 15, 1861. Some paced between and around hundreds of white conical tents. The previous night's campfires smoldered, and smoke drifted straight up into a lifeless sky. Sweat rolled down Foster Swift's face as he knelt to inventory the contents of a wooden box he had pulled out of a wagon. The surgeon attached to the 8th New York Regiment had supplies to check and requisition requests to complete while rumors swirled about where General Irvin McDowell soon would be taking the Union army.

About twenty-five miles away in Virginia, Confederate generals Joseph Johnston and Pierre Beauregard reviewed battle plans. They commanded more than thirty thousand troops who were southeast of Washington near Manassas Junction. Intersecting railroad lines at Manassas offered direct routes to both Washington and the Confederate capital of Richmond. Manassas lay at the crossroad of a war that had yet to erupt on the battlefield.

Swift had heard that the first major land battle of the Civil War probably would take place near Manassas. It was clear that both sides were mobilizing for battle.

In 1861, military medicine was far from ready for battle. Very little medical progress had been made since the end of the Revolutionary War, when the medical corps had been disbanded. By 1802, the military medical corps had shrunk to less than thirty personnel. During the War of 1812, it had been crippled by a shortage of qualified doctors, the absence of a battlefield evacuation system, and military hospitals that were little more than tents and temporary shelters. The practice of bloodletting and ignorance about the causes of disease were as profound as they had been during the Revolutionary War.

Soldiers in the Mexican-American War of 1846–48, which successfully annexed Texas, suffered from a lack of care. The American army of 7,000 men was assigned only 72 medical officers at the outset of the war. When the army grew to 100,000, there were only about 250 medical officers and volunteers. Once again, the medical corps was badly outnumbered and unprepared for the ravages of what became the American army's most deadly war. More than 11,000 soldiers died from illness, about seven times as many as those killed in battle. One out of six soldiers in the Mexican-American War died in combat or from disease. The disease rate in the military was ten times that of the civilian population. Thousands came home from war debilitated by chronic cases of dysentery.

There was no system to evacuate the wounded from the battlefield. Those who made it faced an uncertain future at best. Gunshot wounds that resulted in compound fractures were almost always deadly. Although some soldiers survived amputation and then infection of an arm or lower leg, the closer the wound was to the torso, the more likely it would be fatal. A Navy doctor who accompanied the army to Mexico noted that he did not see a single patient survive a gunshot wound to the thigh that had resulted in a fracture.[2]

Almost nothing had changed by early 1861. At the start of the war, the Union army's entire medical corps numbered only eighty-seven men. Its parsimonious eighty-year-old surgeon general, Thomas Lawson, a veteran of the War of 1812 who died shortly after the beginning of the Civil War, refused to buy them medical textbooks. Many of the doctors supplied by the state regiments had no experience with battlefield injuries, and some had never operated on a patient. Many had never seen the inside of a living patient's abdomen. Yet by July 1861, tens of thousands of young men relied on them for survival.

Sullivan Ballou was a handsome major in the 2nd Rhode Island Regiment. At thirty-two years of age, he was considered an old man in the army, and he was uncommonly accomplished. As a lawyer, he had served as clerk and speaker of the House of Representatives in Rhode Island. Ballou had said goodbye to his wife, Sarah, and two young sons when he volunteered in early 1861.

As Swift inventoried his medical supplies elsewhere in the camp, Ballou wrote his wife:

> *"Indications are very strong that we shall move in a few days, perhaps tomorrow ... I feel impelled to write a few lines that may fall under your eye when I shall be no more ... I cannot describe to you my feelings on this calm summer night, when two thousand men are sleeping around me ... and I, suspicious that Death is creeping behind me with his fatal dart, am communing with God, my country and thee."[3]*

Six days after writing this letter and placing it in his trunk, Sullivan Ballou, surgeon Foster Swift, and more than twenty-eight thousand Union soldiers marched out of Washington, D.C. It took the unseasoned and poorly trained troops two days to hike twenty-two miles toward Manassas and their campsites near Centreville, Virginia. A Union general left twenty wagonloads of medical supplies behind for fear they would slow the tedious advance even further. Undisciplined soldiers often fell out of formation to pick berries before arriving at Centreville and setting up camp.

On July 21, at 0230 hours, under a cloudless sky, twenty thousand Union soldiers moved out toward the Confederate positions. The summer heat was so oppressive that stragglers simply dropped to the ground along the route. Shortly before dawn, thousands of Washington residents climbed into their carriages for a ride out into the country to watch the battle between sixty thousand soldiers. The Civil War was a spectator sport in 1861.

Most were still in their carriages at 0515 when the first Union cannon fired on General Beauregard's headquarters, launching the battle that became known as Bull Run. Three columns of advancing Union soldiers soon ran into logistical and communications problems. Within a few hours, the battle had become concentrated in a small patch of eastern Virginia filled with gentle hills and forested ridges, divided by small creeks and rivers. Isolated stone farmhouses became battlefield landmarks as incessant rifle fire and artillery attacks turned the forests into a landscape barren of cover. Both Union and Confederate troops faced barrages of defensive fire as men fell, screaming for help. Within an hour of the battle's onset, Foster Swift and the rest of the medical corps were treating grisly wounds most had never encountered before.

At 0915, Sullivan Ballou's unit emerged from a thicket of trees and advanced up a hill. The enemy, waiting on both sides, opened fire. A cannonball broadsided Ballou's prized horse, Jennie, killing it instantly and crushing Ballou's leg into a bloody pulp. Blistering pain shot up

Ballou's hip and into his brain. A brief flush of dizziness passed. Lying on the hillside, Ballou grew thirsty as he bled and waited for help. Union soldiers dragged him behind some cover, then carried him to a tall, narrow church that sat atop a ridge, near a creek and sulfur spring. Sudley Church and nearly every other building still standing were quickly converted into field hospitals by both sides.

Foster Swift and other surgeons were ordered to Sudley as dozens, then hundreds, of wounded and writhing soldiers were brought there. Planks balanced across pews became operating tables. Assistants and the walking wounded hauled water from the creek in buckets. Surgeons dipped bloody scalpels in them between operations. Swift and the other Union doctors were unprepared for what confronted them: Weaponry had progressed faster than battlefield medicine.

Their biggest challenge was posed by the Minié ball, a new kind of bullet that cut a wide path of destruction through the human body. Made of soft lead, it traveled 950 feet per second and was accurate to 600 yards when fired by a rifled musket, about 10 times further than the maximum lethal range of a smooth bore musket in the Revolutionary War. Worse, the lead flattened when it penetrated the human body. It shattered bones, destroyed blood vessels, tore through intestines, and severed fingers, hands, and arms. It also had the nasty characteristic of ricocheting within the human body when it glanced off bone.

Surgeons at Sudley Church assessed Ballou's destroyed leg and prepared to cut it off. Far too much damage had been done, and a quick amputation might keep Ballou from life-threatening shock or infection. In less than five minutes, Ballou's leg was tossed onto a growing pile of mangled and severed limbs. Speed was paramount in the face of mounting casualties. The smells of blood, bile, and seared flesh filled the church.

By late afternoon, the Confederates had broken through one side of the Union assault. General McDowell's defensive line collapsed under the Confederate advance. Union soldiers retreated and then ran. They fled back toward Washington, D.C., and collided with the thousands of civilian spectators in their carriages who were escaping to safety. Wounded soldiers were abandoned on the battlefield, left to crawl through the dirt in search of shade to escape the sweltering July heat.

Swift, a handful of surgeons, and some assistants, including Gustavus Winston and Charles DeGraw, chose to stay at Sudley Church to care for more than three hundred wounded men. They performed one surgery after another—nearly all of them amputations—as Confederate troops surrounded them. By 1600 the Confederates had seized Sudley Church. Swift, Winston, DeGraw, Ballou, and the wounded lying on pews and under trees became prisoners of war.

Bull Run was an unmitigated military medical corps disaster. A massive Union army had marched into battle with no practical system or capability for treating its wounded. Bull Run was a huge battle that dwarfed any seen during the Revolutionary War catching both the Union and the Confederate military unprepared to evacuate thousands of wounded off the field of battle. Many military doctors had no or minimal surgical experience. Medical supplies were sacrificed in the interest of expediency. The lack of treatment capability was so acute that some of the walking wounded wandered the nation's capital for days after the battle until one of the city's four general hospitals had room for them.

The fiasco reflected the state of military medicine as it struggled to cope with unprecedented casualties. A chronic shortage of qualified doctors persisted throughout the Civil War. It was especially acute in the South, where nearly all medical schools closed during the war. The shortage created a spirit-crushing burden on doctors in uniform. After one battle, surgeon John Shaw Billings wrote:

"Only [to] say that I wish I was with you tonight and could lie down and sleep for 16 hours without stopping ... [after] ... operating all

day long and have got the chief part of the butchering done in a satisfactory manner."[4]

Billings was one of only two hundred fifty Union doctors available after the battle to treat twenty thousand wounded Union and Confederate soldiers.

Millions of soldiers faced a withering barrage of enemy fire in more than two thousand engagements during the Civil War. The development of a rifled musket significantly extended the range of the dreaded Minié ball ammunition. The battlefield was lengthened even further by the lightweight and portable "Napoleon" cannon, capable of firing a twelve-pound shot up to 1,700 yards and ideal for the hilly country where numerous Civil War battles were fought. The Napoleon also could fire canisters filled with iron balls that sprayed enemy troops, a kind of deadly long-range shotgun. Toward the end of the war, a basic machine gun was introduced, as well as the repeating rifle, which could fire seven rounds in the time a musket could discharge a single shot. Unprecedented numbers of soldiers fell as rifle and artillery fire quickened and grew more efficient. The battlefield's killing zone widened and deepened as a result.

At the outset of the war, a primitive battlefield evacuation system was plagued by incompetent personnel. Unfit soldiers who had been assigned as stretcher bearers became infamous for drinking the medicinal alcohol and hiding from enemy fire.

Assignment to a stretcher team was gut-wrenching duty. Following the Battle of the Wilderness in 1864, Lieutenant Colonel D. Watson Rowe wrote that:

"The stretcher bearers walked silently toward whatever spot a cry or groan of pain indicated an object of their search ... [the cries] expressed every degree and shade of suffering, of pain, of agony: a

sign, a groan, a piteous appeal, a shriek, a succession of shrieks, a call of despair, a prayer to God, a demand for water, for the ambulance, a death rattle."[5]

The destination of stretcher bearers was usually a field dressing station just beyond the range of rifle fire. There, assistants stemmed the flow of blood and gave the wounded a shot of alcohol (and perhaps a dose of opium) to withstand the frequently brutal trip to a field hospital. Often the ride was so rough and painful that wounded soldiers chose to walk if they could stay on their feet. Sometimes located five miles from the battlefield, exhausted surgeons and surgeon's mates established field hospitals in commandeered buildings, sheds, and houses; under trees; and alongside specially designed wagons whose sides folded down to become outdoor operating tables. The wagons held supplies such as mercury-based calomel for intestinal problems as well as arsenic and strychnine for other ailments.

Surgeon's mates doled out opium and morphine to the wounded waiting their turn on the operating table. Because stomach, head, and chest wounds were considered almost always fatal, surgeons prioritized leg and arm injuries suffered by soldiers who still had hope for survival. Even then, thousands of wounded men lay outdoors in congested hospitals for a day or longer before a mangled leg or arm was treated by a doctor.

Pain-wracked patients breathed deeply against rags soaked in chloroform as they lay on a table sometimes chest high to the surgeon. As his predecessors had done in the Revolutionary War, a surgeon often stuck a finger into the wound in search of the bullet. In only a few minutes, he decided whether a leg or arm had to be cut off. If that were the case, one assistant administered more chloroform. Instead of becoming unconscious, sometimes the sedated soldier became agitated, moaning and thrashing on the operating table. Another assistant pressed on a major artery to slow bleeding during the operation, while a third held the limb about to be severed. Practiced surgeons who had grown proficient after hundreds of amputations often earned the nickname "Sawbones."

Surgeons sometimes removed the damaged portion of a leg or arm bone if it was short enough so that the remaining undamaged stubs could fuse together. For example, a surgeon would cut open the length of a forearm, exposing the shattered bone. He then threaded a flexible chainsaw under one end of the bone and pulled back and forth, cutting through. He repeated the procedure at the other end of the damaged bone. Once the shattered pieces were removed, the wound was sutured shut and the limb placed in a splint. If the excision had taken place in a leg and the soldier survived, he would need a modified shoe to accommodate his shortened leg. Many soldiers were left with an upper arm or forearm with no internal support when the bones failed to grow together, a limp appendage that hung useless at their side.

Surgery introduced a second enemy to the Civil War wounded: infection. Almost nothing about surgery was antiseptic. The fact that germs caused infection became known only toward the end of the Civil War, too late to help the estimated five hundred thousand men wounded during four years of fighting. Some surgeons sharpened scalpels on the heel of their boots. Sponges were dipped in a bucket of water hauled from a nearby creek and squeezed damp between operations. In the chaos of combat, cleanliness was considered more of a luxury than a necessary medical protocol.

Shortages forced surgeons to use cotton, silk, and even horsehair for sutures, and they often licked the frayed end before threading a needle. If the operation was an amputation, a flap of skin was folded over the stump of an arm or leg and sutured shut, save for a small drainage hole. Almost every phase of a Civil War operation introduced bacteria into a prematurely sealed wound.

Within a day or two, pus began flowing from the wound, which was thought to be a good sign by doctors who failed to recognize it as a potentially deadly infection. Then, by about the fourth day, the wound dried out, the flow of pus ceased, and a raging fever gripped the patient. Typically he was dead four days after the onset of infection. It might have been blood poisoning, which was 90 percent fatal. Or, it could have been hospital gangrene. Thousands of Civil War deaths were protracted and gruesome.

Military hospitalization proved nearly as lethal as battle. Families near Washington, D.C., often took their sons out of understaffed and poorly equipped military hospitals to care for them at home. Although many Washington hospitals had mosquito netting, sanitation was so bad that patients' unburied excrement and neglected bedpans spawned hordes of flies. Typhoid, dysentery, and malarial outbreaks were frequent. The hospital diet weakened patients further. Men wounded in battle were fed cornmeal and hardtack fried in pork grease. The quality of care wasn't much better. Walt Whitman spent time in Union hospitals and noted that one patient died from an overdose of opium and another succumbed when a wardmaster gave him lead muriate of ammonia, which was supposed to be a foot wash.

Even the wounded with relatively slight wounds might not recover, given their weakened condition when they went into battle. Soldiers in the Civil War faced widespread disease, ignored basic hygiene, and often were malnourished. Civil War recruits typically did not receive thorough examinations by doctors when they joined the military. As in past wars fought by Americans, many soldiers came from extremely isolated areas and had not developed immunity to otherwise common childhood diseases. Those in poor health quickly became ineffective soldiers.

When soldiers fell ill, Civil War doctors were practically unarmed in their fight against epidemics. Ignorant of the organic cause of disease, they treated symptoms with little effect. Quinine, strychnine, and oil of turpentine were prescribed for many of the 1.6 million cases of diarrhea and dysentery in the Union army. Typhoid epidemics raged unabated. Doctors could only control malaria as long as they had adequate supplies of quinine. During the Civil War, disease killed twice as many men as the enemy.

The North's blockade of the South not only prevented munitions from getting through, it also strangled the flow of medical supplies. Confederate doctors relied on ingenuity and holistic medicine. An enterprising surgeon could use a knitting needle as a tenaculum. A pen knife became a scalpel. Eating utensils had a variety of surgical uses, and green tree bark could be used as a tourniquet. A tea made from spicewood was given to malaria and diarrhea patients. Soldiers ate wild onions, mustard, sassafras, and pokeweed, which prevented scurvy. Fresh pennyroyal leaves placed under a soldier's bed warded off fleas.

Gradually over the course of the war, doctors identified a correlation between epidemics and the horrific and unsanitary overcrowding of army camps. A sanitary commission established in 1862 issued regulations to improve hygiene. Soldiers were ordered to dig and use open-trench latrines away from tents and eating areas. Shallow wells believed to be contaminated were avoided. Soldiers were instructed to drink water from the center of a stream, not from a stagnant pool. However, many of the regulations were ignored by officers on the front line, and the men suffered for it. Vermin, black clouds of flies, and other insects plagued overcrowded and filthy military camps.

The battlefield diet also contributed to a weakened soldier's susceptibility to disease. Although it improved later in the war, at Bull Run a typical soldier subsisted on fresh or preserved meat, salt pork, navy beans, coffee, hardtack, and thick crackers frequently infested with weevils. Each man filled his haversack with three days' supply. Army cooks often undercooked and fried most food. It was a diet very low in vitamins. The resulting scurvy was poorly understood and misdiagnosed by many doctors. Some believed that scurvy resulted from poor ventilation, a lack of exercise, and boredom, among other factors.

Many who survived battle with both the enemy and disease ailed long after the end of the Civil War. One study showed veterans suffered from diarrhea and dysentery at fifty-six times the rate found in the civilian population.[6] Heart and circulation problems occurred six times more frequently, and rheumatism developed five times more often than among nonveterans. Untold Civil War survivors suffered for years after America's battlefields fell silent.

Sullivan Ballou was not among them. His leg had been amputated only a few hours after reaching Sudley Church in the early hours of the Battle of Bull Run. Dozens of amputations had taken place before the Confederates took control of Sudley Church late on July 21. They moved the surgeons and surgeon's mates to a Confederate prisoner of war camp. The next day they were returned to Sudley to care for Ballou and the others. Every day the surgeons and their assistants made their rounds, checking on the oozing wounds left by hasty amputations. They removed soaked dressings, rinsed them in dirty water, and reapplied them to wounds reeking of rot. Medical supplies were soon exhausted. The smell of dead and infected flesh mixed with the stifling humidity and hung in the air, even though the few windows still intact had been opened.

Then the fevers began as infections took root. Swift and the medical team at Sudley found themselves powerless as dozens of soldiers grew delirious with fever. They had had no time to meticulously clean wounds or search for bits of skin and clothing that Minié balls had driven deep into legs and arms. They were unable to thoroughly cut away the destroyed and dead flesh to give the body a chance to grow new tissue. Now they could only watch patient after patient grow weaker with each passing hour. After suffering for more than a week, Sullivan Ballou died of his wounds on July 29, 1861, eight days after the Battle of Bull Run.

He was buried near the church. Nearly a year later, when Union troops returned to Sudley, they discovered his body had been exhumed, decapitated, and burned, presumably by Confederate soldiers. They took his remains back to Rhode Island for a permanent burial ceremony that became a citywide celebration of Rhode Island's dead war heroes.

On August 13, 1861, surgeon Foster Swift and the other surgeons and surgeon's mates were released by the Confederates. By that time, Bull Run already had become famous as the first major land battle of the Civil War and one which had ended as a rousing Confederate victory. More than one thousand eight hundred Union soldiers had been wounded, killed, or presumably captured. The Confederates suffered slightly more casualties. The Union and Confederacy would clash again at Bull Run thirteen months later.

By then, Ballou's wife had received her dead husband's trunk. In it was a letter he had written only a few days before Bull Run. "Sarah, never forget how much I love you," part of it read:

> "and when my last breath escapes me on the battlefield, it will whisper your name. Forgive my many faults, and the many pains I have caused you. How thoughtless and foolish I have often times been! … I shall always be near you; in the gladdest days and in the darkest nights … always, always, and if there be a soft breeze upon your cheek, it shall be my breath, as the cool air fans your throbbing temple, it shall be my spirit passing by. Sarah, do not mourn me dead; think I am gone and wait to see thee, for we shall meet again."[7]

Sarah was twenty-four when Ballou died. She never remarried and died fifty-six years later at the age of eighty. She was buried beside her husband. Ballou was one of more than six hundred thousand Americans killed in the Civil War, a mortality rate of about 25 percent. Thousands of survivors were disfigured for life. An estimated sixty thousand amputations took place with a similar 25 percent mortality rate. Yet disease was an even more pervasive killer. It was responsible for approximately 60 percent of Union deaths and 65 percent of Confederate deaths.

Despite these gruesome statistics, the Civil War prompted the first significant era of military medical science progress in America. More than 3 million Americans killing and maiming each other led to the recognition that the medical corps had to play a much larger role. Soldiers could not be expected to fight to the edge of death in the absence of a reasonably staffed medical corps comprised of qualified professionals supplied with the equipment and materials necessary to save as many of their lives as possible. A cornerstone of any army's morale is its perception of how soldiers will be cared for when they fall. The Civil War crystallized the need for a permanent American military commitment to military medicine.

Perhaps the greatest medical innovator of the Civil War was Dr. Jonathan Letterman, who became widely recognized as a pioneer of combat medicine. The horror of the abandonment of so many wounded at Bull Run in part led him to create a battlefield evacuation system using stretchers and specially designed carriages. He established a formal ambulance corps and ordered distinct uniforms and insignia. Letterman made sure the ambulance corps was positioned at the front of the battle, ready to pick up the wounded with its customized horse-drawn carriages as quickly as possible.

After a battle at Fredericksburg in December 1862, Letterman's ambulance corps located and processed all ten thousand wounded Union soldiers within twelve hours of battle's end. After the three-day battle at Gettysburg in 1863, more than fourteen thousand injured Union soldiers were processed by the ambulance corps within one day after the firing ceased. That was a far cry from early in the war when men were left to die on the battlefield.

Letterman also critically assessed the chain of battlefield care. He validated the concept of frontline aid stations that focused on stopping bleeding, bandaging wounds, and treating for pain. A progressive continuum of care, from emergency treatment on the battlefield toward more definitive care in the rear, ultimately became one of the Civil War's most enduring contributions to military medicine. As a result, hospital care improved throughout the war. At the Battle of Antietam in 1862, more than 20 percent of the eight thousand wounded died after reaching a military hospital. Eight months later at Gettysburg, less than 10 percent of the ten thousand wounded died in the hospital.

Four years of war spawned other advances in military medicine that would benefit civilian healthcare in the future. The development of the pavilion-style hospital markedly reduced the spread of disease. It became the basis for hospital design for the next seventy-five years. Tens of thousands of battlefield surgeries also led to trauma-care advances. For the first time, anesthesia was used on a widespread basis as surgeons honed amputation techniques, improved the use of splints, and discovered the value of cleaning wounds and removing dead tissue. Other advances produced far-reaching ramifications. Female nurses joined the military medical corps for the first time. Brutal facial disfigurement led to the emergence of plastic surgery as a specialty.

Both the Confederate and Union military medical corps experimented with specialized hospitals, including psychiatric, venereal disease, and neurological facilities. Thousands of psychologically unstable Civil War veterans led physicians to conclude that individuals could become debilitated from emotional stress on the battlefield. Doctors called it "nostalgia," and symptoms included excessive physical fatigue, poor concentration, a refusal to eat or drink leading to anorexia, and a pervasive sense of isolation. Left untreated, nostalgia could progress to insanity and even become fatal. Nearly ten thousand cases of nostalgia were diagnosed during the Civil War. St. Elizabeth's Hospital in Washington, D.C., built in 1855 for mentally ill patients, became the first facility used for combat psychiatric cases, but its bed capacity paled in comparison with the need. Many psychiatric patients were promptly discharged from the Army during the war, left to fend for themselves in the absence of adequate comprehensive military mental healthcare. Regrettably, the Army closed the psychiatric hospital at war's end, and no books or articles were published on the effects of war on the mind.

A half-century would pass before a new generation of American warriors would return to the battlefield in "the war to end all wars."

Chapter 3

Mechanized War

● ● ● ● ● ● ●

World War I

At sunrise, Weedon Osborne stared out at a sickly wheat field. Blackened bomb craters pockmarked the undulating meadow beside the French forest. An overnight rain shower had filled most of the craters, bent wheat stalks, and muddied the topsoil. Five divisions of German troops in the forest had huddled in their trenches through the surprisingly cold early-summer night. Fires had been prohibited. They would have revealed their position to the 2nd and 3rd American army divisions and the 4th Marine brigade on the far side of the field.

Steam drifted up into the misty dawn on June 6, 1918. A massive, weeklong German offensive toward Paris had been countered by Allied victories at Cantigny and Château-Thierry in recent days. Now the American and French forces intended to push the Germans out of

Belleau Wood. But that would require a suicidal advance across acres of open fields toward the forest under German artillery shelling and machine gunfire.

Dawn's shadows were still long when the Americans began their advance. Almost immediately, German artillery shells rained down with deafening ferocity. The earth trembled under a barrage that staggered the assault. Lead knots of soldiers fell as German machine guns raked across the open countryside. A few screamed for medics and corpsmen. June 6 was the single bloodiest day in the first 143 years of the Marine Corps.

Twenty-five-year-old Osborne had served aboard the USS *Alabama* after graduating in 1915 from Northwestern University's dental school. The Chicago native had arrived in France three months earlier as a replacement dental officer and was sent to the front line at Belleau Wood after volunteering to join a first aid party.

Osborne heard the screams of wounded men. Enemy fire split the air around him as he sprinted out into the field and slid to a stop beside a white-faced soldier gripping his belly, the first of many men Osborne would treat. Later that day, as sweat glued his heavy uniform to his back and his muscles burned, Osborne carried Captain Donald Duncan back to a dressing station. A German artillery shell exploded only a few yards away.

The injuries mounted as the fight for Belleau Wood stretched into the middle of June. After three years of war, the German offensive that had been launched in March 1918—before the American military had fully deployed to Europe—was beginning to look like a major defeat. Slowly, the Allies were pushing the Germans out of Belleau Wood.

Surgeon Orlando Petty had been on the teaching staff at Jefferson Medical College in Philadelphia before the war. On June 11, his unit fought for control of Lucy-le-Bocage, a small village in the Picardy region of France. As he bent over a patient, the enemy's artillery found his dressing station. The blast knocked Petty to the ground, tearing his gas mask. Dazed, he looked around. His station had been destroyed. Body parts littered the ground. Petty carried Captain Lloyd Williams out of the rubble. (Williams, who later died, became famous for saying, when ordered to withdraw, "Retreat? Hell! We just got here!")

With dust still hanging in the air, the surgeon organized those who had survived into an ad hoc first aid station. Petty leaned over a soldier who had been wounded on the battlefield and again by the blast. He decided this man took priority over the others who also had been wounded, but he had little to work with. His wooden box of medical supplies held fourteen dark metal tubes. As he reached for clean bandages, he scanned the tubes' labels: Caffeina citrata for heart stimulation; Sodii bicarbonas, an antacid; Bismuthi subnitras, an internal sedative. There it was: Morphinae sulphas to kill pain. Petty reached for the canvas first aid pouch carried on the soldier's own belt. It contained only two rolled bandages and two safety pins. They were woefully insufficient for the soldier's massive wounds, but they would have to suffice. Petty and Osborne were typical of frontline medical personnel who had minimal supplies to treat the wounded under enemy fire.

The brief Spanish-American War in 1898 had provided America's military medical corps with almost no useful battlefield experience when it mobilized for World War I in 1917. The Spanish-American War was notable primarily for the overcrowded, undisciplined, and unsanitary conditions that plagued the military bases where troops trained. The worst soldiers were still assigned to ward duty; as usual, latrines overflowed, hygiene remained an afterthought among many officers, and medical supplies were still a relatively low priority. Fewer than five hundred soldiers were killed in combat in the Philippines and Cuba, but more than five thousand died from disease, most before they deployed for battle.

America's military medical corps faced a new kind of war when it entered World War I. More than five decades had passed since its medical officers had faced catastrophic death and injury on a massive scale. The Spanish-American War had posed few of the medical challenges that the Civil War had presented. Surgeons had last practiced combat medicine in wagons pulled by horses. Major Civil War battles that lasted three days, such as Gettysburg, were dwarfed by World War I sieges that dragged on for months in Europe. Sweeping advances led by Union and Confederate generals on horseback appeared quaint and outdated in World War I, when massive armies were bogged down in trenches along stationary battle lines that stretched 475 miles from the English Channel to the Swiss Alps.

The shoulder-to-shoulder fighting that characterized the Civil War was replaced by a war waged with artillery, gigantic cannons on railroad cars, machine guns, and tanks. The Germans called it *Materialschlacht*, a war of equipment. The Civil War's Minié ball was rendered obsolete by a jacketed, high-speed bullet that not only greatly increased a marksman's range but also produced shock waves that shattered bones and pulverized organs on its path through a target. Timed fuses ignited overhead artillery bursts, showering troops with shrapnel that resulted in casualties with three or more simultaneous critical injuries.

It was a war that once again had caught America's military medical corps unprepared. The rest of the world had witnessed six major wars, mostly in Europe, in the period between America's Civil War and World War I. During that time, the industrial revolution had created a mechanized battlefield. Huge cannon had expanded the arena from pockets of combat to entire regions of warfare. The enemy no longer had to draw a bead on a single soldier. He could lob shells across miles of territory that exploded into clouds of death among groups of men. Newly stabilized artillery had become far more accurate. Closer to the front line, one machine gunner, firing six hundred rounds a minute, became the equivalent of one hundred riflemen in previous wars.

The lack of recent relevant battlefield experience and preparedness was compounded by a critical shortage of medical personnel when America entered World War I. In 1917 the U.S. Army anticipated a 300,000-man expeditionary force in Europe, but it had only 491 medical officers. Ultimately the Army grew to 2 million men, requiring 20,000 medical officers and a medical department of more than 336,000. Those figures were unprecedented in the medical corps' history and were complicated by the fact that World War I was the first major war fought abroad by Americans. Worse, the medical corps occupied a relatively low position in the military organizational hierarchy and was not considered a high priority when shipping men and resources across the Atlantic. Throughout World War I, the medical corps played catch-up as one Allied offensive followed another, exacting a staggering toll in men.

Fewer lives would have been lost had greater attention been paid to the developments in medical science that had taken place since the Civil War. In the late 1860s, an English surgery professor, Joseph Lister, discovered how to use carbolic acid to clean wounds, kill bacteria, and significantly reduce the rate of infection. His antibacterial practices, which included washing hands, wearing gloves, and even avoiding medical instruments with porous handles, contributed to an emerging era of antiseptic medicine, bacteriology, and immunology.

In the latter half of the 1800s, the German military medical corps pioneered the use of hospital trains to keep pace with armies and to facilitate rapid battlefield evacuation. In addition, German soldiers were the first to be issued sterile first aid kits in an army in which the medical corps was highly valued, something of an anomaly in that period.

By the time America's military medical corps arrived in Europe in late 1918, three years of war had taught French and British doctors brutally painful lessons in wound infection control. The British relied on their medical experience in the Boer War in South Africa, fourteen years earlier. Fought in an arid region of poor soil, that war produced relatively few wound infections. The lessons in proper and meticulous wound cleaning were forgotten. But much of World War I was waged in Flanders, famous for its rich, thickly manured farm fields and naturally damp soil—the perfect ingredients for infection. Thousands of soldiers died from infected wounds that had not been cleaned properly when they were first treated.

Near the end of June 1918, American, British, and French troops finally prevailed at Belleau Wood, the U.S. Army's bloodiest battle since Appomattox during the Civil War. More than 1,800 Americans were killed and nearly 8,000 were wounded at Belleau Wood.

A month after Belleau Wood, the summer heat sucked the energy out of eighty-five thousand American soldiers along the Aisne and Marne rivers northeast of Paris. On July 15, 1918, twenty-three German divisions launched a major attack against the American, British, and French armies. The Germans were intent on splitting the Allied forces in two, but by 1100 hours that day, the last large-scale German offensive of World War I had stalled.

On July 19, the Allies launched a counterattack against German positions in the town of Soissons. Among them were twenty-two-year-old John Balch, a corpsman from a Santa Fe Railroad town on the eastern edge of Kansas, and twenty-eight-year-old Joel Boone, a Navy surgeon from Pennsylvania's coal country. Like many battles in recent days, the advances were minimal as soldiers fell under machine gunfire. Corpsman Balch barely paused at those beyond help, packed the penetrating wounds of some, wrapped the shredded arms or legs of others, and called for stretcher bearers. For nearly sixteen hours, Balch repeatedly left his dressing station and exposed himself to enemy fire, giving the wounded a sliver of hope.

Surgeon Joel Boone was not far from Balch. German gunners pinned down soldiers in open fields. A scream rose above the bone-rattling clatter of a machine gun. Boone left the relative safety of a ravine, sprinted out to the fallen man, and dragged him to cover. Later, Boone jumped on a motorcycle and raced to a field hospital for supplies, making two roundtrips through heavy artillery fire.

The wounded kept coming, one after another. Boone could only buy time for each man he treated. It would be up to surgeons in the rear to utilize a recent development in battlefield wound care.

Three years earlier, Dr. Theodore-Marin Tuffier had developed a surgical technique to thoroughly clean the debris from a wound and remove the destroyed and dying tissue surrounding it, a process called "debridement." Because gaping wounds healed slowly and were easily infected, he used a skin graft to seal the wound so it could heal from the inside out with a lower risk of infection. For the first time, surgeons could treat a badly wounded soldier without resorting to amputation to preempt infection.

Doctors, corpsmen, and medics also faced gas warfare for the first time during World War I. Mustard gas was a stealthy, invisible enemy. Symptoms sometimes took hours to appear. It attacked a man's lungs and interacted with any exposed, moist skin. The concoction released by exploding artillery shells contained an oil agent that sealed the gas against skin. Soldiers learned to dread the onset of a burning throat, coughing, sneezing, and watery eyes. Severe exposure spawned vomiting and blisters on the face or, where the caustic gas burned through damp uniforms, in armpits and on genitals. Although death was relatively uncommon, thousands of weakened soldiers faced infection as well as lifelong disfigurement and blindness.

The horrors of battle only temporarily replaced the terrors of a medic's life in the trenches of World War I. Soldiers lived and fought in miles of seven-foot-deep trenches only three feet wide. Their daily routine began with sentry duty against a dawn attack, followed by weapon cleaning and trench maintenance—which involved draining the trenches of rancid water and mud—then sentry duty at dusk.

At night medics stood ready for casualties from patrols into "no man's land," which often was riddled with barbed wire and land mines. Sometimes, they were ordered to the rear to collect medical supplies or return to the gut-tightening stink of the trenches, which were surrounded by thousands of rotting animal carcasses, decaying soldiers' bodies, and overflowing latrines. Inside the trenches, body odor, cigarette smoke, cooking food, hints of poisonous gas, and gunpowder filled nostrils and coated skin.

Balch, Boone, and others shared their space with countless slugs, frogs, horned beetles, and brown rats. Lice-ridden rats scurried across sleeping soldiers and contaminated food supplies. Sometimes nearly the size of a house cat, these varmints feasted on the eyes and fingers of unburied fatalities. Lice transmitted trench fever that caused chronic leg pain. Soldiers' clothes were steamed at delousing stations, but the eggs that survived in a uniform's seams hatched quickly with the help of a soldier's body heat.

The military medical corps fought an incessant battle against disease in World War I. Although vaccinations controlled smallpox and typhoid, other microscopic enemies were formidable. Trench foot—the development of blisters, open sores, and infection from standing in mud for prolonged periods—was widespread. The worldwide influenza pandemic of 1918 devastated the American Expeditionary Force. Soldiers suffering from influenza occupied 193,000 of the 275,000 military beds available in Europe. At one point, a British military hospital of 40 medical officers and 40 nurses admitted 600 influenza-stricken soldiers a day. The cramped, cold, muddy trenches were as unsanitary as the Civil War's overcrowded army camps.

Doctors, corpsmen, and medics confronted another formidable enemy: shell shock. Known as "nostalgia" during the Civil War, shell shock became more prevalent during World War I because of months-long warfare. For weeks at a time, soldiers endured filthy, stinking trenches overrun with vermin. They lived within range of constant enemy artillery. They saw their friends lying face down in a bomb crater or buried in the wall of a trench after being coated with chloride of lime. Amidst this nonstop barrage of disease, noise, and death, many soldiers developed spasms or tics. Other symptoms of shell shock included delusions, sudden phobias, deafness, stammering, and tremors. Military doctors in the rear tried hypnosis, electric shock, massages, drugs, isolation, and rest. Some men recovered, while experimental treatments failed others who committed suicide or deserted. The British Army recorded eighty thousand shell shock casualties in World War I, equivalent to the total population of modern-day Sioux City, Iowa.

Meanwhile, surgeons faced new and far more complicated battlefield wounds than their predecessors had seen in earlier wars. During World War I, 70 percent of the wounds were from shrapnel and secondary missiles such as wood shards and even bone, resulting in horrific mutilation. Sometimes the wounded could not be evacuated from the battlefield for several days. By the time they reached field hospitals, they were weak from loss of blood, shock, hunger, and dehydration. Maggots or pus sometimes filled their wounds. If a medic had packed a belly puncture wound with dressing, fecal material often poured out of a perforated intestine when a surgeon removed the dressing days later.

Although debridement had replaced amputation as the primary surgical weapon against infection, shock remained a primary killer in combat surgery. World War I surgeons knew that quickly replacing blood and body fluids was vital to warding off shock. Karl Landsteiner had discovered blood types in 1901. But surgeons had no way to store donated blood for more than twelve to eighteen hours for use by the wounded. Early in the war, vein-to-vein transfusions from a donor to a recipient lying next to him were attempted. If the donor's blood was the wrong type, however, there was a chance the recipient would die from a transfusion reaction.

The primary duty of corpsmen and medics in mud-filled trenches was more fundamental: keep soldiers functioning and firing at the enemy.

At Belleau Wood, Lieutenant Weedon Osborne and Captain Donald Duncan were among the one thousand eight hundred Americans who died in battle. German artillery had found the only naval medical officer killed in action during World War I. Osborne posthumously received the Medal of Honor, and in 1919, the U.S. Navy named a destroyer the USS *Osborne*.

Surgeon Orlando Petty survived the destruction of his dressing station near Lucy-le-Bocage. His heroism that day earned Petty the Medal of Honor, Distinguished Service Cross, Silver Star Citation, the French Croix de Guerre, and the Italian Croce di Guerra. After the war, Petty taught at the University of Pennsylvania, and, in 1931, he became Philadelphia's Director of Public Health. He died the following year at the age of fifty-eight.

A month after the battle at Belleau Wood, the Aisne-Marne Offensive in July 1918 became the turning point of the war on the Western Front. It set the stage for a major Allied counteroffensive the following month. By that point U.S. troops were fully deployed in Europe. America's manpower and mechanized resources helped turn the tide against Germany after four years of war on the European continent.

Corpsman John Balch kept treating wounded soldiers out in the open at Aisne-Marne. A few months later, on October 5, 1918, Balch again defied death by establishing a critical advance dressing station under brutal shellfire. More than 900 of the 2,300 Marines fighting the Germans suffered casualties in that attack. Many survived because of Balch's willingness to die if it meant saving the lives of wounded Marines. Balch received the Medal of Honor and an honorable discharge in 1919.

In 1942, he reenlisted in the Navy, and retired as a commander eight years later. John Balch died in 1980, at eighty-four years of age.

Surgeon Joel Boone also survived the assault on Soissons in the Aisne-Marne Offensive and received the Medal of Honor for his valor. Boone became the personal physician to Presidents Warren Harding, Calvin Coolidge, and Herbert Hoover. He commanded naval hospitals later in his career, and represented the medical corps during Japan's surrender ceremony aboard the USS *Missouri* in 1945. Vice Admiral Boone died on April 2, 1974, at the age of eighty-five. He was buried in Arlington National Cemetery.

Their valor typified a fundamental shift in the scope and role of America's military medical corps. Doctors, corpsmen, medics, and even dentists had joined the troops on the front line. Army medical personnel received 265 Distinguished Service Crosses, and two stretcher bearers were awarded the Medal of Honor. The Navy's 331 medical personnel who accompanied the Marines were given 684 citations for bravery. Six earned the Medal of Honor. The corpsman became the most decorated rank in World War I.

An estimated 60 million men fought in World War I. More than 7 million were killed, 19 million were wounded, and 500,000 suffered amputations. On average, 900 French soldiers and 1,300 German soldiers were killed every day during the course of four years of war. In just one day in 1916, the British Army suffered 60,000 casualties. By contrast, America's relatively short participation produced 53,000 battle deaths, 200,000 wounded, and 63,000 noncombat fatalities, nearly all from disease.

The human devastation drove home both old and new lessons in battlefield medicine. World War I surgeons confirmed that near-immediate debridement improved a wounded soldier's chances of survival. American doctors, corpsmen, and medics also adopted the

French method of treatment called *triage*, literally meaning "to sift or sort." They learned to assign each wounded man to one of four groups: those who were beyond help; casualties needing immediate treatment; wounded who could wait for treatment; and those with minor injuries. It was the critical first link in a chain of progressive battlefield care that became the basis for casualty care in future wars.

When an American soldier fell wounded in a trench or field during World War I, stretcher bearers—sometimes nicknamed "body snatchers"—carried him as far as several hundred yards through enemy fire to a dressing station. Some stations were little more than medics with first aid packs huddled in a ravine. Others could handle as many as two hundred patients but were equipped with only a single operating table for the most critical abdomen, chest, and severe-fracture wounds. Ambulance drivers stood nearby, ready to take the more seriously wounded to field hospitals about five miles behind the front. Although that usually placed the field hospitals out of range of most artillery, churches commandeered closer to the battlefield for use as field hospitals made easy targets.

Mechanized transportation revolutionized battlefield evacuation. Ford ambulances were prized for their ability to plow through mud. Wounded soldiers who needed more comprehensive care were driven another twenty miles to the rear to evacuation hospitals established along railroad lines. These generally were operated by the American Red Cross, which had created and mobilized university-based hospital teams prior to the war. Their ability to train together in the United States and be ready for deployment to Europe as a single unit on a few weeks' notice ultimately saved thousands of lives. The Red Cross dramatically increased hospital capacity, which became critical in a war of unprecedented scale.

Late nineteenth-century advances in civilian medicine became evident in military hospitals during World War I. X-rays, discovered in

1895, were utilized for the first time, typically on soldiers with multiple wounds in order to help surgeons determine which were most serious. Advances in diagnostic bacteriology enabled surgeons to ascertain when it was time to close a gaping wound with a skin graft without fostering infection. For decades, surgeons unknowingly had been closing infected wounds prematurely, ignorant of the bacterial origin of infection. By 1917, one battle that produced twenty-five thousand wounded soldiers generated only eighty-four cases of gas gangrene. Progress also was made in the war against shock. Intravenous saline transfusions became common in military hospitals, and blood transfusions on the battlefield were introduced on a limited basis.

These advances led to dramatic increases in wound survivability. Surgeons Orlando Petty, Joel Boone, and others returned 78 percent of wounded soldiers to the front after hospitalization. Only 6 percent died—less than half the 15 percent mortality rate of the hospitalized wounded in the Civil War. Wound survivability also was attributable to the first comprehensive battlefield evacuation system implemented in war. By the end of the war, 21 hospital trains had carried 197,000 wounded men to treatment. The United States had nearly 7,000 ambulances at its disposal in Europe and had built 333 hospitals with more than 275,000 beds.

Disease remained America's deadliest enemy. Pneumonia and influenza killed more young men than the enemy, while typhoid, diphtheria, malaria, smallpox, and measles accounted for fewer than one thousand deaths. The first large-scale use of the tetanus antitoxin reduced a fatality rate of 90 percent in the Civil War to less than 1 percent in World War I, despite battle conditions that had greatly increased the potential incidence of tetanus.

Both offensive and defensive armor led to the advent of reconstructive surgery on a large scale during World War I. Steel helmets inadvertently contributed to devastating facial ricochet wounds.

Glancing strikes by bullets slammed the steel edges of helmets into foreheads, cheeks, and eyes. Early in the war, surgeons were ill equipped to handle these critical facial wounds. Some of these soldiers were transported lying down, and died from suffocation. Later in the war, prosthetics, such as eyeglasses built into fake cheeks and atop hand-crafted noses, developed into a subspecialty practiced by those who cared for the wounded when they returned to America. Thousands of maimed soldiers benefitted.

Once again, however, the military medical corps had vastly underestimated the traumatic casualties that a major war would produce. New killing technology had overwhelmed peacetime advances in medicine. In some hospitals, one doctor was assigned to as many as two hundred fifty wounded soldiers. Frontline treatment for the slightly wounded was so inadequate that many were forced to occupy badly needed beds in field hospitals. Convalescent hospital capacity fell well short of the demand that was created by American casualties.

That lack of preparation led to military medicine's principal accomplishment in World War I: administration and organizational development. In only eighteen months from the start of U.S. involvement in World War I, the Army Medical Department grew to more than 336,000 personnel, including approximately 25 percent of all American physicians. The Red Cross was incorporated into this expansion, as the equivalent of reservists responsible for base hospital operation. In addition, the fledgling development of mobile field hospitals became the precursor to acute-care mobility, which would prove invaluable in the future. That mobility would prove critical more than thirty years later when warfare emerged from the trenches to span thousands of miles across the Pacific Ocean.

Chapter 4

Fighting Infection

● ● ● ● ● ● ●

World War II: The Pacific

The wail of the air raid siren froze the work detail on the deck of the submarine. Exposed topside on the USS *Sealion*, the knot of sweat-soaked men in blue dungarees squinted into the noonday sun. They swept the blue sky for specks that might grow into Japanese bombers, even though for two days they had jumped at sirens that had yielded nothing. Pulses quickened when the drone of enemy aircraft washed over them. Several sailors glanced over at another sub, the USS *Seadragon*, and a minesweeper, the USS *Bittern*, alongside to see if their crews also had been caught in the open. All three ships were lashed together at the Machina Wharf at Cavite Navy Yard in the Philippines on December 10, 1941.

Two groups of twenty-seven enemy bombers converged on the largely undefended Navy base and leisurely formed up for bombing runs at defenseless ships and buildings. The first stick of enemy bombs missed the two submarines by one hundred fifty yards. The enemy bombers circled, seemed to pause, and then made another run. The *Sealion* shuddered when the bombs hit. One destroyed a machine gun mount that had been vacated only seconds earlier, exploding just outside the sub's control room where most of the crew had gathered. Another bomb hit at almost the same instant, exploding deep inside the sub, killing four men. Shrapnel skittered through the *Sealion*, slicing skin and scalp.

Within seconds, the *Sealion* listed hard to starboard as seawater filled the ruptured aft engine compartment. As the sub settled into the mud, a short, skinny corpsman from New Castle, Virginia, escaped through the forward torpedo hatch into the bay as explosions rocked the burning Navy yard. Wheeler Lipes treaded water in a circle, shocked at the near-total destruction of the Navy base. When a rescue party finally pulled him out of the water and took him to one of the few remaining piers, Lipes treated soaked, bleeding, and burned men.

That night, after a hot dog and sauerkraut dinner, Lipes collapsed on a cot aboard a tender that had survived the attack, oblivious to the smell of burning rubber and rubbish that wafted through the ship. As he closed his eyes, "Wheeler Lipes, report to sick bay" blared from the ship's loudspeakers. The sound of men arguing pierced Lipes's exhaustion as he approached the compartment. The USS *Seadragon*'s corpsman had been wounded during the attack, and the Navy needed a replacement before the submarine put to sea. Several men shouted over each other, trying to convince a confused officer that they deserved the transfer.

"Look, I've been here longer than you! An' you know I got more medical training than you," said one.

"Yea, and how many times you been late from liberty? Just last Saturday the MPs had to drag your sorry ass aboard," said another.

"Enough!"

The senior medical officer looked Lipes up and down as he entered. "How would you feel about another submarine?" he asked Lipes, whose scalp laceration still ached.

"I'm ready now, sir," said Lipes.[8]

Over howls of protest from men senior to Lipes, the matter was settled. Wheeler Lipes, a young man who always had his nose to the grindstone, was the only candidate present who had completed all the qualifications for transfer to submarine duty as a corpsman. Soon he would head out to sea.

America's military medical corps was poorly prepared and undermanned when the Japanese attacked Pearl Harbor and the Philippines in 1941, even though President Franklin D. Roosevelt had begun mobilizing for war two years earlier. The Army's medical department totaled 11,000 doctors, 7,000 nurses, and 107,000 enlisted personnel. The entire U.S. Navy medical department numbered only 13,500. Rapid medical corps expansion became paramount as America sent 16 million men and women to war over four years. That required the military medical corps to more than quintuple in size, ultimately numbering more than 800,000 by 1945. That expansion created a variety of options for bright and ambitious young men.

Wheeler Bryson John Charles Lipes had always been a serious young man. Standing five feet, six inches tall and weighing about one hundred twenty pounds, Lipes had small feet and small hands. He had wanted to be a doctor for as long as he could remember, especially after working in a Norfolk, Virginia, naval air station dispensary, where he served patients their evening meals, punched capsules in the pharmacy, and typed patient records.

The family bragged that his aunt had been Virginia's first woman pharmacist, but it was his mother, Ida Mae, who set the example he would follow. As a child, Lipes had watched excitedly as some taffy syrup boiled on the stove. When he accidentally stuck his hand in the syrup, he suffered horrific burns. Ida Mae refused to let doctors amputate the badly burned hand, and she slowly restored it to health and dexterity. Another time, while sitting on his mother's lap, Lipes unexpectedly flinched, startling her. She was holding a toothpick and accidentally poked him in the eye. Weeks of daily care slowly but fully rehabilitated his eye. Wheeler Lipes might have grown up with one eye and one hand. Instead, his family's patient ministering instilled a deep sense of responsibility, self-reliance, and ingenuity that would define his life.

Lipes dropped out of high school and enlisted in the Navy in 1936. Within weeks, the former Eagle Scout found himself on the USS *Nitro*, bound for hospital corps school in San Diego. Corpsman training came easily to Lipes. Anatomy classes that confounded others were a snap. The body was a road map and all a man had to do was study it, he often said.

Several months later, Lipes headed for corpsman duty at a Navy hospital in Philadelphia. Over the next three years, he constantly sought physicians who didn't mind teaching young corpsmen. "I want to learn everything I can,"[9] the single-minded young man told them. Lessons often extended well beyond the boundaries of corpsman duty.

Rain pounded the *Seadragon*'s periscope, blurring Captain William Ferrall's view of the South China Sea whitecaps. The sub had departed Fremantle, Australia, sixteen days earlier on August 26, 1942, on its fourth patrol of the war. The next day it reached its assigned station. Secret Operation Order 49-42 directed the *Seadragon* to pursue and destroy enemy shipping.

The *Seadragon* had spotted an enemy sub and a destroyer, evading both as it headed for a shipping lane often filled with Japanese troop transports and supply ships. After completing a watch assignment, Lipes headed for the crew compartment in the battery section of the sub.

"Hey, Doc, I don't feel very good," Seaman first class Darrell Dean Rector said to Lipes. On the youngster's nineteenth birthday, a dull ache in his belly made it impossible to stand up straight. For three days the stomach pain had persisted, and now his temperature was 102.4 degrees. "I think I need a laxative."

Lipes wasn't so sure. "You lie down, and I'll go stand your watch for you." Two hours later Lipes returned.

"Jeez, Doc, my belly's really hurting. Bad. Gimme me a coupla pills or some mineral oil or somethin'. Maybe I just need to take a dump."[10]

Lipes paused as a frown creased his face. "Why don't you just get in this bunk and we'll see how you do." The corpsman was thinking several moves ahead:

"There isn't a qualified physician for more than a thousand miles. We're in the middle of the South China Sea in Jap waters and I've got a sailor beginning to act like he has appendicitis. He's pulling his right leg up toward his chest, trying to ease the pain that looks like it's localized on his right side."

When Lipes touched Rector's abdomen, the crewman nearly jumped out of his bunk. Sailors heard his scream several compartments away.

Lipes left to see the captain. "What do you think is wrong with him?" Ferrall asked.

The corpsman had assisted with appendectomies before transferring to the submarine service. "I think he has appendicitis. He needs an appendectomy."

Ferrall and Executive Officer Norvell Ward blanched. They were weeks away from a friendly port, and appendectomies even in hospitals were far from routine. Deadly infections were common in the prepenicillin era of 1942. Ferrall, Ward, and Lipes headed for the bunk where the sailor squirmed in pain. No position brought relief as Rector looked up at concerned faces. Ferrall turned to Lipes. "What are you going to do?"

"Sir, I can't do anything," Lipes replied.

"Son, we're out here in enemy waters. We do the best we can every day. When I fire torpedoes, I know sometimes they'll miss. But we all have a job to do. You tell me this sailor's got appendicitis. Now, can you do an appendectomy or not?"

Only the engines' rumble through the metal deck and a distant clang broke the lengthening silence.

"Yes, sir, I can do it, but everything is against us. Our chances are slim. But if that's what I'm ordered to do, that's what I'll do," said Lipes as he, Ferrall, and Ward looked down at Rector, his face red with fever.

"Son, what do you think?" Ferrall asked Rector.

"Whatever the doc feels has to be done, it's okay with me," said the sweating Kansas native.

Only twenty-three years old, Lipes's heart pounded as he considered his orders. No one had performed an appendectomy on a submarine before, largely because no surgeons served on them. A corpsman with modest basic training stood between Rector and a ruptured appendix that would kill him. Worse, Lipes realized he lacked the tools he had seen surgeons use when he had assisted in the Philadelphia Naval hospital.

Color drained from his face as he looked around the *Seadragon's* cramped officers' wardroom. It was so small, even the diminutive Lipes could not stand up straight. Lipes lacked the necessary equipment to take Rector's blood pressure. There was no way to do a blood count to assess the patient's condition. No intravenous fluid. No equipment to administer anesthesia. Wheeler Lipes's patient faced death unless he operated, yet the corpsman lacked the most basic equipment found in many physicians' offices.

Lipes, though, possessed an intuitive gift, intelligence, and a passion for learning. Years earlier, he had bought *The Merck Manual*, a massive technical guide to the human body. He considered it one of the greatest books ever published, second only to the Bible.

Captain Ferrall ordered the *Seadragon* down to one hundred twenty feet, to get below the stormy South China Sea swells. The *Seadragon's* helmsmen would have to keep the submarine perfectly level for as long as the surgery required. Lipes began to improvise. A desk drawer pulled out extended the wardroom table to accommodate the six-foot-tall Rector. Sailors rigged floodlights, normally used for night loading, for added illumination in the dim wardroom. Others piled battle lanterns and flashlights on a nearby bench. Lipes pricked Rector's ear and used a torpedo stopwatch to time how long it took the blood to clot to make sure Rector wasn't a hemophiliac.

Pajamas sterilized in torpedo alcohol served as surgical gowns. Five tablespoons with handles bent backward became retractors. Lipes would have to monitor Rector's pulse rate by watching blood vessels pulsing in his opened belly. Sailors ground sulfa tablets into powder for sprinkling into the patient's stomach to fight infection.

Infection had always been a major killer in war. During World War I, 1.8 million Allied soldiers died from battlefield wounds—after reaching a military hospital.[11] Infection accounted for an estimated 10 percent of all German deaths in World War I. Military doctors understood the necessity of cleaning wounds and used a weak bleach solution to sterilize them, but they had no broad-spectrum, systemic antibacterial drugs to fight infection from within the body. As a result, wound infection was so common it often was called a "military disease" and barely rated a mention in leading surgery books written between the Civil War and World War I.

For many soldiers who survived the battlefield, hospital gangrene led to a gruesome death. A fever developed a few days after being wounded. Vomiting and diarrhea followed. After the wound became swollen, it typically turned black and fetid. Then tissue began to fall off, exposing muscles. As gangrene progressed, the muscles separated while vomiting and diarrhea increased. If that didn't kill the wounded man, eventually veins and arteries disintegrated until he bled to death and his pitiful screams ceased. Hospital gangrene was a weeklong hell.

Gerhard Domagk, a German researcher, saw the horrors of wound infection as a medical assistant in the Ukraine during World War I. Under brutal operating conditions, he watched surgeons insert dirty magnets into entry wounds in search of shrapnel. He was powerless as half the men in his postop ward died of gangrene. Domagk survived the war, intent on making medicine his career.

At Bayer, a German pharmaceutical company, Domagk began testing chemical dyes used to stain invisible bacteria so doctors could monitor infections. If a poison could be attached to the dye, perhaps it could become lethal to the many bacteria species that caused a wide range of infections and diseases. Both had killed more soldiers in war than the enemy.

Wheeler Lipes was twelve years old on Christmas Eve, 1932, when Domagk made a startling discovery. Four days earlier, Domagk had given a red dye called Prontosil to a group of mice infected with streptococcal bacteria. By Christmas Eve, every mouse treated with Prontosil was free of infection. All the mice in the untreated control group had died. Domagk was stunned. He replicated the test time and again, with similar results.

At one point he gave Prontosil to his daughter who was very ill. She recovered completely. Domagk had discovered sulfonamide, the world's first antibacterial drug. His discovery sparked worldwide research into different types of sulfonamide, which proved to be effective against pneumonia, streptococcal infections, common types of meningitis, and other diseases. On the eve of World War II, newly developed mass production capability made sulfa drugs a potent new weapon against wound infection in the hands of surgeons, corpsmen, and medics.

In 1939, Domagk received the Nobel Prize in physiology, but it was awarded in absentia. The Gestapo had arrested the researcher to prevent him from accepting it in person because Domagk had refused to support the Nazis.

By 1941, every corpsman and medic carried a supply of sulfa. Soldiers' first aid pouches included sulfa powder and tablets. Five grams of crystalline sulfanilamide powder were to be sprinkled over open wounds. Sulfadiazine tablets were taken orally, except in cases of stomach or throat wounds. Sulfa was known to cause nausea and abdominal cramps, but its advantages more than outweighed these nuisances. For the first time, corpsmen and medics had a battlefield weapon against infection.

If Rector survived Lipes's crude surgery, the ground sulfa tablets might give Rector a fighting chance at staving off infection, even considering the primitive surgical tools that would be used in largely unsanitary conditions. Lipes didn't know how long it would be before Rector reached a proper Navy hospital.

Lipes's surgical team included communications officer Franz Hoskins, who would act as an untrained anesthesiologist; yeoman H. F. Wieg, who would hand the bent spoons to Lipes; Ward, who would assist Lipes by positioning the retractors inside Rector to separate tissue and muscle; Ferrall, who would keep track of the sponges and spoons inserted in Rector's abdomen; and the engineering officer, Lieutenant Charles Manning, who would monitor the patient's circulation. The surgical team gathered around Rector in the *Seadragon*'s sweltering heat and incessant, vibrating hum.

Lipes pulled on alcohol-drenched gloves whose fingers were too long. He looked like Mickey Mouse in his oversized gloves, a blue blouse taped tightly around his neck, and white duck cap. He inverted a tea strainer and covered it with gauze. It became the patient's mask, through which Hoskins administered ether. A sailor notched the stopper in the ether bottle so Hoskins could dribble the liquid onto the tea strainer. The ether was so caustic that another sailor smeared petroleum grease on the patient's face to keep it from burning.

At 1046 on September 11, 1942, corpsman Wheeler Lipes began operating. The first incision barely creased the skin. Lipes cut deeper, to the fascia, then through the fascia to separate Rector's stomach muscles, and another incision through the peritoneum. Lipes kept peeling away Rector's abdomen until his patient's organs appeared.

The air in the crowded wardroom grew stale. Then Lipes noticed an odd smell enveloping the surgical team. He looked at Rector's face and immediately saw that the notch in the ether bottle's stopper was too large. The ether overdose threatened to anesthetize the surgical team where they stood, while the patient received inconsistent doses. As ether fumes wafted through the compartment, Lipes felt Rector's stomach muscles tighten, then go limp as Hoskins struggled to drip more ether into the tea strainer. "Give him more!" Lipes ordered as Rector grimaced.

Once Hoskins had the ether administration under control, Lipes made the last incision. He expected the appendix to pop up, probably blackened with inflammation, but nothing happened. It wasn't there. *Oh, God*, thought Lipes, *does this guy have* situs inversus? *Is his appendix on the opposite side of where it's supposed to be? Just my luck*, as he frantically searched for Rector's gangrenous appendix. Finally, there it was, coiled, engorged, black, and attached in three places to the caecum, a pouch that forms the first part of the large intestine. Rector's appendix had adhered to the inside of his abdomen.

Okay, take it one small cut at a time … don't rush it … look it over, look again, then make the cut. Slow and careful … don't hurry it … just like they did it in Philadelphia. … Lipes knew that if he punctured the appendix, Rector would die. If Rector died on the *Seadragon*, it would be from an appendectomy performed in slow motion, not at the hands of an untrained corpsman frantic to close Rector as quickly as possible.

One step at a time, take double notes to be sure nothing is left behind. Make sure the seventy sponges we've used are accounted for. Make sure the sulfa is ground finely enough that it can be sprinkled inside Rector as we close. Two hours and fifteen minutes after the first incision, Lipes completed the operation. It had taken nearly three times as long as it would have for a practiced surgeon.

Lipes and the others peeled off their sweat-soaked surgical gowns and sat down with mugs of coffee. Word raced through the crew. It was over. Rector had survived, but now Lipes and the rest of the crew had to wait to see if he would recover.

"I'm still in there pitching," Darrell Rector said forty-five minutes later when he regained consciousness. In the following hours, Lipes regularly checked on Rector. An initial fever spiked and then ebbed as the *Seadragon* resumed its patrol and the surgical team disbanded. Two days later, a pair of sailors helped Rector to his feet. He took his first few tentative steps as the *Seadragon* assumed its assigned position in the South China Sea. Five days after, the sub's cook complained to Lipes that Rector "was eating like a horse." A week later the *Seadragon* engaged a Japanese heavy cruiser and two destroyers and survived a depth charge attack.

"One Merchant Ship. One Oil Tanker. One Successful Appendectomy," read the cryptic report from the *Seadragon*'s skipper. To *Chicago Daily News* reporter George Weller, it smelled like a story. The journalist had escaped after being held by the Gestapo for two months in Greece in 1940, and now was assigned to cover the war in the Pacific. Weller was based in Australia, where he had taken refuge after the Japanese had chased him out of Singapore and Java.

Weller paced the dock as the *Seadragon* pulled into Fremantle on October 20, 1942. He had asked Admiral Charles Lockwood for permission to interview Lipes and his surgical team, eager to decipher the sanitized, curt summary of the *Seadragon's* fifty-nine days at sea.

"I'm sorry, sir. I thought the captain wanted to see me," stammered Lipes to the stranger in the wardroom after the *Seadragon* had tied up.

"Are you Lipes?" Admiral Lockwood inquired.

"Yes, sir."

"Well, you fellows had an exciting time," the admiral said as he wrapped an arm around the corpsman's shoulder.[12] They talked for five minutes, Lipes adding details to the skipper's report. When he finished, Admiral Lockwood asked George Weller to come in. Weller looked Lipes up and down as the two sat in the same wardroom that had been an operating room weeks before. As Lipes recounted his experience, Weller furiously took notes, flagging some he would check when he later met with nearly fifteen crewmen who played various roles in the Rector operation. Weller knew when to give an interview subject plenty of rein and let him run with his story.

"Somewhere in Australia—'They are giving him ether now,' was what they said back in the aft torpedo rooms. 'He's gone under, and they're ready to cut him open,' the crew whispered, sitting on their pipe bunks cramped between torpedoes. One man went forward and put his arm quietly around the shoulder of another man who was handling the bow diving planes. 'Keep her steady, Jake,' he said. 'They've just made the first cut. They're feeling around for it now.' 'It' was a little group of anxious-faced men with their arms thrust into reversed white pajama coats. Gauze bandages hid all their expressions except the intensity in their eyes. It was an acute appendix inside Dean Rector of Chautauqua, Kansas. The stabbing pains had become unbearable the day before, which was Rector's first birthday at sea. He was nineteen years old."[13]

George Weller's story gripped the nation, and the reaction stunned Lipes. The corpsman who had been trained as an electrocardiographer hadn't bothered to mention the appendectomy in letters to his wife. He simply assumed he was doing his job and knew he had been following orders. One day his wife's sister pointed out a brief article in a Philadelphia newspaper headlined "Sailor Removes Shipmate's Appendix in Submarine" that didn't specifically name Lipes. His wife said, "That's the kind of thing Johnny would do." Soon the complete story made national headlines and reporters were pounding on her door for comment.

Not everyone marveled at Lipes's audacity.

"You should have let that man die!" sputtered the Navy physician. He had grabbed Lipes by the shirt after the corpsman had been introduced to him in Australia. Lipes paled as the young doctor swelled with rage and shook him by the shoulders. As the one-time recreational boxer recovered from the unexpected assault and prepared to throw an overhand right, others pulled them apart. The doctor thought it despicable that anyone other than a surgeon dare perform any kind of surgical procedure. Better to protect the integrity of the medical profession than to allow such rash behavior, no matter the circumstance or consequence. What would happen if other corpsmen took it upon themselves to operate at sea?

"Is this operation over yet?"

Submarine corpsman Thomas Moore cringed at the question. George Platter had awakened as Moore searched inside Platter's belly for a bleeding vein. The Texas native was in the midst of removing Platter's appendix when his patient roused early from a spinal tap. Moore had wanted to be an electrician in the Navy but decided on the spur of the moment to take the corpsman test to avoid a sudden inspection of his gear by his commanding officer. To his astonishment, he had passed, and on December 21, 1942, he found himself operating on Platter one hundred feet beneath the surface of the ocean.

Four days earlier the USS *Silversides* had sailed out of Brisbane, Australia. The sub's captain, Creed Burlingame, refused to request a PBY amphibious plane to evacuate Platter when his belly pain had intensified. Sighting several Japanese aircraft through *Silversides*'s periscope made a radio message too dangerous. He dared not risk revealing the submarine's position.

Moore had no choice. As Platter moaned and squirmed on the USS *Silversides*'s wardroom table, the crew retrieved a can of ether from sick bay. Moore had heard about Lipes's appendectomy four months earlier and remembered his use of a tea strainer lined with gauze for the ether. Initial doses proved inadequate, when Platter awoke shortly into the operation. As sailors held Platter's open abdomen stationary, Moore showed a senior officer, Roy Davenport, how to drip the ether steadily into the gauze. When Platter quieted down, Moore resumed his search for the bleeder. Half an hour later, he found it and finished what became the third successful appendectomy aboard a submarine in three months. Only a week earlier, corpsman Harry Roby had performed an emergency appendectomy aboard the USS *Grayback* in the South Pacific.

These operations fueled a debate within the Navy that had been spawned by Lipes's appendectomy. Lipes's commanding officers had reeled in shock that a corpsman had successfully conducted surgery behind enemy lines. On October 20, the day the *Seadragon* had returned to port, the commander of Submarine Squadron Two had written, "It is hoped that his [Lipes] success on this occasion will not encourage others to take unnecessary risks ... treatment with sulfa products would appear to be the more sound procedure except in unusual cases."[14]

Yet two days later, Thomas Walsh, the squadron's medical officer, had cautiously praised Lipes:

"While it is by no means desirable to encourage major surgical procedures on naval personnel by other than qualified surgeons, yet, in this particular instance, it appears that deliberation and cautious restraint preceded the operation; that the operation was performed under difficult circumstances and with pioneering fortitude and resourcefulness; and that the result was entirely satisfactory."[15]

A few days later, the Pacific fleet commander, Admiral Charles Lockwood, had noted Wheeler Lipes was being recommended for promotion to "Pharmacist, U.S. Navy," adding "his skill and willingness to assume responsibility for performing a major operation is outstanding."[16] The view from Washington, D.C., however, was entirely different.

"This is not to be tolerated! You understand me? I don't give a damn what you do, but make sure there are no more appendectomies! What the hell do they think they're doing out there? I don't care what you do, no more!"[17]

Ross R. McIntire, Surgeon General of the Navy, slammed both fists onto his desk. Before him sat the medical officer of the submarine service, Chuck Shilling.

The day before, McIntire had read a report detailing Thomas Moore's successful appendectomy. Three appendix removals by corpsmen in three months could not to be tolerated. As McIntire saw it, Shilling had to rein in his submarine corpsmen who apparently felt free to remove inflamed appendices without any surgical training. So Shilling developed new protocols for corpsmen, designed to ease their patients' discomfort and buy time until they could be evacuated off a submarine or until the sub reached a port with a surgeon. As a result, for the remainder of the war, some sailors lived with excruciating pain and risked death for weeks before a "proper" appendectomy could be performed ashore.

Meanwhile, a hushed smear campaign against Lipes slowly swelled within the Navy medical community. Some doctors felt threatened by the corpsman's pioneering heroism. In wardrooms and naval hospital cafeterias, they whispered that Lipes really hadn't removed the appendix. That he saw a man in pain as an opportunity to open him up, close, and claim the removal in order to catapult his career. Others speculated that he somehow removed the appendix, but that the removal had not been necessary. The appendix really wasn't "hot." The latter was particularly specious because Lipes had saved the appendix, and laboratory analysis in Australia confirmed the blackened organ had swollen to nearly twice its normal size. Darrell Rector almost certainly would have died from its rupture.

For weeks after Weller's story first appeared in the newspaper, bags of mail from across the country arrived daily for Lipes. "I didn't want my son to go into the Navy, but when I read this story of how you care for the patient, it makes me feel better,"[18] wrote one mother. But nothing was forthcoming from the Navy's medical service. Wheeler Lipes did not receive a decoration for his ingenuity and daring. Instead, he received two quick promotions to warrant officer, which took him off submarines and the duty that he loved. In January 1943, he transferred to a naval hospital in Philadelphia. Lipes remained a celebrity some Navy doctors wished would go away.

"Darrell Rector is dead." Wheeler Lipes swallowed deeply at the news. On October 24, 1944, Rector had been aboard the USS *Tang*, a submarine preying on Japanese supply ships near the China coast. In a night attack, the *Tang* had sunk several Japanese ships. As soon as the crew fired the *Tang*'s last torpedo, they knew the sub was in trouble. The torpedo arced left, broached the surface, and "porpoised" as it turned back toward the submarine. The torpedo buried itself in the *Tang*'s stern, the explosion deafening the crew. Men flew across compartments, breaking legs and arms. The Pacific poured in through the hull, pulling the *Tang* toward the seabed, one hundred eighty feet below the surface. Only nine members of the crew had managed to escape and remain afloat until they were picked up the following morning by a Japanese warship. Darrell Rector had gone to the bottom in the crippled *Tang*.

By that time, the sulfa drugs that had helped save Rector's life had been replaced by a new antibiotic whose efficacy was being proven on the battlefield: penicillin.

Penicillin's roots extended back to World War I, when bacteriologist Alexander Fleming witnessed the horrors of rampant wound infection in combat hospitals. Lipes was nine years old when Fleming accidentally discovered mold that appeared to be killing bacteria in a Petri dish. He published a paper about his observation, but it garnered little attention when Fleming failed to adequately replicate the bacteria-killing mold.

While Lipes honed his corpsman skills in 1939, a team of Oxford University researchers headed by Australian pathology professor Howard Florey and German refugee biochemist Ernst Chain turned their attention to Fleming's decade-old observation. Remarkably, only two years later, in mid-1941, they had found a way to reproduce enough of the antibacterial mold for experimentation, completed the first round of human testing, and laid the groundwork for its mass production. Penicillin was used in combat for the first time in North Africa in 1943. Doctors called it the "magic bullet."

Penicillin became a national medical priority. In 1943, U.S. drug companies produced 21 billion units of the antibiotic. In excess of 1.5 trillion were produced in 1944, more than enough to protect the Allies during the Normandy invasion.

Millions of wounded and sick soldiers owed their health and even their lives to antibiotics. During World War I, 8 percent of the wounded had died of their wounds, a mortality rate that declined to less than 5 percent in World War II. In World War I, a battlefield surgeon reported that 70 percent of amputations were due to infection rather than anatomical destruction. During World War II, the military medical corps effectively replaced amputation with antibiotics as the first line of defense against infection. Although a higher percentage of amputations took place in World War II, that was due to improved battlefield evacuation procedures that delivered more gravely wounded patients to field hospitals. Antibiotics had an even more profound impact on disease in war. Only 0.1 percent of the 14.3 million soldiers who fell ill died during World War II.

Wheeler Lipes stayed in the Navy after the war, although it seemed that an invisible black mark had blemished his name. He resumed his education: he finished high school and began attending university classes. A lifelong student of the world around him, Lipes was a highly principled man who didn't fit in a bureaucracy as political as the Navy. He fearlessly identified policies, rules, and protocols he thought were ill advised. He had a very strong sense of right and wrong, and he always spoke his mind—for which he paid a price.

Lipes's peers quickly overtook him. They were promoted repeatedly, while characterizations of arrogance and stubbornness dogged Lipes. In 1957, he was asked to be the technical advisor for an episode of *The Silent Service*, a popular television series about Navy submarines. Admiral Thomas Dykers produced the episode called "Operation Seadragon," which was based on Lipes's successful appendectomy. Lipes refused to endorse the program. He felt the producers had taken too much dramatic license with the facts and believed the result presented an inaccurate portrayal of what had happened fifteen years earlier. No matter what Dykers said, Lipes refused to endorse the final cut. Even a summons to the Pentagon didn't sway Lipes. "Operation Seadragon" went on the air without his blessing, another black mark on his name. When it aired one Sunday night, a boy sat mesmerized by the story.

More than forty-five years later, Jan Herman would play a pivotal role in Lipes's life.

In 1962, Lipes retired as a lieutenant commander after twenty-six years in the Navy. His Navy retirement letter became a poignant capstone to his career. It made no mention of Lipes's willingness to follow orders to perform the first appendectomy aboard a submarine. No mention of his passion for learning that made it even remotely possible for a man who had never spent a day in medical school to cut into another man's belly, remove an inflamed organ, and give that man a second chance at life.

In 2003, Herman, historian at the U.S. Navy's Bureau of Medicine and Surgery (BUMED), attended an officer's retirement ceremony that left him unsettled. The man had received the Legion of Merit when some believed he was wholly undeserving of the honor. They felt that bestowing it simply as a lovely parting gift belittled those who had legitimately earned the recognition in years past.

History was irreplaceably precious to Herman. Its preservation came in many forms, from oral histories to books to documentaries. Awards and medals served as history's mile markers in measuring a person's contribution. The standards by which medals were bestowed were sacrosanct and born from years of considered application in a spirit of fairness.

Herman remembered watching *The Silent Service* on television and marveling at a corpsman performing an appendectomy with little more than a spoonful of faith. As the BUMED historian, he had met and interviewed Wheeler Lipes to record his life story for posterity. The two had grown so close, their relationship was beyond friendship; it approximated that of a father and son. Herman believed that Lipes had gone unrecognized for too long. Something had to be done.

"Admiral, there has been a stain on the Medical Department since 1942,"[19] Herman said at a meeting with then Surgeon General of the

Navy, Admiral Michael Cowan. As Herman launched into a recitation of Lipes's heroics, Cowan cut him short. Everyone at BUMED knew the story. But Herman was just building up a head of steam. "You, sir, need to make it right. If I can document what Lipes did and nominate him for a medal, will you sign it?"

"You bet I will," promised Cowan.[20]

Herman embarked on a complicated scavenger hunt. He researched BUMED's archives and the U.S. Navy's records. Second-hand reports, however, were not enough. He had to find witnesses to the appendectomy, more than sixty years after it occurred, who remembered the details and who were willing to sign an affidavit. Most of the officers in the wardroom that day in 1942 were no longer alive. But Herman found the executive officer, Norvell Ward, living in Florida. Ward remembered the incident and signed the necessary paperwork.

His research complete, Herman submitted a medal nomination to the awards board of the Chief of Naval Operations and anxiously awaited the panel's decision. He knew some medical officers in the Navy still clung to the belief that Lipes's actions had merited a court-martial rather than an award. Others remained convinced that it was a hoax of sixty years' standing which had originated at a time when America desperately sought good news about the war in the Pacific—a sham best forgotten.

Not so, ruled the awards board. Admiral Cowan called Lipes as soon as he received word that the Navy stood ready to correct one of its longest-running omissions of recognition. Wheeler Lipes had earned the Navy Commendation Medal.

Then pancreatic cancer struck Lipes. At the age of eighty-three, he somehow survived an eight-hour surgery and faced a long recovery. Nearly eighteen months later, in February 2005, the Navy brought the awards ceremony to Lipes, holding it at Camp Lejeune, not far from his home. Family and friends filled the auditorium as corpsmen stood at attention. More than one hundred fifty people attended the brief presentation. None was surprised to hear Lipes brush aside any talk of heroism.

Although Lipes began a new series of cancer treatments two days later, the ceremony marked the closing chapter of his life. He faded fast. On April 17, 2005, Wheeler Lipes passed away.

Lipes had spent a lifetime caring for others, becoming the chief executive officer and president of large hospitals in Tennessee and Texas after retiring from the Navy. One day, while flying to a medical convention, he noticed a man next to him reading an edition of *Ripley's Believe It or Not*. The book sat open to a passage and cartoon about Lipes's appendectomy. The man noticed Lipes gazing at the page, his face blank.

"Look at that," the man said. "Can you believe somebody could do something like that?"

Lipes didn't miss a beat, shook his head, and said, "Don't believe a word of it."[21]

Wheeler Lipes, along with thousands of doctors, corpsmen, and medics, had helped save more than 670,000 wounded sailors and soldiers during World War II by using sulfa drugs and pencillin to ward off infection. The wounded survived enemy fire, wounds, and the threat of infection. Millions more also had survived another ageless nemesis on the battlefield: disease.

Chapter 5
Defeating Disease

● ● ● ● ● ● ●

World War II: Tarawa

The American convoy cut into the endless green South Pacific swells in November 1943. As Japanese submarines silently patrolled below, more than eighteen thousand American soldiers on battleships, cruisers, and transports waited and wondered. Some faces blanched with fear, while others affected a false bravado to guard against the uncertainty ahead. Many were at sea for the first time and discovered seasickness was made worse by taut nerves. Their destination was an island called Betio in the Tarawa Atoll, so small it would fit within Central Park in New York City.

The Japanese garrison on Betio knew the American battle group was heading directly for it. Their admiral claimed that a million Americans could not drive his men from the island in a thousand years. Every

Japanese soldier had been trained to drive the enemy into the sea or die when the invasion force reached Tarawa. Both invaders and defenders had nowhere to retreat on isolated islands in the Pacific. Either the Japanese or the Americans would be decimated in the coming showdown.

Ray Duffee had just enrolled at the University of California, Davis, when the Japanese bombed Pearl Harbor. He decided that school would have to wait.

Although school officials had told him it was his patriotic duty to stay in college, restlessness pulled at Duffee. He had seen how news of the Pearl Harbor attack had devastated his Japanese college classmates. Not knowing exactly why, Duffee felt it imperative that he serve his country. On March 25, 1942, Duffee and his aunt drove to San Francisco to talk to Navy recruiters.

As he stood in a long line at the recruiting office, a recruiter walked past and asked Duffee about his background. He described his part-time work in a veterinarian's office and mentioned that he had a Red Cross certificate. The recruiter pulled him out of the line and sent Duffee to corpsman school at the U.S. Naval Hospital in San Diego's Balboa Park, an expansive complex on a ridge overlooking San Diego Bay.

Corpsman training in the summer of 1942 was basic, and much of it was based on common sense, it seemed to Duffee. He was taught how to assess patients and monitor their condition, and he knew just enough to discern when to call for a doctor. He also learned that disease had always been the most lethal enemy on the battlefield.

For thousands of years, disease had determined the victors of numerous wars. Epidemics ravaged the Roman Empire's armies and contributed to its demise. Typhus crippled Napoleon's attack on Russia. Raging disease epidemics led to a three-year stalemate in World War I: there simply weren't enough soldiers to wage war. From 1916 to 1918, one British army unit of 124,000 men suffered 162,500 cases of recurring malaria compared to 24,000 men killed in action. A French army of 120,000 men suffered a malaria rate of 80 percent.

In 1935, Army maneuvers in Panama had been cancelled due to an outbreak of malaria. As long as the U.S. Army stayed out of regions ravaged by disease-carrying mosquitoes, its soldiers remained relatively healthy. In 1939, the malaria rate among soldiers was five per thousand men, the lowest since the Revolutionary War. That changed in 1941 when America went to war. Malaria decimated American troops in the Pacific throughout the first year of World War II. On New Guinea in late 1942, the malaria recurrence rate was four thousand per one thousand men. This was shocking, considering that the medical corps had an effective weapon against the disease: Atabrine.

Atabrine was a synthetic alternative to quinine, which had been used for hundreds of years to treat malaria. Atabrine was developed by German researchers Walter Kikuth, Hans Mauss, and others in the early 1930s after Germany found itself without a supply of quinine during World War I. Early in World War II, the Japanese seized control of the only major source of quinine, the cinchona plantations in Java, Indonesia. Atabrine became the Allies' only widely available antimalarial drug.

Some soldiers who began taking it after reporting aboard ships bound for the Pacific theater suffered nausea and vomiting, so they stopped their doses. They may have associated seasickness with Atabrine. Once they joined their units in the Pacific, they found many officers who considered disease control a distraction to "killing Japs." Enforcement of the daily dose of Atabrine was lax at best. Some soldiers also considered hospitalization for malaria preferable to combat duty.

Although effective, the small yellow tablets tasted extremely bitter. Atabrine also gave the skin a sickly, pale tint. Complaints grew so rampant that some corpsmen and medics stationed themselves at the head of mess hall lines to make sure everyone took his Atabrine every day.

Once his corpsman training was complete, Duffee and hundreds of others reported to downtown San Diego's Navy Pier 11A and boarded the *Bloemfontein*, a Dutch transport bound for the Pacific.

When Duffee arrived in New Caledonia, the young corpsman began treating exhausted and mangled Marines who had been shipped off Guadalcanal. The island assault in late 1942 was one of the war's first prolonged battles of attrition in which disease was far more debilitating than the Japanese. Nearly two thirds of the Marines suffered from malaria, while 25 percent had been wounded by the enemy. In November, there were 1,800 cases of malaria (including recurrences) per 1,000 Marines. New Caledonia had been selected for recuperation in part because the anopheline mosquito that spread malaria wasn't found there.

The second year of World War II became a critical turning point in the military's undeclared war against disease. In 1943, the British decided that troop health was the responsibility of the officers, not just the medical corps. At one point, three British commanders were dismissed for lack of health and sanitation standards enforcement. Once combat officers were held accountable for the health of their men, enforcement became far more stringent. In the United States that year, medical supplies that once languished on docks became a top priority for oceanic transport. Specially trained disease control units began shipping out to the war theaters as well.

In early summer 1943, Duffee's transfer to McKay's Crossing near Wellington, New Zealand, brought him closer to war. Assigned to the 2nd Marine Regiment, he had his hands full as malaria swept through the ranks while they healed, rested, and resupplied after Guadalcanal was secured in February. Sanitation was lax, and officers allowed troops to bivouac in mosquito-infested areas when safer campsites were less than two miles away.

In New Zealand, Duffee learned the value of ingenuity in treating tropical diseases. A man's temperature had to hit 104 degrees before he was sent to the hospital for two or three days' treatment with quinine, if it was available, or Atabrine. Duffee discovered the gel caps shipped from the United States often melted in transit, making it impossible to fill them with the medicine. So Duffee calculated the proper dosage of powder, wrapped each in toilet paper, and ordered the Marines under his care to wash it down with grapefruit juice.

Slowly, the Marines regained their strength as they speculated on their next assignment. The combat veterans knew they would not be told until they were already on their way to the next battle. No one looked forward to more island assaults where the Japanese had built nearly indestructible defenses in caves on hillsides above the Marines' landing sites.

The Japanese high command knew the Pacific war had begun to turn in the Americans' favor. The standoff in the Coral Sea in May 1942, followed by the decimation of the Japanese fleet at the Battle of Midway the following month and the American victory on Guadalcanal in early 1943, forced a change in Japanese plans. They developed *yogaki*, a defensive strategy along an imaginary line stretching from the Aleutians in the north down to the Marshall Islands, about two thousand miles southeast of Japan. This became the outer line of defense for the Japanese empire in the face of America's island-hopping advance toward their homeland. The Gilbert Islands, consisting of sixteen scattered atolls in the central Pacific more than two thousand miles from Hawaii, were considered crucial. The Gilberts could not be lost to the Americans because the airstrip on Betio in the Tarawa Atoll of the Gilberts would put American bombers within range of the Marshalls.

As Duffee and the 2nd Marines began serious training exercises in July, the Joint Chiefs of Staff ordered Admiral Chester Nimitz to develop a plan to capture the Gilbert Islands. "Get the hell in and get the hell out," Nimitz ordered his admirals.[22] Only a few weeks later, the Japanese ordered a rear admiral trained as an engineer, Keiji Shibasaki, to take command of the Gilberts and prepare for the widely expected invasion. The airstrip on Betio at Tarawa must be defended to the last Japanese soldier. The Japanese knew they had to stop the American invaders on the beach. If the Marines established a beachhead, their overwhelming number of men and weapons ultimately would destroy the Japanese defenders.

When American planners spread out a map of Betio in the Tarawa Atoll, they saw what resembled a dead bird lying on its back. Less than three miles long and no more than eight hundred yards wide, the center of the island bowed northward like a bird's chest with a long, thin tail to the east, and a small promontory, shaped like a bird's beak, to the west. There was no natural elevation of more than ten feet. Betio was a flat, narrow spit of coral sand covered with palm trees. Admiral Shibasaki intended to turn it into an impenetrable killing zone.

A shallow reef surrounded the island, in some places stretching nearly 800 yards from shore. At low tide, the water could be only a few inches deep, making an amphibious assault extremely risky. Admiral Shibasaki immediately installed steel tetrahedrons interspersed with barbed wire and mines across the reef. Betio had only three landing beaches on the north side, each about 600 yards across. Shibasaki built his underwater defenses on the shallow reef so that American amphibious craft would be driven into channels of crossfire from more than 500 Japanese pillboxes filled with snipers and machine gunners. They were part of a force of more than 4,800 men, 2,600 of whom were highly trained Imperial Japanese Marines.

When Admiral Nimitz ordered Plan 13-43, codenamed Operation Galvanic, on October 5, 1943, a massive showdown became a certainty, a clash that would produce one of the most brutal and shocking battles of World War II.

"Okay guys, we're headed for Efate for a couple of days of practicing amphib assaults. Get your gear ready."[23]

When Duffee heard the order from an officer, he had assumed he would be back in New Zealand in time for a dance that had been scheduled in Wellington. A few days at Efate shouldn't be a big deal— probably some contusions and maybe a broken leg or two to take care of.

Duffee reported to the transport ship USS *Harry Lee*. The living conditions onboard terrorized the nine hundred Marines. Bunks were stacked five high, with the top bunk having only sixteen inches of clearance from the bulkhead. The air grew hot and stultifying, filled with the smell of sweat and vomit. The vibrations from a slightly unbalanced propeller rumbled throughout the ship. Ammunition lay in stacks a few feet from Duffee's bunk. Death in a dimly lit compartment filled with putrid air would be quick if a Japanese submarine found the *Harry Lee* in its sights.

The Marines conducted two landing rehearsals at Efate. They were less than realistic as their support aircraft had been excused from participating. Veterans of previous island campaigns knew that coordination with air cover was critical to a successful amphibious assault. The Marines' armada did not turn back for Wellington. The massive assault force set a northerly course as clusters of men tightened and voices hushed when talk turned to what lay ahead.

As Task Force 53 approached Tarawa, the troops spent their days reviewing maps and plans. The Marines learned that the most concentrated bombing in history would precede their landing. Nearly three thousand tons of shells would be lobbed onto 291 acres. They wondered whether there would be an enemy to fight after that. The men around Duffee grew silent. Some never seemed to stop sharpening their knives, oblivious to the rhythmic grate of metal. Others endlessly disassembled and cleaned their rifles. Many wrote their last letters home or watched a second-rate movie, *Marry the Boss's Daughter*. Some worried more about suffering a crippling injury than death.

Men wilted under the pressure. On the eve of battle, corpsman Duffee saw how fear drove some Marines to desperation. A number of soldiers had avoided battle on Guadalcanal by not taking their Atabrine in the hopes of getting malaria. As the invasion force approached Tarawa, Duffee learned to smell the armpits of men reporting to sick bay. He knew a man sometimes put lye-laden soap under his arm to raise his temperature. A first offense prompted a stern warning from the corpsman and a promise to report it if it happened again.

On November 19, a blazing tropical sunset on Betio reddened the sky. As the twilight air cooled, Admiral Shibasaki looked out across the mine-studded reef. The promised Japanese scout planes had failed to arrive. Military intelligence on what might be approaching was limited to his instincts and imagination. "I feel it in my bones … in a day, maybe less, we will be fighting for our lives," he said before he issued the final battle order to his troops:

"I order you, in the emperor's name, to defend to the last man all vital areas. Should the enemy attempt a landing, destroy him at water's edge. I know you will not fail our emperor, Hirohito, the Son of Heaven! Banzai! Long live Japan!"[24]

Hours earlier, just over the horizon, a message from the command ship USS *Maryland* had been flashed to the American task force: "It is not the Navy's intention to wreck Betio. We do not intend to destroy it. We will obliterate it from the face of the earth."[25]

Ray Duffee jerked awake to reveille at forty-five minutes past midnight on November 20. Tradition held that Marines eat steak and scrambled eggs as a last meal before battle. Duffee never saw it. Instead "shit on a shingle"—chipped beef on bread—landed on his tray. He encouraged everyone to eat lightly. Corpsmen didn't want full intestines emptying out onto the sand in a few hours after bullets ripped open a man's abdomen.

After landing craft came alongside the troop transports, Duffee and thousands of others climbed down the cargo nets hanging over the side of the ships and jumped into their amphibious craft. Duffee heard four things as he climbed down the rope ladders: sloshing water, a periodic muttered prayer, the landing craft's engine, and Marines retching onto the deck.

At 0500 hours, Betio exploded. Dozens of American warships simultaneously opened fire. Within seconds, a curtain of smoke, sand, and coral dust hung over Betio. The entire island disappeared in balls of fire as spasmodic volcano-like eruptions marked ammo dump detonations. More than seventy-five landing craft circled offshore, watching one of the most intense bombardments of World War II.

"Maybe they pulled a Kiska," said a Marine in one landing craft, referring to the Japanese abandoning Kiska Island in the Aleutians in the face of a U.S.–Canadian assault. "Yea, right," said another. "Whether they bugged out or not, they'll be flattened when the battleships are finished," promised another.

"The earth shook and the sky was a fiery red ball," wrote one Japanese soldier. "I thought of my family as the shells slammed around us ... we were flung like rag dolls ... I thought of honor and courage and the Mikado ... this was the acid test."[26]

Captain John Moore of the USS *Indianapolis* marveled at how the attack decimated the island. "Fires were burning everywhere. The coconut trees were blasted and burned and it seemed that no living thing could be on the island."[27]

Despite the massive bombardment, Admiral Shibasaki's preparations on Betio withstood the assault, in part because American warships had moved in too close. Many shells skipped off Betio and detonated harmlessly on the reef on the far side of the island. Hundreds of others found their mark, yet proved largely ineffective against Shibasaki's concrete bunkers, which were reinforced with mounds of sand and layers of coconut logs.

The waiting had seemed endless to Duffee, as shells sounding like freight trains thundered overhead. As his group circled outside the reef with dozens of other landing craft, the prelanding assault already had been bungled. Communication between Navy ships disintegrated when the command ship USS *Maryland*'s communications went down with the initial barrage.

Finally, orders came at about 0900: "Head for the beach." The boats turned south toward three landing zones. Duffee's boat headed for the middle landing zone on the north side of Betio, alongside a five-hundred-yard pier. The water over the reef boiled white in the landing craft's wake. As they approached the beach, palm trees shredded by shrapnel emerged from the hazy smoke, looking like a grotesque, twisted picket fence. The smell of smoldering palms, sulfur, and rubber floated out over the lagoon as black smoke drifted over Betio.

Many of the advancing landing craft ground to a halt at the edge of the coral reef far from shore. They had "high centered" on coral heads. Assault planners had known there would be only a fifty-fifty chance the tide would be high enough to allow the amphibious Higgins boat to navigate over the coral reef. Senior officers had rolled the dice, betting the lives of hundreds of Marines assigned to the boats—and lost. The Marines paid with their lives. They either stayed in the stranded boats hundreds of yards from shore and became targets for the enemy or took a deep breath, prayed, and climbed out to wade ashore.

Duffee and others who were lucky enough to be in another type of landing craft that could cross extremely shallow water plowed ahead. Artillery, small arms-, and machine-gun fire erupted as the amphibious craft climbed up onto the shallow reef for the agonizingly slow six-hundred-yard trip to shore. Explosive bullets pierced the boats' thin armor, then ricocheted among the Marines, who wore no armor. One man after another slumped to the side, motionless. Soon, hundreds of Marines who had been wading ashore were floating face down among thousands of dead fish. The coral reef turned pink with blood. The smell of burned and torn flesh wafted over the lagoon. Boats smoldered.

Duffee's landing craft made it to Betio's twenty-foot-wide beach and tried to climb over a five-foot-high, coconut-log wall that ringed the island. On the other side, the enemy waited. The amphib raised high on its haunches and, belly exposed, stalled. Someone yelled "Everybody out!" Duffee and two others climbed over the side onto the beach. Duffee flattened on the sand. Next to him lay two buddies shot dead as they rolled over the side of the amphib.

The cacophony stunned the corpsman. Screams stretched between the explosions and gunfire bursts. Men only ten feet away moaned, some of them gasping "Doc!" with what might have been their last breaths. As his eyes and ears focused, his training took hold. Duffee, hunched forward with rounded shoulders like a snail, immediately began treating the wounded men on the sand. In the roar of war, treatment became strangely clinical. Duffee didn't actually see that a teenager from Milwaukee was crippled by shrapnel that exploded his kneecap and shredded a hamstring. It was simply a clear-through wound, so cinch it with something—a belt, anything—sprinkle sulfa, smother the torn flesh with a battle dressing, inject morphine, attach the Syrette to the uniform, stay low, and get to the next man. Fast. Duffee hoped stretcher bearers like Irwin Dunlap and Harry Shanker would find the wounded he had treated and carry them to an aid station up against the coconut-log wall. There was no time to look back.

Nearly invisible enemy machine guns erupted twenty-five yards away as waves of men reached the narrow beach, exhausted and exposed. The Japanese-built coconut-log wall at water's edge offered scant cover to men unable to advance inland or retreat back to the sea. Hundreds of Marines waded onshore, some of them cut in half in an instant.

It quickly became an assault measured by the length of a dead soldier. Betio was so narrow the Japanese had no place to retreat. Nearly the entire battle would be fought within one hundred yards of the water. The Japanese had positioned concrete gun emplacements, bunkers, trenches, fire pits, machine-gun nests, infantry trenches, and rifle pits with interlocking fields of fire. Men kept falling everywhere. At 1330, the commanding officer ashore, Colonel David Shoup, radioed a status report to the USS *Maryland*: "Still encountering strong resistance, issue in doubt."[28] The last part of the message stung. It contained the same phrase used two years earlier by the Marines at Wake Island just before it fell to the enemy. Operation Galvanic was in trouble.

Duffee dove from one wounded man to the next on the beach with no time for small talk. Those who were conscious usually asked, "Have you seen my buddy?" Duffee's answer rarely varied: "Sorry. No." He knew how long a Marine had been ashore. Newcomers slithered on the sand on their bellies. A few minutes later, they scrambled for safety on their hands and knees. Minutes after that, they ran to their positions hunched over, resigned to what fate held in store.

The blood-red summer sun hovered over Betio on the afternoon of November 20. For six hours, wave after wave of Marines had braved horrific enemy fire. By sunset, nearly 1,500 of the 5,000 Americans on Betio had been wounded or killed. Many were corpsmen. A Marine had fallen dead or wounded every twenty-four seconds. Some had been incredibly unlucky. An American dive-bomber had attacked a Japanese ammo dump as an American Sherman tank drove by. The massive ammo explosion blew up the tank, incinerating the men inside. The whirling shrapnel from the blast also gutted a Marine assault that had begun minutes before the dive-bomber struck.

At water's edge, the narrow slit of beach had become a massive, confused medical ward. Red Cross flags stuck in the sand marked aid stations where emergency operations took place in the open. Corpsmen arranged the wounded in exposed rows, easy targets for Japanese infiltrators with grenades. One Japanese soldier wearing a Marine uniform nearly made it to the rows of bodies before a sharp-witted sentry spotted the impostor by his Japanese lace-up boots and shot him dead.

Duffee moved a few yards inland from the beach. Close to sunset, he joined a mortar squad near Betio's airstrip. His legs and arms were red and burned from crawling on hot sand for most of the day, moving from one wounded man to the next. He knew dehydration soon would become a concern.

"Duffee! We got a man wounded out there," an officer yelled. "Maybe thirty-five yards out and to your left. Get out there and see what you can do. Now!"[29]

Legs lead-heavy with fatigue, Duffee sprinted out in front of the American line to the man and dove into a shell hole blasted in the coral. The Marine refused morphine. He realized that Duffee couldn't drag him back to safety, so he needed to stay alert for the inevitable Japanese night assault. The corpsman knew that if the wounded man survived the night in the crater, infection would become the enemy. He tore open an envelope that held five grams of sulfanilamide crystals. He had slowed the bleeding enough to sprinkle the wound with sulfa. After he secured a sterile battle dressing to the red-raw flesh, Duffee opened a small carton containing peppermint-flavored sulfadiazine. "Chew these!"[30] The wounded Marine needed to ingest the anti-infection pills within five minutes of Duffee's application of the crystals to his wound.

As the light dimmed, Duffee patted his patient on the shoulder. "Keep your eyes peeled tonight."[31] Crouching as low as he could manage, Duffee raced back to his mortar squad. Sometimes a corpsman treated a man only to buy time and hoped it was enough.

Soon another Marine went down forward of the mortar company. Without hesitation, Duffee commandeered several stretcher bearers who ran with him among the splintered palms to rescue the Marine. Japanese gunners waited for the rescuers to load the injured Marine onto the stretcher. Duffee's team had barely begun the slow trek back to safety when a Japanese grenade detonated near their feet, injuring a stretcher bearer. Duffee grabbed a stretcher handle and helped carry the wounded man forty yards back to his mortar company as Japanese gunners filled the air with fire.

As night fell, Ray Duffee crawled into a shell hole, hoping to sleep. The fighting eased as it grew dark because the flash of a gun revealed a man's position. A new kind of horror gripped corpsmen in the eerie, black silence. The Japanese began calling for corpsmen in nearly perfect English. Their cries for help tore at American "docs," lying flat in shallow trenches. The Guadalcanal veterans had reminded everyone to ignore pleas that surely had to be phony.

Hunched down in his shell hole, Duffee discovered the knots of fear and tension in his stomach made it impossible to eat. He and others dozed through the night waiting for the expected predawn Japanese counterattack as Betio's land crabs crawled over sleeping soldiers. The attack never came. If it had, the Japanese likely could have pushed the mauled landing force back into the sea. Instead, the bloodletting resumed when gunfire greeted the dawn.

Offshore, amphibious craft filled with a second Marine landing force circled. Communication breakdowns had left a group of Marines outside the reef for twenty-four hours without food or water, waiting for the word to hit the beach. Most were seasick, dehydrated, and angry, as their landing craft finally turned toward shore.

They smelled the death on Betio. The bodies of men killed the day before had bloated and reeked. As they headed toward shore, withering enemy fire ripped them apart. During the night, Japanese snipers had sneaked out onto shipwrecks in the lagoon. The Marines coming ashore effectively had been surrounded before they even reached the beach. Badly coordinated American aircraft that drove toward the beach, attacking the shipwrecks with machine-gun fire, also tore into Marines before the pilots aborted the attack. The Japanese continued to shoot from three sides.

Within minutes, another two hundred dead bodies floated across the coral flat. Only about half of the six-hundred-man landing force made it to shore intact. Even the Marines who had fought months earlier on Guadalcanal had never seen such sudden, wholesale death.

The cries from men slogging through thigh-high water across the reef reached Ray Duffee on the beach. Some were wounded, many exhausted. Either way, without help they soon would die. Unarmed and with his back to the enemy, Duffee left the relative safety of the coconut-log wall. After a few strides, he hit the water and ran toward the bloodied men out in the lagoon. Up, over, and down coral heads, he pushed toward the nearest Marine paled by shock or exhaustion. His every few steps were met with a burst of gunfire. Defenseless, the next burst might boil the water around him or might rip into his back. As his thigh muscles burned, Duffee kept moving toward men out on the reef who had become nearly stationary targets.

"Hold on! Hold on! I'm coming," he yelled to each Marine as he drew close. Gunfire often cut him short. Then, "Come on! Let's go! We can do it!"[32] Duffee yelled as he looped the man's arm over his shoulder and pulled him back to shore, closer to enemy fire. He brought the Marine to other corpsmen hunkered down in the sand. Duffee sucked a couple breaths of salty humid air, turned, then headed back out onto the reef. *No time to treat, others had to do that. Just get those guys out of the water!* Duffee kept telling himself.[33]

The Marines, many of them wounded and lying on the beach, marveled at Duffee's bravery and determination. Many were tethered to a plasma bag that had been attached to the butt of a rifle that was stuck bayonet down into the coral grit. More than a dozen times Duffee dared the enemy as he made his way out across the reef to a Marine, grabbed him around the upper chest, and hauled him back to shore. No time for reflection. *There's another one! Gotta go*, thought the young man who had wanted to be a veterinarian.[34] Torn, bleeding men needed him.

After nearly two days of rescuing and treating wounded Marines, Duffee reported to an aid station, exhausted. He stopped for his first cigarette in more than twenty-four hours. But he shook so badly, he couldn't smoke. He ground the cigarette into the coral before he gathered his gear. He knew his place was back out there with the Marines.

"You! Duffee!" yelled an officer. "Get over to that mortar squad at the wall. They're going to cross over to the other side of the airstrip to the south, cleanin' out those friggin' snipers. Get going!"[35]

As Duffee moved across the airstrip, he spotted a dead Marine's K-rations. A putrid, gassy smell surrounded the bloated body. It was the first and last time Duffee thought of food until the battle ended.

By 1600 hours the second day, the Americans were beginning to gain the upper hand. After thirty-six hours of devastating losses, a landing force had secured the western beach so reinforcements and badly needed supplies could come ashore. A U.S. troop ship finally sailed into the lagoon to take aboard the wounded. Its five-man surgical team treated more than five hundred fifty critically injured men during the next three days, using ether when they ran out of sodium pentothal.

On land, the Marines' noose tightened around the remaining Japanese soldiers. Admiral Shibasaki had been isolated in his bunker. The Navy's bombardment had destroyed his hardwire communications system, eliminating his ability to coordinate Japanese counterattacks. He sent his final message to Japan: "Our weapons have been destroyed and from now on everyone is attempting a final charge. May Japan exist for ten thousand years!"[36]

Meanwhile, the first genuinely positive American report was radioed out to the command ship: "Casualties: many. Percentage dead: unknown. Combat efficiency: we are winning."[37]

By the third day, Ray Duffee was unrecognizable. Black grime mixed with coral dust had caked on his arms, hands, and face. His shoulders hung low from numbing fatigue. He and thousands of Marines had gone without food and very little water because poorly cleaned oil drums contaminated the water they held. While mop-up operations continued at the eastern edge, the battle for Tarawa Atoll had been won as the final elements of Japanese resistance melted on Betio and the surrounding islands. By that point, more than eighty corpsmen had been killed, and nearly three dozen more had been wounded in action.

The worst had passed for the surviving corpsmen. Some were lucky. At one point, a corpsman walked toward a regimental aid station. He flinched as if he had been shot. He reached into his pocket and pulled out a Japanese bullet that had lodged in his pack of cigarettes. It didn't even leave a bruise on the humbled corpsman.

Another found a body next to the pier near where Duffee had landed. The corpsman took a pack of Lucky Strikes, a soaked wallet, ID card, and stamped letter from the body. He risked needless grief because it would confuse his identification if he were killed later. But for many corpsmen, the risk was worth it if they could send something home to a grieving family.

Single gunshots periodically broke the sullen silence that hung over the dead bodies lying on the beach. Japanese survivors committed suicide in their bunkers, wedging their Arisaka 7.7mm rifles against their foreheads and firing them with their big toes. The Japanese had not been trained to improvise. They had expected to repel the Marines at water's edge. When that failed, a lack of communication and an inability to adjust tactics doomed them to the only defeat they could accept: death.

On November 23, the battle for Tarawa ended. It had taken 75 hours and 42 minutes before the 5,000 assault Marines had finally secured Betio and its vital airstrip. The cost staggered the survivors: 990 Marines had lost their lives fighting for 291 acres of coral sand. The Navy identified only 565 of them, and 200 of those were buried at sea. The Navy brought home for burial only one in four Marines killed on Betio. Almost 2,300 had been wounded. Except for 129 Korean laborer prisoners and 17 Japanese prisoners of war, the 4,856-man Japanese force had been wiped out.

Duffee smiled when he received orders to head for the north beach on the way out to a troop transport. He barely noticed the equipment necessary for digging graves for the dead. Nearly six thousand Japanese and American soldiers were buried on Betio in long, sandy trenches backfilled with ground coral. In the brutal tropical heat, many corpses already had exploded from decay. Burial details wore gas masks to keep from gagging in the pockmarked, moon-like landscape.

Once Duffee reached the transport, he went straight to the galley, slathered two pieces of bread with butter and ham, and washed it down with a bowl of coffee. Seconds later, he raced topside to throw up. Once the retching eased, he returned to the galley to try again, slower this time.

On Duffee's way to Hawaii two days later, the galley served Thanksgiving dinner. Men, still pale and shaking, ate in numbed shock. Years later, many couldn't remember that 1943 Thanksgiving Day dinner aboard a ship crowded with wounded men in the rolling Pacific. Once Ray Duffee reached Hawaii, indications that he might be headed back into battle surprised him as he had anticipated reassignment stateside. But a nagging pain suspected to be appendicitis soon erupted into a full-blown ulcer. It became Duffee's ticket back to the United States, back to the Navy hospital in San Diego. He never returned to the Pacific.

A soft breeze rolled up Broadway off San Diego Bay on August 15, 1945. Japan had surrendered. Duffee stood on a balcony of the U. S. Grant Hotel, watching a mass of sailors' white hats floating on a shoulder-to-shoulder sea of dark blue uniforms celebrating VJ Day.

Ray Duffee received the Navy Cross for his heroism on Betio. Embarrassed by the award citation, he didn't remember many of the specifics before it concluded, "By his courage, determination, and untiring devotion to duty, he saved many lives." His award entitled him to a discharge earlier than other corpsmen whose service was being extended. Postwar America still needed corpsmen.

Ray Duffee became a reluctant war hero—another honored corpsman who thought he simply had done his job. Before receiving his discharge, he had sheepishly participated in a vaudeville-style war bond tour by giving speeches in small-town theaters and to large employers throughout Arizona and California. But all he really wanted to do was go home, enroll at a junior college with an eye toward becoming a veterinarian, and get used to the idea of looking forward to tomorrow again.

But Raymond Duffee never became a veterinarian. The twists in his life's path led him to a career as an insurance agent in rural Iowa, where people called each other by their first names on the street and at the country club. Names like Everett, Chuck, and John—solid Midwesterners who looked forward to Pufferbilly Days and were proud of their libraries and city parks. Most didn't know the self-effacing man down the street was a war hero. After the war, many were content to look ahead with resolute confidence and eternal optimism. As one who valued self-reliance, Ray Duffee fit right in.

World War II brought unprecedented advances in wartime disease treatment and management. This included the military's recognition that the troops' health was the responsibility of frontline officers. Training and education became a strategic military priority and no longer the sole province of military doctors as new weapons against disease were developed. Medical supplies and preventive medicine specialists became a priority as well.

The insecticide DDT made its appearance in the latter half of World War II. A Viennese chemistry student had first synthesized the compound in 1874. In 1939, Swiss chemist Paul Müller discovered its remarkably effective insecticidal qualities. By the end of the war, DDT was widely used to rid soldiers and prisoners of war of head and pubic lice as well as to control disease-carrying insects. A vaccine late in the war was an effective new weapon against typhus, a disease that had been the scourge of armies for centuries. A broad spectrum of antibiotics and synthetic alternatives to quinine enabled Duffee and thousands of corpsmen and medics to effectively treat the sick for a wider variety of illnesses than in previous wars.

In World War II, disease deaths amounted to only 40 percent of the 291,000 killed in action. That reflected a remarkable decline from World War I, when disease had killed more men than the enemy. Battlefield survivability increased substantially even as the lethal power of World War II weaponry reached new heights. The race toward survival for many of the wounded soldiers, sailors, and Marines began with an unprecedented fast evacuation off the battlefield, which was only possible through the valor of corpsmen and medics such as Raymond Duffee.

For thousands of soldiers wounded in Europe, survival lay in the hands of equally courageous corpsmen whose families were were incarcerated in American internment camps.

Chapter 6
Mobile Combat Care

● ● ● ● ● ● ●

World War II: Europe

Kenzo and Fuyu Okubo's nine children were in danger. So, too, were many of their friends in Bellingham, Washington. Anger swept across a terrified America in the months following the Japanese attack on Pearl Harbor. Many Americans turned that anger inward. Japanese Americans—whether U.S. citizens or foreign-born—became targets of unprecedented racism in the name of national security. Washington Attorney General Smith Troy openly worried about mob violence and wanted all Japanese Americans moved out of the Pacific Northwest. "The government should initiate instant and drastic orders sweeping all aliens, foreign and native born, so far inland that we can forget about them for the duration [of the war]," opined a *West Seattle Herald* editorial on February 26, 1942.

Thousands of Americans of Japanese descent, called *Nisei*, suddenly faced a future filled with uncertainty and even incarceration. They might lose their homes and businesses. Older children might have to abandon college. Younger siblings, who pledged their allegiance to the American flag every day, could be yanked out of the only neighborhood school they had ever known. Families spread across different communities might be permanently splintered. Americans turned on their own.

President Franklin Delano Roosevelt made their nightmares real. With little opposition, on February 19, 1942, he signed an executive order mandating the relocation of more than one hundred thousand Japanese Americans living in the western United States into ten internment camps scattered from California to Wyoming. They were sent to some of the bleakest, least hospitable places in America.

In early April 1942, eviction-notice posters appeared on telephone poles throughout the Seattle area. Nearly ten thousand Japanese Americans were forced to leave their homes, businesses, and farms on only a few days' notice. When the Okubo family was assigned to Tule Lake, California, Kenzo and Fuyu hoped they would be able to keep their sprawling family together.

One of their sons, James, attended nearby Western Washington University. A lackluster student until he decided to go to college, James was a slight, soft-spoken youngster whose quick smile made him approachable. He had spent summers in high school working with salmon trappers in Alaska to support his family, and he had joined the ski club when he entered college.

Beginning in May 1942, thousands of Japanese-American families passed through the entrance to the Tule Lake internment camp in northern California. Outside the barbed wire, sagebrush stretched forever. Rounded, featureless hills undulated on a hazy horizon that surrounded the dry lakebed chosen as the new home for fifteen thousand Nisei. A small hospital and school separated the camp's administration building from identical rows of hastily constructed wooden structures twenty feet wide and one hundred feet long that contained one-room living units. When the Okubos reached their unit, they found only a few beds and a wooden stove for the entire family. Camp rules prohibited them from cooking their own food, and a howling wind forced them to keep their door closed.

Shortages dictated life in the compound. Students shared textbooks in the makeshift school; taking books home was out of the question. A lack of medical personnel crippled the camp's hospital. A patient died while having a seizure because his epileptic condition had not been noted on his chart. A pregnant woman bled to death because there were no available surgeons. The hospital became a place to avoid.

By the first anniversary of the attack on Pearl Harbor, Tule Lake had schooled the Okubos and thousands of other Japanese-American citizens from California, Hawaii, Oregon, and Washington in the life of inmates. Endless days strung together, filled with constant boredom, menial work, and frustrating waits in lines.

A year of war also had taught the military medical corps that several reorganizations in the two decades following World War I had still failed to prepare them adequately for this war. Blitzkrieg and island warfare battle lines crossed continents and oceans. Hospitals had to become mobile to keep pace with advances and attacks. The stagnant fronts of World War I had become as obsolete as the previous century's shoulder-to-shoulder fighting.

Distance to treatment could not be the yardstick by which the chain of medical care was measured. Instead, time to treatment became paramount in a mobile war that required fleets of ambulances, hospital ships, amphibious field hospitals, and medical trains. Combat medicine's goals were to get critically wounded soldiers to emergency surgery at a clearing station within five hours of being hit and to stage the less serious cases for delayed treatment. This could be as long as eighteen hours later at an evacuation hospital in the rear for those with minor wounds.

The nature of the fighting in World War II, however, posed new challenges to the time-to-treatment standard. Battles on remote islands and deep in jungles made it impossible to establish traditional military hospitals nearby. In early 1942, Army Colonel Percy Carroll developed a new kind of hospital that met the needs of this new kind of war. It contained twenty-five beds with basic equipment, a few surgeons, and a handful of assistants who could relocate quickly and operate in the far reaches of the Philippines, Burma, and New Guinea. They were limited by a lack of equipment for major surgery and bed capacity for postop patients. Many of the young and inexperienced surgeons in the rapidly expanding medical corps could not handle the brutal jungle duty. Regardless, the new hospital represented progress toward the kind of combat care required in the remote settings of World War II. By the end of the war, this hospital model was in use throughout the U.S. Army.

Later in 1942, the Allies launched their first major offensive against Germany in North Africa. America's traditional military hospital system proved inadequate. Hospitals were too far removed from the battlefield, forcing front-line clearing stations to perform surgery within range of the enemy. The military medical corps needed fresh ideas as much as it needed fresh young men to execute them.

America turned to the Japanese Americans it had incarcerated for more than a year. On February 1, 1943, President Roosevelt announced the formation of the 442nd Infantry Regimental Combat Team, composed entirely of soldiers of Japanese heritage. The segregated units would be commanded by white officers.

"No loyal citizen of the United States should be denied the democratic right to exercise the responsibilities of his citizenship, regardless of his ancestry," said the President. "Americanism is not, and never was, a matter of race or ancestry."[38] He made no mention of the one hundred thousand Americans who had been confined without due process for nearly a year already solely because of their race.

More than twelve hundred young Japanese-American men volunteered for the U.S. Army from internment camps. Their draft status as "4-C Enemy Agent" no longer mattered. They joined the more than six thousand Hawaiians who had enlisted and been assigned to the segregated combat regiment. James Okubo was among them. He volunteered on May 20, 1943, just ten days short of his twenty-third birthday. He left for Camp Shelby, Mississippi, a world apart from the Pacific Northwest.

Tarpaper, wet forest undergrowth, moldy plywood, stagnant water, and sweat enveloped the new recruits at Camp Shelby. Nearly everything was foreign to the volunteers, most of whom were away from home for the first time. They faced a diet without rice and cringed when they saw such unfamiliar foods as beef brains, tongue, and liver on the menu. Lunch became a favorite meal: a peanut-butter-and-jelly or bologna sandwich and a piece of fruit.

Forced four-mile marches proved brutal for the smaller Asian Americans who struggled under full combat gear to keep up with their long-legged white officers. Drills in sticky spring mud gave way to summer hikes in suffocating humidity in forests where the shade often harbored snakes. At night, the recruits collapsed on worn cots in drafty barracks with broken windows and leaky roofs. Training deep in the South prepared them for war.

After three years of war, the medical corps had been fully integrated into combat operations, sometimes with disastrous results. In February 1944, during fighting on the Anzio beachhead, German aircraft and artillery pounded military hospitals. Doctors, medics, nurses, and patients alike all had been killed.

In the Normandy invasion on June 6, surgical teams had been aboard gliders that touched down in German territory. More than fifty amphibious landing craft had been modified to become coastline operating rooms for wounded troops. As the Allies pushed inland across northern France toward Germany, field hospital platoons advanced along the front line. Evacuation hospitals of one hundred beds or more were not far behind. Three dozen vehicles could transport the entire facility, though a lack of trucks and supplies sometimes hampered mobility throughout the war.

James Okubo and the rest of the 442nd arrived in Italy on June 10, 1944, and joined the Allied effort to drive the retreating Germans north of the Arno River. After ten weeks of battle, the 442nd boarded transport ships and sailed into Marseilles, France. The combat-hardened regiment had been combined with the similarly segregated 100th Battalion composed of Japanese-American draftees. They formed part of the southern pincer designed to advance northeast from southern France toward Germany. It would be up to each regiment's medical detachment to keep pace with the combat troops as they fought through forests and negotiated mountain ridges. Okubo had been trained as a medic and, as part of the 442nd's medical detachment, was assigned to K Company.

In late September, Okubo, K Company, and the rest of the combat team were hiking deep in the Vosges Mountains, home to dense forests that were often wet and dark even at midday. They navigated with the help of maps provided by the French underground. The 442nd neared its objective, a small pocket of French mountain towns—Bruyeres, Belmont, and Biffontaine—on the doorstep of Germany.

The enemy was prepared for the Americans. German defenders had to stop the Allied advance in the Vosges at all costs. Retreat into Germany was out of the question.

Okubo and the 442nd reached the front lines on October 15. They heard American artillery shelling German defenses in Bruyeres and Biffontaine. The rain and fog that had been near-constant companions since the regiment had arrived in France worsened. Okubo's medical gear never dried. Every infantryman was soaked to the skin. Their foxholes filled with water faster than they could dig. As they pushed through dense stands of timber toward the enemy, Okubo faced widespread trench foot in his company. Left untreated, trench foot led to gangrene and the loss of a leg.

On October 16, after four years of occupation by Waffen-SS troops, Bruyeres was liberated by units of the 442nd. K Company moved through the devastated town that had been hit at least fifteen thousand times by Allied artillery. Okubo and other medics frequently stopped to treat wounded French residents who had somehow survived the Germans and the incessant shelling. As they chased the retreating German soldiers into the Belmont forest toward Biffontaine, enemy positions high on ridges forced K Company to move through heavily mined valleys, where machine gunners waited silently. Once the Americans were exposed, machine guns that fired twelve hundred rounds a minute and were lethal to two thirds of a mile unloaded on them.

Men screamed for a medic as bullets pounded into their shoulders, chests, and thighs. Loaded down with a medical bag on each hip and two canteens on his belt, Okubo crawled from soldier to soldier, ticking off a triage checklist in his mind. His thought process went something like this: *Check his breathing: is it a "sucking" wound? No. Lungs probably okay. At least slow the flow of blood. First, sprinkle sulfa into that gash. Don't worry about it being packed with mud and pine needles for now. Stabilize him. Battle dressing. Give him a quick Syrette of morphine. Good. Tag him and call out for stretcher bearers. The rest will be up to the aid station down the hill. Okay, stay low, and get over to that guy down in the creek bed. Gotta stay low. Ignore that machine gunner. Can't worry about the bouncing betties. Go! Go! Go!*

Nicknamed "bouncing betties," the enemy's s-mines carpeted the forest floor. If a soldier didn't step on the trigger, he might trip a wire strung from the buried mine to a downed tree trunk. When he did, he had half a second to drop to the ground and pray as a charge propelled the mine up to about chest height before it exploded. Small steel rods, scrap metal, and sometimes as many as three hundred sixty ball bearings flew out in every direction. Each could kill a man twenty-five yards away and injure others up to one hundred yards away. A single tripped mine could wound or kill a dozen soldiers.

By October 24, the Nisei liberated Belmont and Biffontaine, but they had paid a horrific price. In eight days of combat, Okubo and the other medics had treated twelve hundred casualties. When all three battalions of the regiment moved into Belmont, the exhausted men, many of them wounded but still on the front line, were sure the troops would be given perhaps a week to rest and patch their wounds. Maybe their anger would subside during that time.

Pushed beyond all expectations, the Nisei began to resent their Caucasian officers. Hills had been taken at a great cost in blood—and then abandoned to the enemy when orders changed unexpectedly. Were the Japanese-American soldiers being sacrificed in a mad drive into Germany? Many Nisei were starting to wonder whether they were more expendable than "American" soldiers.

Yet duty compelled the exhausted troops to follow orders, regardless of how many men they had lost and despite the bleak prospect of success. The rain remained relentless. Trench foot became epidemic as feet grew numb, turned blue or red, and swelled just before blisters burst and open sores ate into exposed flesh.

Not far from the 442nd, the 1st Battalion of the 141st Infantry Regiment blocked the enemy's retreat. Originally composed of men from the Texas National Guard, the battalion had driven six miles into enemy territory, deep into the forest. As night fell, they dug in on a hilltop near a small French town, La Houssière. The next morning disaster struck. The Germans had reinforced during the night and at dawn counterattacked, trapping more than two hundred fifty soldiers. The Americans had used so much ammunition the day before that they were nearly powerless to stop the assault on their position on Hill 351.

James Okubo had only two hours to get his medical gear ready when the alert came at 0200 hours on October 26. His unit wasn't told the mission would be to rescue the "Lost Battalion" that was in serious trouble. The battalion had endured two days of enemy shelling. It had run out of food. Soldiers drank green water filled with algae, which they collected from a pond halfway down the hill. Those who volunteered to fetch the rancid drinking water risked death. German snipers picked off dozens who tried to reach the pond or break through enemy lines. Time was running out.

At 0400, Okubo's K Company moved out into a fog so thick each man gripped the shoulder of the soldier in front of him. When one slipped on the slick muddy trail, ten others often might fall with him. Crusty mud soon caked their uniforms as the forest lightened and German 88mm shells began pounding them. Ahead, enemy machine-gun nests waited to rake across their path. Okubo spent much of the day on his belly in the mud, dragging bleeding men behind tree trunks and patching them up with damp battle dressings. As stretcher bearers carried them back to aid stations, Okubo struggled to keep up with the rest of K Company, which took the brunt of the enemy's attack.

As darkness fell, the rocky forest floor made digging foxholes nearly impossible. Most Nisei looked for the slightest swale in the ground and curled up as best they could for a long, bone-chilling night. A few pine boughs on top of the mud were a bonus. Unseen tanks and heavy armor rumbled through the forest. The enemy reinforced its positions as the mist thickened.

Okubo ached with exhaustion after two days of the relentless German assault. He was barely upright at 0630 on October 28 when the sky brightened with flashes of enemy artillery. The ground exploded as men dove for cover. The enemy had zeroed in on K Company's position. One soldier lost an eye; another lost his hand. Others collapsed when red-hot shrapnel lodged in their spines. Soldiers slowly advancing on thin trails detonated mines buried under leaves and disappeared in a flash of flesh and forest debris.

Even those who ducked behind trees, boulders, or fallen timber suffered attacks from above. Enemy mortar and artillery shells that exploded up in the trees showered the ground with deadly splinters and shards sometimes a foot long. Foxholes became useless in the deluge of wooden shrapnel. Okubo not only faced flesh torn by metal but found men with chunks of wood buried in chests, legs, and bellies.

With each thunderous explosion, Okubo saw more men writhing on the forest floor. As he climbed a hill, the quiet medic spotted a wounded Nisei more than the length of a football field away. Somehow the soldier had gotten well ahead of the slow advance and had fallen, bleeding, only forty yards from the enemy. Okubo immediately started crawling toward the injured man. Machine-gun fire ripped the air just over his head. He ignored blasts that stung his eardrums. The soft ground buzzed with vibrations from enemy machine guns only a few trees away.

It seemed hours had passed before Okubo finally reached the wounded Nisei, who was still alive. He shielded the bleeding soldier with his body, staunching the flow of blood before he turned and dragged the man back to safety as mortar shells exploded around him. Through it all he heard the screams: More Nisei had fallen with broken arms, shredded abdomens, and sliced faces. Okubo crawled back onto the battlefield, treating one soldier after another. He hoped there were enough stretcher bearers behind him to take the wounded out of the German killing zone. Evacuation had to be left to others—evacuation that ultimately could carry a soldier all the way back to America.

James Okubo was the first link in a refined method of battlefield care that had changed significantly during the course of the war. Although the Russians used aircraft to evacuate the wounded as early as 1941, America had no medical air evacuation capability at the start of the war. By 1943, however, the first class of flight nurses had graduated, and they were aboard customized aircraft transporting critically wounded men out of war zones. Airborne medical troops were tested in the Sicily campaign. Medics began parachuting with the 82nd Airborne Division. Hospitals, too, were evolving into a fluid chain of care that extended from a French battlefield to a military hospital stateside.

For the overwhelming majority of men fighting in Europe, medical care began when a medic like Okubo braved enemy fire to get to them. Medics applied immediate triage and called for stretcher bearers to take the wounded to an aid station, typically located about five hundred yards from the heart of the battle. Sometimes the stretcher bearers took the wounded to a waiting jeep on the far side of a ridge; other times they carried the wounded all the way to the aid station, under fire for much of the distance. There, a few doctors and assistants waited. A quick diagnosis was made, field dressings replaced, and, perhaps, plasma or morphine administered. There were no beds. Treatment often took place on dirt that quivered when artillery hit nearby and as the dust of battle hung in the air.

Jeeps took the wounded away from battle to a clearing station, which was a cluster of tents, a commandeered church, or an abandoned home. Clearing stations were manned by surgeons, a few dozen enlisted men, a chaplain, and sometimes a dentist who doubled as an anesthesiologist and surgical assistant. Emergency surgery was performed under primitive, largely unsanitary conditions if critically necessary. Sometimes for the third time on the same day, the wounded soldier faced another trip by ambulance to a field hospital.

The four-hundred-bed field hospital was mobile and could be broken down into one-hundred-bed units. Flexibility was crucial as war moved across Europe, Africa, the Pacific Ocean, and the Far East. The wounded were taken to a receiving tent. It was a surprisingly quiet place. Most patients were in shock. Some mumbled about the moment they were hit. Surgeons knew that about a third of the wounds would be to the chest, a third to the belly, and a third to the extremities. Shrapnel made multiple injuries common and sometimes a mystery until blood-soaked bandages were removed and wounds examined.

Few soldiers remembered the operating tent. Dim lights were reflected onto the patient off white liners on the inside of the canvas tent. Surgeons often operated while standing in mud or worked bare-chested in the jungle. Then the wounded were moved into a postop tent. Inside, floor-mounted poles held bags of plasma or glucose with plastic tubes connected to patients' arms. Drainage tubes snaked out of chests, bellies, and bladders to various containers on the floor.

Further to the rear, evacuation hospitals with seven hundred fifty beds were more permanent installations, often situated near railroads. Medical trains carried the wounded to general hospitals, convalescent hospitals, and sometimes to waiting hospital ships and medical transport aircraft. By 1944, the medical corps ferried the soldier off the battlefield along a route that ended only when he reached the level of care demanded by his wounds.

As the hours passed, men kept falling in a blizzard of shrapnel as the 442nd's advance slowed and then stalled. James Okubo rescued and treated wounded soldiers within a few yards of the enemy. He ignored grenades exploding only a few feet away and somehow escaped whirling shrapnel. Finally, the forest quieted at sunset. While they speculated about the events of the day, the men's banter would fill the air:

"Did you hear what's up?"

"No. What?"

"This is a rescue mission! More than two hundred guys have been surrounded up on Hill 351 for five days. They're outta food and water. Almost no ammo! That's why they're pushing us so hard. As soon as it's light, we're movin' out again."

Word spread from foxhole to foxhole among the Nisei early on the morning of October 29. Some had been surrounded a few weeks earlier near Biffontaine and knew what it was like to face Germans on every side.

In the driving rain, fixed bayonets at the ready, Okubo and the few remaining men of K Company moved straight up the spine of a ridge, directly into the heart of the German position. It was the only path to the surrounded regiment. The frontal assault on the narrow ridge nearly became a suicidal banzai charge as K Company troops fired from the hip at the enemy.

More Nisei soldiers fell. Okubo applied a battle dressing, gave a quick morphine shot, and placed a sulfa tablet in a wounded man's mouth. Sometimes he had to short-circuit his corpsman training. As he raced up to another injured man, a strange gurgling sound told him right away that the soldier had a chest wound. With each breath, the soldier sucked air into his lungs through the open wound. Training called for Okubo to close the edges of the chest wound with safety pins or sew them together with needle and thread, but he had no time for such precision. He placed a sterile dressing into the chest wound, hoping it would restore a semblance of internal pressure.

Eight times that day, Okubo pulled a wounded soldier through the mud and under enemy fire back to safety. Adrenaline fought numbing exhaustion as the mud thickened on his boots, his muscles burned, and the semisweet smell of blood filled his nostrils. Meanwhile, Lieutenant Colonel Alfred Pursall called headquarters for help:

> "We have no officers left in K Company. We are up on the hill but we may get kicked off. There's a roadblock and we're having a lot of casualties … We've lost the K Company command post and have many casualties. How 'bout some infantry help?"[39]

The plea over the battlefield radio sounded shrill against the steady barrage of artillery explosions.

"I can only give you engineers," replied General John Dahlquist.[40] K Company was on its own.

As night descended on October 29, Okubo and the surviving soldiers of K Company dug shallow foxholes, knowing German outposts were within yards of their position. Okubo had treated and rescued twenty-five Nisei soldiers in two days, most of them well in front of the American line of assault. As he dug his foxhole, the forest chill deepened. Exhaustion failed to stem the searing pain that radiated from his elbows and knees, left raw from crawling along the debris-strewn ground to reach his fellow Nisei.

James Okubo awoke to snow flurries, but the weather had no bearing on the advance. With two battalions on their flanks, K Company and the remainder of the 3rd Battalion pushed closer to the enemy. Finally, by late afternoon, the relentless will of the 442nd and 100th overcame the last of the German resistance to liberate the Lost Battalion. The surviving 211 exhausted and starving soldiers of the 141st Regiment stared in disbelief when Nisei soldiers walked up to their position. Voices failed many of the mud-encrusted survivors of the six-day siege. They managed just a thin grin and a nod when their Nisei rescuers offered them cigarettes.

The 442nd had suffered devastating losses. Soldiers and medics had been in constant battle for nearly two weeks. Sometimes they had engaged the enemy in hand-to-hand combat as they advanced uphill against the well-entrenched Germans who held superior, elevated firing positions. Through extraordinary heroism, daring, and a willingness to pay a deadly price for each yard of forest, they had saved the Lost Battalion. Only 78 soldiers of the original 200 in K Company remained able to fight. Of the 2,000 Nisei ordered to rescue the Lost Battalion, nearly 1,000 had been killed—among them were more than a dozen medics—or wounded. Medics had treated more than 800 wounded soldiers in the brutal Vosges Mountains campaign, none more inspirationally than James Okubo.

Yet almost as soon as the Lost Battalion had been rescued, K Company was ordered to move out once more. Morale plummeted, as the Nisei grumbled that white officers pushed them into the teeth of the enemy without adequate rest, supplies, or personnel.

Men trained as engineers were the only replacements available. As they moved up to the front line, many picked up a rifle from a dead Nisei infantryman. Medical provisions also had to be carefully conserved, as the wounded far outstripped available supplies.

Sherman tanks led the infantry's push toward Germany. At one point on November 4, Okubo spotted a smoldering tank only a few yards from the enemy. Again, he ran ahead of the front line—this time seventy-five yards beyond the nearest fire support—dodging small-arms fire as he neared the tank. He heard the moans of a tank crewman inside. As gunfire ricocheted off the tank, he pulled the crewman out and carried him back to the front line before treating his wounds.

Finally, on November 9, fresh combat units relieved Okubo's unit. It had fought since October 15 with only two days' break.

In May 1945, the Nisei gathered to honor James Okubo for his heroism. His commanding officer had recommended the Medal of Honor for the medic who required little supervision, was well liked by the grunts, and repeatedly ran into enemy fire to rescue and treat soldiers who otherwise would have died. But the nomination for the Medal of Honor was stamped "Approved for Silver Star." Maddeningly, someone up the chain of command believed the highest honor "a noncombatant medic" could earn was the Silver Star.

James Okubo received his Silver Star at a memorial service in Novi, Italy, that honored nearly seven hundred dead Nisei and saluted the nearly ten thousand who had been wounded. Three days later Germany surrendered.

The organizational lessons learned in World War I in part had enabled the Army by April 1945 to support its 3 million soldiers in

Europe with 258,000 medical personnel. They represented the largest and fastest expansion of the military medical corps in history. By the close of the war in Europe, the Army had established 318 hospitals whose capacity exceeded 250,000 beds, or one bed for every 12 soldiers.

If World War I was the first mechanized war, World War II was the first massively mobile war. The mobilization of military medical care paid enormous dividends. The full integration of medical personnel into the Normandy invasion enabled 97 percent of the men wounded in the assault to survive. The mobile army surgical hospital, particularly the version developed in the Far East, became the basis for MASH units that would define military medicine in future wars.

The evolution of expedited battlefield care beginning with medics like James Okubo and extending through hospital echelons ultimately enabled 231,000 seriously wounded men to be evacuated by air or hospital ship to the United States. As many as 100,000 per month were transported by air to the care they needed. By 1945, their mortality in flight dropped to only 1.5 per 1,000 patients. General Dwight Eisenhower believed the development of medical evacuation by air ranked alongside the availability of antibiotics, whole blood, and plasma as vital to saving hundreds of thousands of lives in World War II.

The Army's medical detachment treated 2.3 million noncombat casualties and 393,000 battle casualties. Only 12,500 of those wounded soldiers died, resulting in a mortality rate of 3 percent, the lowest ever achieved by the medical corps to that point.

It came at a steep price to the corpsmen, medics, nurses, doctors, and surgeons who served. More than 14,000 casualties were suffered by the medical corps in Europe, of which nearly 12,000 were wounded and 2,700 died. Six medics earned the Medal of Honor, three of them posthumously.

Medic James Okubo and the other Nisei soldiers returned home to hostility and sometimes unconcealed racism that had festered throughout the war. As Japan neared defeat in 1945, Oregon Governor Walter M. Pierce made it clear that some Americans had yet to make peace with neighbors of Japanese descent:

"Their ideals, their racial characteristics, social customs, and their way of life are such that they cannot be assimilated into American communities. They will always remain a people apart, a cause of friction and resentment, and a possible peril to our national safety."[41]

Yet some Americans rose to the defense of the Nisei. "The Nisei bought an awful big hunk of America with their blood," said General Joseph Stilwell:

"You're damn right those Nisei boys have a place in America's heart, now and forever. And I say we soldiers ought to form a pickax club to protect Japanese Americans who fought the war with us. Any time we see a barfly commando picking on these kids or discriminating against them, we ought to bang him over the head with a pickax. I'm willing to be a charter member. We cannot allow a single injustice to be done to the Nisei without defeating the purposes for which we fought."[42]

When James Okubo was discharged in December 1945, he reunited with his family and enrolled at Wayne State University. He married Nobi, a Wayne State student, and upon graduation decided to study dentistry at the University of Detroit. They started a family and had two sons, John and William, and a daughter, Anne. When he received his degree, he joined the faculty at the University of Detroit and established a part time-dental practice. Quiet and industrious, James Okubo struck his colleagues in much the same way as neighbors in Bellingham had seen him: a hard-working young man with a smile that put others at ease.

He rarely mentioned his Silver Star and revealed little about the horrors of the Vosges Mountains.

In the early 1990s, the 442nd Veterans Club, Oahu AJA Veterans Council, and others began campaigning for a review of 442nd and 100th Battalion battle records. In 1996, Hawaii Senator Daniel Akaka sponsored legislation that required a Pentagon review of Japanese-American service records. Approximately sixty thousand Asian Americans had served in World War II, yet only two had received the Medal of Honor. Also, 1.2 million blacks had served in World War II, but none had been awarded the Medal of Honor. However, more than 430 Medals of Honor were awarded to white soldiers. It was clear that American soldiers of color had been denied medals for valor that they had earned.

In 1997, a Senior Army Decorations Board recommended that twenty-one Asian Americans' Distinguished Service Crosses be upgraded to the Medal of Honor. Once federal legislation was passed waiving a time limit in Okubo's case, he was added to the list of Americans who had been denied proper honor. Only seven of the twenty-one were still alive by 2000. James Okubo was not among them. He had died in an auto accident in Detroit in 1967 when he was forty-seven years old.

The haunting notes of Aaron Copland's "Fanfare for the Common Man" swept across the enclosed pavilion outside the White House on June 21, 2000. Seven old men shuffled toward reserved seating under a massive American flag, accompanied by other Japanese Americans. President Bill Clinton and other government officials waited patiently for them.

As James Okubo's award citation was about to be read, his diminutive widow, Nobi, stood before the president. When the reading was completed, he handed her an open wooden box containing James's Medal of Honor.

"They did more than defend America," President Clinton told the audience. "They helped define America at its best ... Rarely has a nation been so well served by a people it has so ill-treated."[43]

In fewer than two years of combat in World War II, the 442nd fought in seven major campaigns and earned seven Presidential Unit Citations. More than 18,100 individual honors were earned by 18,000 men, including 21 Medals of Honor, 42 Distinguished Service Crosses, 588 Silver Stars, more than 4,000 Bronze Stars, and almost 9,500 Purple Hearts. Although some Army units saw desertion rates of 15 percent, there were no reported cases of desertion among the Nisei.

Far away in the Pacific, hundreds of corpsmen found themselves marooned on island atolls where evasion and retreat were impossible.

Chapter 7

Overcoming Shock

● ● ● ● ● ● ●

World War II: Peleliu

The yellow quarter moon slowly rose in a darkening desert sky over ridges dotted with sage and creosote bush as quail and brown birds scratched the baked earth. Tonopah, Nevada, quieted in the early summer night as the yard lights at the Y Service Station cast a humming white glow over the gas pumps.

A few blocks away, three teenagers stood at the cusp of manhood. Hours before, Sammy Petrovich, Bob Warren, and Joe Marquez—the town's entire high school senior class of boys in Tonopah—had graduated at a time when war defined young men's dreams. In June 1943, they faced a simple choice: stay in Tonopah to become a miner, bartender, or grocery store clerk or go to war.

Called the "Three Musketeers" by friends at school, they gathered in a shed behind Sammy Petrovich's house to drink wine, smoke cigarettes, and celebrate their graduation. Sammy typified Tonopah. His Yugoslavian family hailed from a long line of miners, back in the old country and then at a copper mine in Ely and finally in Tonopah. Five-foot-seven Sammy matured early. He affected the hallmarks of miner manhood, smoking cigars and playing poker in the backroom of the Skunk Dive.

Bob Warren loved music. He learned the piano at an early age and soon added the saxophone. Before school each morning, he practiced on his home's screened porch. His notes rode the breeze up the canyon and across town as men headed for the mines. He played in a high school Dixieland band, with Sammy on the trombone.

Joe Marquez lived at the edge of Tonopah. The son of divorced parents, he was raised by his grandparents. His grandfather and uncles worked in the nearby mines. They lived on credit from one silver strike to the next, paying off the old debt with a big paycheck only to begin a new one. Joe worked a succession of jobs starting in the third grade, selling newspapers, working in a laundry, and tending the gas station. Mining was a family heritage. As an eighth grader, he started hitchhiking to Los Angeles to see his father, who became a paraplegic after a mining accident. Before returning to Tonopah, sometimes he gazed out at the Navy ships moored at San Pedro and Long Beach. About six feet tall and whisper thin, Joe overcame his modest early schooling with a natural charisma and innate athletic ability. He was the captain and most valuable player of the school basketball team as well as student body president. Everyone liked and respected the Hispanic kid from the other side of town.

On graduation night, Joe Marquez, Bob Warren, and Sammy Petrovich knew they soon would be drafted, so all three planned to enlist, after spending one last night in Sammy's shed.

"I heard that one out of three guys shipped out overseas gets killed," said Sammy.

"I dunno, that seems a little high," said Joe.

"You sure about that?" Bob asked.

"Well, that's what I heard. So I guess one of us won't be coming back," Sammy replied.[44]

Silence followed as the three teenagers contemplated their futures. They decided to draw straws. Whoever drew the short straw would be the one to get killed in the war, so the other two would know they would survive and return to Tonopah. Each drew a straw. Each took its measure and glanced at the others. All three wondered whether fate would abide by a teenager's game of predicting the future.

Sammy Petrovich decided to enlist in the Marines. Bob Warren opted for the Army. Joe Marquez joined the Navy. When asked for his preferred duty, Marquez first listed yeoman because of business classes he had taken in school. Having worked nights at a gas station earning $40 a week, he made "mechanic" his second choice. His third option was "anything else."

One day as Marquez got into formation on the boot camp's parade ground, an officer walked up. Without explanation, he ended Marquez's boot camp a week early and sent him to corpsman school, fulfilling that third option of "anything else." He didn't know what a corpsman did when he headed up to Balboa Park, a fourteen-hundred-acre oasis at the northeastern edge of downtown San Diego. Some of the park's buildings a few blocks from the nearby Navy hospital had been converted into barracks for corpsmen. Training there would be the first step down a path that might lead to hospital duty, assignment to a ship, or possibly transfer to the Marine Corps.

As Marquez finished his hospital training, a clerk tacked the official list of Marine Corps corpsman assignments on a hallway bulletin board. Marquez found his name halfway down. Visions of combat patrols on beaches and islands with Marine platoons immediately appeared. The first stop would be Camp Elliott, just north of San Diego, where sweaty marches replaced mundane hospital ward duty.

Navy corpsmen became Marines at Camp Elliott, a vast expanse of scrub-covered ridges separated by arroyos filled with Mexican sage, sumac, prickly pear cacti, and rattlesnakes. They learned to crawl through ditches covered with barbed wire as machine-gun fire blasted the air just inches overhead. They were taught how to jump into the water carrying full medical gear and how to survive an oil slick on fire. Corpsmen toughened for battle.

By Thanksgiving 1944, Marquez eagerly anticipated transfer to the war zone. The tide had turned, and the United States had forced Japan into retreat. One morning, an officer announced that Marquez's unit would ship out to the South Pacific. They cheered at the prospect, young men who had left home eighteen months earlier, anxious to make their mark.

The Marines choked on the stench of rotting coconuts on Pavuvu Island. Marquez had been assigned to the 1st Marine Division, a unit famous for the vicious island battles it fought in the march toward Japan. Pavuvu was supposed to be a place to rest, replenish, and train for the next assault on a little-known island called Peleliu.

Peleliu is part of the Palau Islands, a group of 100 islands and atolls 600 miles east of the Philippines and nearly 2,500 miles south of Tokyo. The island is shaped like a lobster's claw, its pincers pointing toward the northeast. About six miles long and only two miles wide, its dense jungles, rock-hard coral ridges, invisible caves, and mangrove swamps made it nearly impenetrable. The Japanese had built a triangular airfield in the southwest corner of the island, not far from a handful of ridges, called the Umurbrogol Mountains, which rose five hundred feet above sea level. Vegetation covered them so completely that they were nearly invisible from the air.

In early 1944, Peleliu became the focal point of a heated debate among America's most senior war planners. General Douglas MacArthur pleaded for the opportunity to fulfill a very public promise to retake the Philippines, which he had evacuated two years earlier. He viewed securing Peleliu's airfield as crucial to protecting his eastern flank. However, Admiral Chester Nimitz pointed out that American forces already had bypassed Peleliu as they advanced from the Gilbert Islands to the Marshalls and on to Guam and Saipan. He argued for a continued advance toward Iwo Jima, Okinawa, and ultimately the Japanese homeland. Should the thrust into Japan come from the southeast, a single island at a time—with no need for taking Peleliu? Or should MacArthur be authorized to lead America's charge up from the south through New Guinea, the Philippines, and then mainland China?

General MacArthur took his case to President Franklin Delano Roosevelt in July 1944. MacArthur prevailed. The 1st Marines received orders to secure Peleliu and its airfield in September to protect the general's flank. For Joe Marquez and thousands of Marines, the road to Peleliu went through Pavuvu.

Everyone hated Pavuvu. Many officers considered it too small for maneuvers and training exercises. Its massive coconut groves had been unharvested since the start of the war. Legions of rats swarmed over the rotting coconut carpet as battled-scarred veterans tried to rest and heal. The stench of rotting coconuts and putrid coconut milk soaked into everything: clothes, food, and the water. Men choked on the stink. Even more despised were the thousands of coconut land crabs that roamed the island at night. The spiny creatures, as large as a man's hand, often climbed into boots, under cots, and among personal belongings. Hordes amassed by the thousands during mating season. Men cringed at the sound of steady crunching under boots and vehicle wheels.

Marquez's first assignment on Pavuvu was the "soak tent," where Marines covered with fungus arrived for treatment. America's warriors had never faced tropical diseases and parasites on such a massive scale as they confronted in World War II. Marquez slathered gallons of calamine lotion on backs, arms, legs, and faces. Sometimes the medical staff applied a potassium permanganate solution to Marines who were so blanketed with fungus that eating and sleeping had become impossible. Fungal infections the Marines called "jungle rot" in armpits and on ankles tormented malnourished soldiers.

The food dampened the Marines' spirits even further. They were fed dehydrated eggs, oatmeal, and Spam, washed down with a fake lemonade concoction they called "battery acid."

Worst of all was Pavuvu's lack of fresh water. Limited water supplies had to be shipped to the island and rationed. The mess hall commanded top priority for the water, followed by sick bay. Personal hygiene depended on stripping and running out into a rain shower, soaping up, and waiting for the next thunderstorm to rinse off.

Preventive medicine was a priority for corpsmen and medics. Marines frequently stood in line for a shot, especially boosters, as they recovered from a jungle bug or built up immunity before their next invasion. In an era before disposable needles, a corpsman sometimes spent hours filing needle points after they dulled with repeated use. On more than one occasion, a corpsman gave a shot, pulled the syringe away, and discovered the well-used needle remained lodged in the Marine's arm.

Once training was completed, crowded transports carried Marquez, other corpsmen, and the massive assault force toward Peleliu. Marquez grew certain that he would be wounded in battle. He didn't know if it would be on Peleliu, but he knew he'd be hurt. "God, don't let me be disfigured," he prayed one night:

"Don't let me be disfigured. If I have to get hurt, maybe an arm or a leg. Maybe if I have to lose something, please let it be a leg. My

dad did okay without his legs. Please, God, if it has to be, let it be my legs."[45]

Men whispered similar prayers as the American armada approached Peleliu.

Three days before their arrival, underwater demolition teams cleared a path across the island's reef. On the surface, five battleships and five heavy cruisers pounded Peleliu. Attack aircraft from three carriers, five light carriers, and eleven escort carriers screamed over the island, blasting it from one end to the other. After two days of uncontested assault, Admiral Jesse Oldendorf claimed he had run out of targets. He called off the bombardment, believing Peleliu had been bombed into easy submission.

He wasn't alone in his belief. General William Rupertus told his Marines to expect a two- or three-day operation, similar to the landing on Tarawa, which had been an intense and bloody but short assault the previous November. Hit the beach fast, move inland on the double, and destroy what was left of the enemy after the pre-invasion bombardment.

On the eve of the invasion, Marquez and other corpsmen reviewed everything they had learned from a handful of weeks in corpsman school.

"What do you do for a sucking chest wound?"

"What's the first thing you do for a gunshot wound?"

"What's the minimal equipment you need to give the wounded plasma? How can you improvise a transfusion to keep a man from going into shock?"[46]

Shock had plagued the medical corps in every war. Civil War doctors had thought that shock and severe hemorrhaging were different conditions. Little had changed by World War I, although by that time military doctors suspected blood loss was a complicating factor for what they called battle shock.

Low blood pressure, cold legs and arms, a fast pulse, and nausea were common early indicators of shock from blood loss and dehydration. Shock was common in men badly wounded, but sometimes it also surfaced after minor wounds. It made a soldier a poor candidate for surgery. The prevailing thinking in World War I had been to first treat shock with rest, warmth, and medication and then to treat the soldier's wounds after he "came out of it."

That posed a conundrum for military doctors. If they waited for a severely wounded soldier to stabilize from shock, he was less likely to survive his wounds. In World War I, the mortality rate for a soldier with nontransportable wounds was 10 percent if he was treated within an hour of being wounded. If doctors waited eight hours to treat him, the mortality rate increased to 75 percent. Shock, simply by delaying definitive treatment, could be as deadly as the most severe battle wounds.

Military doctors knew to treat shock with blood transfusions. They also understood that matching recipient and donor blood types was critical. Austrian physician Karl Landsteiner had developed the classification system of blood types in 1901, but the World War I medical corps was poorly equipped for blood transfusions. The military had a limited ability to reliably preserve, store, and transport perishable blood. In the absence of blood-typing capability near the battlefield, some British doctors in 1916 attempted direct transfusion from healthy soldiers lying next to wounded men. Fifteen out of sixteen wounded soldiers died from receiving incompatible blood. Later in World War I, doctors collected blood between battles and stored it in iceboxes. They gave a wounded soldier a small amount of donated blood, and if he didn't show an adverse reaction after two minutes, they administered the remainder. The inability to administer intravenous fluids and blood on a widespread basis contributed to thousands of wounded men dying from shock and hemorrhaging during World War I.

In the decade preceding World War II, remarkable progress had been achieved in understanding the role and use of blood in war. In 1928, a Russian doctor, Serge Yudin, successfully used cadaver blood for the first time to resuscitate patients. By 1932, he reported more than one hundred successful transfusions of blood that had been stored at least three weeks. By 1936, that figure had ballooned to nearly one thousand.

Then in 1940, an American, Dr. Charles Drew, made blood a viable battlefield weapon against shock. Drew developed a method that separated plasma from whole blood. Plasma is whole blood's liquid component. It contains blood cells, glucose, dissolved proteins, clotting agents, and hormones. Plasma could be dried into a powder for easy transport, storage, reconstitution, and use on the battlefield.

Drew also pioneered methods of reliably preserving, storing, and shipping whole blood. His motivation at the time had been to provide needed blood for Britain in its war against Germany. Drew's Blood Transfusion Betterment Association of New York, with support from the American Red Cross, began soliciting blood donations in August 1940. Within five months, more than fourteen thousand units of blood were donated and more than ten thousand units of plasma were shipped to Britain. The concept of the blood bank had been established.

Military medical personnel were armed with a valuable new weapon. Joe Marquez and other corpsmen and medics on the front line were issued pairs of small tins filled with the plasma powder and distilled water for reconstituting it. But plasma had limitations: it couldn't fully replace all the components of blood a man lost when seriously wounded.

Long before the sun rose at Peleliu on D-Day, September 15, 1944, reveille sounded on the pitching transports. Marquez gathered his gear and balanced it on his back for the climb down the cargo net into a Higgins boat. He had two large medical kits, one attached to each hip. He carried a .45 pistol and two clips of ammo along with a backpack and trenching shovel. As the temperature soared past ninety degrees within two hours of sunrise, the boat's exhaust seemed to settle inside the boat. A thickening blue haze made men woozy as they waited for word to head for shore.

As soon as his amtrac touched sand on the southwestern end of Peleliu, someone yelled "Everybody out!" Marquez rolled out to help another corpsman unload a box of plasma. Within seconds, a mortar shell detonated only yards away. Knocked off balance with a foot injury, Marquez heard "Corpsman!" over the noise of constant explosions. Head down, he limped toward an injured Marine lying on the sand bleeding from the ears, nose, and mouth. Marquez's first casualty neared death, and he didn't know what to do.

"There's nothing you can do for him," said a veteran corpsman who had come up behind Marquez. "Move on!"[47] Marquez returned to his unit without looking back at his first patient. He never saw him again.

As Marquez helped establish a battalion aid station, the Japanese pounded the beach with well-hidden artillery. Again, Marquez heard a weak call, "Corpsman!" He ran to a Marine who had lost his right arm and left leg to a mortar shell. Blood drained from his body.

"Don't do any more for him," the battalion doctor told Marquez. "Just ease his pain." Marquez gave him morphine, hoping it would numb both stumps. In a thick Southern drawl, the Marine asked Marquez to dig a photo out of his wallet and show it to him. Two minutes later, he died, looking at the photo of the infant son he never held in his arms.

A cascade of enemy fire greeted the landing force as it came ashore. One Marine stopped to stare at a buddy whose stomach had been blown away. Only a sliver of skin on either side connected the torso with the man's hips. Not far away, a Marine hunkered behind a jeep, trying to smoke a cigarette even though his upper lip had been torn from his face. Nearby, another jeep disappeared in an explosion. A Marine wounded in the blast watched a corpsman stagger toward him, missing an arm that had been blown away. The corpsman apologized to the Marine, saying he didn't think he could help him. The corpsman then collapsed dead on the sand, as one artillery explosion blurred into the next.

Based on what they had learned from defending islands against earlier American invasions, the Japanese had designed deadly crossfire alleys and pinpoint artillery barrages. The eleven thousand Japanese on Peleliu, under the command of Colonel Kunio Nakagawa, also had adopted a new defensive tactic called *fukakku*. Instead of attacking and fighting to the death at water's edge, Colonel Nakagawa had deployed his troops on the beach's flanks in honeycombed caves and behind natural defenses. The days of wasted defensive Japanese banzai charges had passed. Meanwhile, the Americans had stuck with the same tactic of nearly identical beach assaults that relied on massive pre-invasion bombardment, which usually proved ineffective.

By the end of D-Day, the assault had bogged down. Marines hunkered down for the night, speculating on a Japanese counterattack under the cover of darkness. They stuck their Ka-bar knives into the sand within arm's length, just in case. Veterans from previous campaigns told first-timers not to take their boots off. If the enemy attacked, no one wanted to fight on ground coral in socks.

The next morning, as Marquez gathered his gear at the battalion command post for the hike inland to the front line, a Japanese machine gunner opened fire. Bullets fractured the air as Marines fell on the coral gravel.

"Corpsman!"

"Corpsman!"

"Goddamn it, CORPSMAN!!"

Marquez scrambled to his knees, ready to sprint out to a fallen Marine.

"Don't go," said Bob Lovell, Marquez's tentmate on Pavuvu. "You're with battalion aid. Let the company corpsman handle it."

"I can't," Marquez told Lovell. "I just can't do that. I have a job to do."[48]

Marquez skittered out to the wounded man under friendly covering fire and helped him back to the battalion aid station. Adrenaline, horror, and gore blurred his world just before he threw up. It would be the only time nausea overcame the corpsman. Meanwhile, his patient was transported out to a fully equipped hospital ship offshore.

As the battle on Peleliu stretched into weeks, Marquez's hands and face blackened with oil, grease, and an oily mosquito repellent called "skat." His uniform had paled from the coral dust that covered every fiber that hadn't frayed from crawling on his elbows and knees toward the wounded.

Coral made life miserable for Marquez and his fellow troops. A soldier couldn't dig a hole in rock-hard coral to do his business. Marines gagged at the smell of human excrement. When hunkered down in a foxhole for the night, a soldier was forced to use an empty can, which he simply threw over the side. Burying his waste wasn't worth getting shot.

The stench of death was everywhere. In sweltering humidity, a body bloated and putrefied within hours. As American and Japanese fatalities reached into the thousands, burial became impossible. Grotesque bodies slowly cooked on the coral sand, the smell grabbing at the back of a man's throat.

Blowflies, shiny green creatures, feasted on rotting food, human excrement, and corpses. They grew so bloated they couldn't fly. Marquez and others shook their food to rid it of the flies, taking care that they didn't fall into the drinking water that had been brought in five-gallon cans on a two-wheel trailer. Rust turned the lukewarm water brown.

By early October, enemy resistance remained only in the Umurbrogol Range of coral ridges, a tiny area that measured about four hundred yards wide and nine hundred yards long. The Umurbrogols caught the Marines by surprise. Somehow intelligence officers had concluded that Peleliu was flat. But the Japanese had blasted a honeycomb of connected caves inside sharp ridges that forced naked assaults by handsful of Marines on one cave at a time. Nicknamed the "Pocket," the area controlled by the Japanese was riddled with steep coral ridges. American attack aircraft taking off from Peleliu's airfield didn't have time to retract landing gear before they were over their Umurbrogol bombing targets.

On October 13, Marquez checked his gear carefully before he headed up into the Umurbrogols. He joined a battered unit of thirty men trudging up the coral spine to an elevated covering position, as other units directly assaulted nearby caves. Just before dusk, Marquez encountered a unit that had suffered so many casualties that a first class private had taken charge. Marquez's unit stopped on a barren ridge for the night. In a space a little larger than an average living room, the Marines bedded down, as a handful of sentries stood watch. The coral was so hard that it took hours to chip out a small depression for a man's hips so he could lie on the ground more comfortably.

It must have taken the Japanese infiltrator hours to shimmy up the coral ridge before he got within range of Marquez's exhausted unit. At 0300 hours, he lobbed a grenade into the group of men. It bounced and rolled to a stop on the coral. The dud failed to explode. Panicked, the infiltrator pulled another from his belt, armed it, and threw again. A blinding explosion knocked Marquez on his side and yanked his leg upward. Coughing in the dust, trying to regain his bearings, Marquez thought back to the Marine he had seen on the first day, the soldier missing a leg and an arm. At that instant, the corpsman didn't know if he remained whole. He had neither the time nor the inclination to look.

"I'm hit! I'm hit!" a Marine yelled next to him. Marquez rolled over to him, his bloodied leg useless.

"I'm hit, too," he whispered as he clamped a gritty hand over the young Marine's mouth. "Now calm down. I'll take care of you, but you

115

gotta calm down."[49] A howling soldier became a target for the enemy at night. Silence gave the Americans a chance at surviving the attack.

Other men moaned in the darkness. The grenade had landed in their midst, spraying flying shrapnel and spinning chunks of razor-edged coral in every direction. Marquez couldn't worry about how many Japanese might be within grenade-lobbing range. As he settled the first Marine, Marquez crawled across the coral to another wounded man. It was Ken Bluett, another corpsman. Shrapnel had shredded the side of his chest. Bluett needed plasma.

Plasma wasn't the cure-all for shock that doctors had hoped it would be. In 1942, military doctors had been dismayed at how soldiers wounded in the North Africa invasion had died even after they had been given plasma. It didn't always enable them to withstand anesthesia and surgery. Too many relapsed and died. Regardless, Army Surgeon General Norman Kirk believed whole blood in battle wasn't necessary, that transporting it was impractical, and that plasma was what the wounded required most. But wounded American soldiers continued to die. By 1944, American military doctors concluded that plasma wasn't enough to revive a badly injured soldier. Whole blood was critical to survival in battle. American doctors looked to their British colleagues who were using whole blood to treat shock and to promptly replace massive blood loss.

The Army had established an air transport program to deliver whole blood to the European theater. The Navy sought the same for the Far East, even though the war there was being fought more than seven thousand miles from home. On November 16, 1944, the first refrigerated shipment of one hundred sixty pints of perishable blood left San Francisco. Six days later when it arrived in Leyte—only three days before the end of Marquez's four-month battle on Peleliu—there were no established medical blood teams to receive it. It sat on trucks in the tropical sun, uninsulated. Poor communication and coordination led to its spoilage.

Ultimately, the ability to collect, process, store, transport, and then utilize whole blood and plasma on the battlefield only minutes after being wounded saved thousands of soldiers, sailors, and Marines in World War II. It was one of the great military medical advancements in the war. Of nearly 600,000 Army soldiers wounded in battle, nearly 575,000 survived.

In four years, the American Red Cross collected 13 million units of blood and produced more than 10 million units of dried plasma. Marquez, like most corpsmen in battle, only had plasma at his disposal.

Marquez focused on getting Bluett the plasma he needed. It was so dark that Marquez botched the "stick" when he tried to get the reconstituted plasma into Bluett. His needle had missed Bluett's vein. He crawled over to the company's commanding officer, a man he knew only as "Meatball."

"Sir, can we get a flare? I can't see the men to treat them."

"You're in charge, doc," said Meatball.[50]

Marquez radioed for a flare and under the greenish-white starburst he successfully inserted a needle into Bluett's vein to get the plasma flowing. Ignoring the searing pain from his own damaged leg, Marquez pulled himself to another man, this one bleeding profusely. His hands sticky with the soldier's blood, Marquez yanked a battle dressing package open.

"I'm a corpsman. Can I help you?" said a voice somewhere behind Marquez. Perhaps there was another unit in the area that had come up to provide support.

"Yeah. I've got a lot of wounded here. Go to it," said Marquez, not bothering to turn away from his patient.[51] There were too many injured for niceties.

Marquez dragged himself from one wounded man to another for the next several hours, leaving a smeared bloody trail on the coral. He ignored his right foot, which was full of shrapnel and coral chunks. The quiet returned, broken only by the crunch of Marquez crawling from one casualty to the next.

As the sun rose to warm a cloudless sky, a string of Marines reached Marquez's decimated unit high on the ridge. "You took care of all these men?" asked a corpsman who had arrived with the reinforcements.

"Not just me. Another corpsman showed up last night, and I put him to work," Marquez replied.

"That's impossible," said the corpsman. "There are no other units in the area, no other corpsmen. I don't know who you were talking to, but it wasn't another corpsman."[52]

Confusion spread across Marquez's face. He clearly recalled hearing another corpsman offering help, but when he thought about it, he didn't remember seeing the corpsman treating Marines later. Marquez turned to the unit's lieutenant for orders on whom to evacuate off the ridge.

"You're in charge, doc," said Meatball.

"That's all the stretchers we got," said the corpsman, as twelve stretcher bearers gingerly snaked their way down the ridge with three injured men. Marquez had treated eight injured men through the night. His arm draped over a Marine's shoulder for support and his lower leg wrapped in a bloodied bandage, Marquez walked off the ridge before collapsing at the battalion aid station. He never found the corpsman he thought had helped him through the predawn hours of hell.

Approximately 1,300 Marines died on Peleliu before it was finally secured after 73 days of fighting. More than 5,400 had been wounded. Their numbers paled against Japanese losses. An estimated 11,000 had been killed. Only 19 Japanese and 183 Korean laborers survived.

In 1945, Marquez was awarded the Navy Cross for his valor on Peleliu, but the Navy gave the corpsman little time to reflect on his award. He received orders to report aboard the USS *Mascoma*, a floating gas station that resupplied battle groups at sea.

More than two thousand miles away, on May 12, 1945, shadows lengthened across the deck of the USS *New Mexico* as it steamed toward its night anchorage. A day of fire support for the Marines ashore on

Okinawa was nearly over when Sammy Petrovich began to relax. He had been assigned to a 20mm gun on the twenty-six-year-old battleship. It was grueling duty that had begun almost two months earlier when the *New Mexico* first arrived off Okinawa.

Two enemy aircraft approached the *New Mexico*. When they turned toward the battleship, Petrovich's gun pounded the sky. The aircraft dropped low and straight toward the center of the ship. The kamikazes intended to send the *New Mexico* to the bottom of Hagushi Bay.

In the Philippines, Bob Warren "shot" patients. An X-ray technician in the Air Force, he had been training to become a pilot when he learned that the military needed medical personnel more than it needed aviators.

Petrovich, Warren, and Marquez tried to keep in touch with each other after enlistment, but wartime letters were sporadic and slow at best. News of a buddy's exploits was always out of date. They each knew one was a corpsman, another a gunner assigned to a battleship gun tub, and the third an X-ray technician, all in the Pacific theater.

On September 2, three months after the *New Mexico* had survived the kamikaze attack, Joe Marquez sailed into Tokyo Bay for the formal Japan surrender ceremony. As the USS *Mascoma* prepared to refuel the USS *New Mexico*, Marquez yelled across the rail to a group of sailors standing on a catwalk.

"You guys know a guy named Sammy Petrovich? He was on the *New Mexico* a while back," hollered Marquez.

"Sure do," answered one, who then told Marquez about Petrovich's duty on the battleship, the marathon assault to take Okinawa, and how it had returned to action after battling the kamikazes.[53]

The bus slowed as it climbed into Nevada's San Antonio Mountains. The world had known peace for only a few months when Joe Marquez returned home in late 1945. Brakes squealed as the bus slowed to a stop at the Tonopah bus station. No one had come to greet the war hero.

Young men who had left hometowns as boys returned home every day on nearly every bus. Marquez pulled his duffle bag from the luggage compartment and started walking toward his grandparents' house.

A week later, Marquez returned to the bus station to greet one of his high school buddies. There was so much to talk about. It had been more than two years since they had been together, drinking and drawing straws on graduation night. When the bus door swung open, Bob Warren stepped out into the sunlight. Marquez started toward him. He stopped when Warren raised a hand, his faced clouded.

"Don't ever speak of that night again," said Warren.

Awkward small talk briefly broke the silence before each turned for a solitary walk home.

Sammy Petrovich never joined them. The two kamikazes had crippled the USS *New Mexico* four months earlier. One had crashed into it amidships. A massive explosion had instantly killed more than fifty men, including Sammy Petrovich, the suave Yugoslavian who had drawn the short straw two years earlier.

Shock wasn't the only enemy on the battlefield. Only a few months following Peleliu, four heroic corpsmen confronted unspeakable conditions on a tiny island called Iwo Jima. Corpsmen would treat the searing physical wounds of battlefield burns and an invisible enemy so entrenched that he was within killing range of nearly every man on the island.

Chapter 8

Battle Burns

● ● ● ● ● ● ●

World War II: Iwo Jima

The old man could barely walk. He shuffled on stick-thin legs onto the cavernous hangar deck of the USS *Midway* aircraft carrier in San Diego in the summer of 2006. He immediately noticed the carrier's "breath," a mixture of hydraulic fluid, oil, grease, and fuel. It is a smell unique to U.S. Navy ships. After forty-seven years of active service, the longest of any U.S. aircraft carrier in the twentieth century, the USS *Midway*—now a museum—was no different. More than 200,000 *Midway* sailors had inhaled the same smell.

It carried George Wahlen back to another life. To a time when he tried to ignore that very smell, compounded with sweat, body odor, and vomit as his ship approached a stark, little-known island called Iwo Jima. Although the *Midway* was docked at San Diego's Navy Pier,

Wahlen remembered the rhythmic swells and troughs of the Pacific. It seemed unnatural to be aboard a Navy ship and hear the sounds of families instead of men cleaning and snapping their weapons back together again.

Wahlen was only twenty years old in 1944 when American forces were pushing the Japanese back toward their homeland, one island at a time. After the United States had secured air bases in the Mariana Islands, American B-29s began bombing Japan. But the bombing run was a long, three-thousand-mile roundtrip, and the Japanese had installed a large radar station on Iwo Jima, a small, eight-square-mile island about four hundred fifty miles from the mainland. Radar detection of incoming American aircraft provided Japan with two hours' advance warning. The Japanese sent fighter planes from Iwo Jima's two airfields to confront the American attackers. Intelligence reports revealed Japanese engineers were building a third airfield on the island to increase its defensive capability.

Capturing Iwo Jima offered several strategic advantages: American fighters based there could escort the heavy bombers to Japan. The island also could serve as an emergency landing area for B-29s too badly damaged to make it back to the Marianas. And driving the Japanese off their own territory would deal Japan a powerful psychological blow.

American aircraft took thousands of air reconnaissance photos of Iwo Jima, revealing a barren outcrop of volcanic ash and sand. Shaped like an upside-down pear, the rocky island was anchored at the southern end by Mt. Suribachi, which provided multiple lines of defensive fire on the beaches below. Officers reviewed the lessons from the overwhelming losses they had sustained earlier on Tarawa and other Pacific islands. The assault on Iwo Jima would require a seventy-thousand-man invasion force to pry an estimated twelve thousand Japanese defenders out of bunkers and pillboxes. American invasion planners anticipated a casualty rate as high as 5 percent in the first few days on Iwo Jima's exposed beaches. Corpsmen, aid stations, division hospitals, and offshore hospital ships would play a key role in the invasion.

Some of the young men reporting to field medical training camps in North Carolina and California would be assigned to the Marines destined for Iwo Jima. They began training alongside Marine riflemen and grenade launchers, flamethrowers and snipers, without knowing they'd be fighting an invisible and vastly underestimated enemy. George Wahlen was among them. The slightly-built hospital corpsman with a long, thin face and narrow shoulders had volunteered for duty with the Marines after discovering he hated the routine of hospital duty after he had become a Navy corpsman.

Born in 1924 in Fairmont, Utah, a place of hardscrabble farms west of Ogden, Wahlen belonged to a family that struggled to make ends meet. They lived on land owned by his mother's parents, and when the Depression struck, they moved to property that belonged to his father's grandparents. Wahlen hunted night crawlers after dark and sold them by day to help with family expenses.

A month before the attack on Pearl Harbor in 1941, Wahlen had convinced his father to allow him to drop out of high school to attend a private aviation mechanics school. When he graduated in 1942, he enlisted in the Navy, confident he would be working on Navy aircraft. But the Navy sent him to corpsman school. On December 10, 1943, he reported to Camp Elliott about ten miles northeast of downtown San Diego. There, Wahlen met a quiet young man with a quick smile and a broad, open face. John Harlan Willis had grown up in Columbia, Tennessee. As a youngster, Willis had lived with his grandparents and was the most popular newsboy for the local *Democrat* newspaper. The oldest of nine children, he also worked in local grocery stores and helped with barnyard chores to support his large family. A man of faith, he often practiced preaching to his friends while standing on a tree stump. His favorite prayer was "Oh, God, give us those things which you think we ought to have." Willis arrived at Camp Elliott the day after Thanksgiving in 1943. He wrote letters to his hometown sweetheart, Winfrey Morel, and considered getting married before shipping out to the Pacific.

On January 31, 1944, another young corpsman arrived at Camp Elliott. Born in Harrison, Arkansas, Jack Williams was raised in the Ozark Mountains. The son of a blacksmith, he tended the family's chickens on a small, rented farm. He hauled water from a nearby spring to a farmhouse that lacked indoor plumbing. He liked to play marbles, and he stashed money he earned from odd jobs in a violin case after he had abandoned music lessons. The country boy with narrow eyes and crooked teeth enlisted in the Naval Reserve. Six months later, he completed basic and corpsman training. He had been promoted to hospital apprentice first class when he began training with the Marines at Camp Elliott.

When Jack Williams transferred to the Marines' 5th Division headquartered at Camp Pendleton just north of San Diego on April 1, 1944, he joined George Wahlen and John Willis, who had arrived two days apart in early February. The 5th Division was new, established for a Pacific campaign shrouded in secrecy.

The Marines' 4th Division had left Camp Pendleton six weeks earlier, on January 13. Francis J. Pierce was one of the corpsmen assigned to the division. He had volunteered the day he turned seventeen, a week after the Japanese attacked Pearl Harbor. A native of Earlville, Iowa, he was an avid hunter. When he trained with the Marines at Camp Pendleton, he became so proficient at firing a submachine gun that the Marines nicknamed him "Angel with a Tommy Gun."

More than two dozen troop transport ships left Pearl Harbor on January 27, 1945, carrying twenty thousand Marines. Nervous boredom preceded battle at an unannounced destination. Some men did calisthenics on deck to kill time. Others repeatedly took apart and reassembled their weapons.

Meal time was good for standing in line, wasting at least an hour before being served. Young men facing the uncertain prospect of killing and being killed were crammed in transports that reeked of fear.

In late January, senior medical officers called their corpsmen together. They pulled tarps off models and unfurled maps. Few knew anything about Iwo Jima. The officers knew the island was in the midst of an unprecedented seventy-day pre-invasion bombardment. No one dared repeat the pre-invasion mistakes made on Tarawa when the gunfire from poorly positioned ships had skipped off the island's interior harmlessly before detonating in the lagoon.

"I could not forget the sight of Marines floating in the lagoon or lying on the beaches at Tarawa, men who died assaulting defenses which should have been taken out by naval gunfire," wrote General Holland Smith, commander of the Marines' amphibious forces in the Pacific.[54]

The marathon bombardment of Iwo Jima concluded with a massive, three-day pounding delivered by Navy battleships as the final prelude to the landing on February 19. Ship loudspeakers blared updates:

"Hear this, now hear this. Before landing, intensive air strikes and surface bombardment will smash this tiny island with nine thousand tons of steel. To date, no other island target has been so favored. The enemy will be so demoralized that it will be an easy task to secure the island in three days or less. Then we'll reboard our transports and proceed to Okinawa."

One of Japan's top admirals, Tadamichi Kuribayashi, had been ordered to repel the American assault force. He had amassed nearly twenty-three thousand troops, almost as many as had defended Saipan, which was nine times larger than Iwo Jima. He had devised one of the most ingenious defensive positions in modern warfare. Working through the night to avoid American photo reconnaissance planes, his troops had dug more than fifteen miles of tunnels that connected approximately fifteen hundred gun emplacements, concrete pillboxes, and observation posts. He had made it clear to his island's defenders that they were expected to die, but not before each killed at least ten American soldiers. Tactically, suicidal banzai charges would not be employed. His troops had been trained to allow the Americans to land and concentrate their forces on the beach before showering them with rockets, mortars, and bombs.

On February 19, thousands of Americans were positioned to come ashore from the southeast. Their goal was to cut off the five hundred fifty-foot Mt. Suribachi from the rest of the island, secure the high ground, then move north to force the Japanese defenders into the sea.

John Willis, Jack Williams, and George Wahlen had been assigned to different regiments in the 5th Division that would be making the initial assault. Wahlen's unit would be held in reserve, but that only meant he would go ashore in an assault wave following the initial invasion. Corpsmen checked their gear one last time in the final pre-invasion hours. They carried a pouch over each shoulder. The bag on the left held sulfa powder, burn dressings, and battle dressings. The pouch on the right contained morphine syringes, iodine pencils, tags, ammonia, scalpels, and hemostats. The pouches marked corpsmen as a priority target for the enemy.

Dozens of landing craft that had been circling offshore in the last hours of the final bombardment turned toward Iwo Jima at 0900 hours. It was eerily quiet as the assault force reached the beach. Ramps were lowered, and thousands of Marines gathered ashore, ready to move inland. But the jet-black volcanic sand mixed with volcanic ash had the consistency of wet coffee grounds. Soldiers sank to their ankles. Jeeps, ambulances, trucks, and artillery equipment disappeared up to their axles. Men and machines were stuck in the muck when, suddenly, thousands of rounds of artillery, rockets, and mortars began blasting the surf and pulverizing the beach. Screams rent the air.

Two terraces, one hundred and two hundred yards inland, from five to ten feet high, made progress almost impossible after the Marines had pulled themselves out of the muck. Casualties mounted as enemy artillery found clumps of soldiers huddled in craters for protection. Just as had happened on Tarawa and Peleliu, the pre-invasion bombardment had failed. Instead, it had alerted a well-entrenched enemy to their approach.

The Marines kept coming ashore. Corpsmen crab-ran from one casualty to the next in the surf and across the narrow beach. Four battalions landed in the first hour of the assault. Although that would provide substantial firepower if the force could somehow get inland, it also exposed to the enemy a large mass of soldiers crouching nearly shoulder to shoulder on the beach. Some were out in the open for more than an hour as Japanese gunfire raked across the shoreline. Shredded corpses floated among discarded packs, crates, body parts, and wrecked equipment.

Many Marines had covered their faces with a white cream to guard against burns as they waded ashore. They had expected the Japanese to detonate submerged drums filled with gasoline. Several were defenseless when a Japanese mortar found a pile of artillery shells on the beach. The flash burns seared skin instantly.

A generation earlier, explosive weaponry in World War I had produced burn wounds the likes of which had not been seen in earlier wars. Military doctors used bicarbonate of soda dressings on the burns, a treatment that had changed little from the previous century. There was scarce understanding of how the body reacted to a severe burn.

Frank Pell Underhill was a chemical warfare specialist in World War I. He discovered that the sticky liquid that leaks into a severe burn site is similar to the plasma in blood. Burns that weep copiously rob the body of critical fluid. If left unchecked, blood cells become concentrated and out of balance. Cells cease functioning properly, which leads to shock. Underhill realized that promptly restoring fluid to the burned soldier to ward off shock before multiple organ failure was as important as treating the burn wound.

Following World War I, researchers sought treatments for burns that were more effective than soda-based dressings, salt solutions, and honey. A hospital intern in Detroit, Edward Davidson, developed a tannic acid treatment that covered raw nerves and eased searing pain. It also enhanced the healing process. When Britain went to war in 1939, the medical corps scrubbed burns with sodium bicarbonate, rubbed them with bleaching powder, and then applied tannic acid compresses for two to three weeks. Tannic acid, however, often permanently puckered the wound site. For example, badly burned hands that had healed were left permanently half-clenched.

By mid-1941, Dr. Robert Aldrich had created a new antiseptic coagulant called triple dye that reduced infection, a frequent complication of burns. Aldrich believed that a wounded soldier should be treated for shock for the first seventy-two hours and then receive three sprays of aniline dyes that reduced pain, killed bacteria, and allowed new skin growth with less puckering than that caused by tannic acid.

The American military medical corps had both tannic acid and triple dyes to treat victims of the attack on Pearl Harbor, half of whom had been burned, but they were not satisfied with either treatment. Shortly after Pearl Harbor, physicians began spraying on burns a wax film composed of paraffin, sulfanilamide, and cod-liver oil. The wax covered raw nerves to ease patient pain, allowed wound inspection, and could be applied quickly in mass casualty situations. It could be washed off daily, reapplied, and did not require a dressing. The treatment eliminated the need to clean a burn site.

If the corpsmen on Iwo Jima could stabilize the badly burned so that they could be evacuated to the hospital ships offshore and to Navy hospitals in Guam and Saipan, they stood a far better chance of survival than their counterparts in World War I.

Caspar Wistar and most physician's assistants in the Revolutionary War were volunteers with little or no medical training. Some became doctors after the war in an era when there were no physician licensing standards. *(University of Pennsylvania Archives)*

Men wounded at Fredericksburg lie under a tree, waiting for medical treatment in a country estate that had been commandeered by Union troops and converted into a makeshift hospital on the eve of battle. Unprecedented Civil War casualties often overwhelmed army medical departments. *(National Archives)*

A great deal of medical care took place outside during the Civil War. Scores of wounded men lying under trees and huddled along creek beds were a common sight following a battle. *(National Archives)*

As medical director of the Army of the Potomac, Dr. Jonathan Letterman's creation of military medicine's first dedicated ambulance corps such as this was one of the Civil War's most profound medical advances. *(National Archives)*

An exhausted corpsman on Saipan checks a wounded soldier. A corpsman's work doesn't end when the fighting stops. For many corpsmen, surgeons, and nurses, the most intense work comes once the battlefield becomes quiet and hundreds of wounded need attention. *(USMC)*

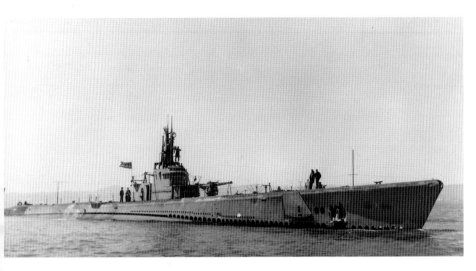

Crews in World War II submarines such as the USS *Seadragon* made extensive deployments into combat without a doctor aboard. They typically relied on a single corpsman for all types of routine and emergency medical care. *(U.S. Navy, Bureau of Medicine & Surgery Archives, Wheeler Lipes Collection)*

Darrell Rector (left) showed off his appendectomy scar after Wheeler Lipes (right) performed the first emergency appendectomy by a corpsman aboard a submarine in World War II. *(U.S. Navy, Bureau of Medicine & Surgery Archives, Wheeler Lipes Collection)*

Corpsmen on Tarawa treated thousands of wounded Marines while exposed to enemy fire after the U.S. Navy's pre-invasion bombardment stripped the atoll of nearly all vegetation. *(USMC)*

Tarawa's narrow strip of sand along the lagoon became clogged with hundreds of wounded Marines who were treated by corpsmen prior to evacuation by amphibious landing craft. *(USMC)*

Corpsmen were exposed to enemy fire when they dragged wounded Marines over a coconut-log wall near the water's edge on Tarawa that provided their only protection. The Marines' invasion force was pinned down on the narrow beach after enduring brutal enemy fire as they crossed the lagoon in exposed landing craft. *(Ray Duffee Collection)*

War heroes like Ray Duffee often were pulled off the battlefield to make speeches at home, urging civilians to buy war bonds to support the war effort. *(Ray Duffee Collection)*

In World War I, the medical corps became fully integrated with the front line troops. They provided prompt care that stabilized thousands of badly wounded patients so they could be transported by ambulance and rail to field and evacuation hospitals in rear areas. *(National Archives)*

Marines paid a steep price in World War II's Pacific island assaults. Many amphibious landings resulted in so many wounded Marines that some had to wait more than a day until an amphibious landing craft was available to evacuate them to hospital ships offshore. *(USMC)*

Makeshift aid stations sometimes were established in river beds, abandoned vehicles, or behind natural cover. *(U.S. Army)*

Thousands of Japanese Americans were sent to internment camps in the months following the Pearl Harbor attack. Later, many volunteered for a segregated Japanese-American army battalion that became one of the most decorated units in World War II. *(U.S. Army)*

Medic James Okubo was one of twenty-two Asian Americans who were awarded the nation's highest award for valor, the Medal of Honor, more than fifty-five years after the end of World War II. Okubo's award was posthumous. He had died in an auto accident more than thirty years earlier. *(U.S. Army)*

Few planned to become heroes when they enlisted. Most, like Joe Marquez, felt an obligation to serve their country and leave their childhood home behind as they stood at the edge of adulthood. *(Joe Marquez)*

Barren coral ridges, called the Umurbrogols, on Peleliu were honeycombed with caves used by Japanese snipers to ambush exposed American troops and medical personnel. *(USMC)*

A corpsman on Iwo Jima shook an injured man's hand. A soldier wounded in battle rarely had the opportunity to thank the corpsman or medic who may have saved his life on the battlefield. *(USMC)*

Left: John Willis was one of four corpsmen who earned the Medal of Honor on Iwo Jima. Fourteen Medals of Honor were awarded for valor during the thirty-six-day battle, the most for any single engagement in World War II. *(U.S. Navy, Bureau of Medicine & Surgery Archives)*

Right: Corpsman Jack Williams was shot three times in the belly and groin while treating a wounded soldier on Iwo Jima. He treated his own wounds before crawling under enemy fire to another wounded soldier. Williams tended to that soldier's wounds as well, before an enemy sniper killed Williams. *(U.S. Navy, Bureau of Medicine & Surgery Archives)*

By afternoon of the first day, the Americans had advanced a few hundred yards inland. Some regiments suffered a 33 percent casualty rate that day, far more than the invasion planners had predicted for the entire campaign.

Corpsmen raced from one wounded soldier to the next, first checking for life and then assessing medical condition. The top priority was the sucking chest wound. Without immediate medical care on the battlefield, a man could drown in his own blood if a bullet or red-hot piece of shrapnel had punctured his lungs. A corpsman had to jam a battle dressing into the wound to seal it from the outside and give the soldier a shot of morphine. Then he wrote a large "M" on the soldier's forehead with an iodine pencil so medical personnel at the battalion aid station would know the wounded man had been given morphine. Next the corpsman filled out a tag with as much information as he could read from the soldier's dog tags and tied it to the soldier's uniform. Then he called for a stretcher team and moved on to the next injured man. A wounded soldier's fate sometimes was determined by a corpsman who spent perhaps two minutes with him.

Stretcher teams didn't always arrive immediately to take a patient to the rear. Usually, the least experienced privates were assigned as stretcher bearers. Sometimes they drew straws to determine who had to head up to the front line, knowing they would be easy targets for Japanese snipers. Hearing "*pffftt, pffftt*" as they ran was a good sign: snipers' bullets were missing them.

The following morning, the sun rose over the carnage. The beach had become a junkyard of twisted cranes, abandoned equipment, and overturned tanks. Scattered among the wreckage were bodies that had been half-buried in the black sand by the incoming tide.

That day and for many thereafter, the Marines measured their progress in feet. Some of the thousands of caves and dugouts concealed fifty-five-gallon drums (called "spider holes") with Japanese snipers hiding in them, bent on suicidal sneak attacks from behind as the Americans pushed forward.

After a week of intense warfare, the 5th Division had crossed Iwo Jima to the western shore and had turned northward toward three hills with the same elevation, designated 362A, 362B, and 362C. They had made tedious headway along paths through minefields that engineers marked with tape and white streamers.

On February 26, George Wahlen accompanied his platoon as it moved out across a small, open plateau. Once the platoon became fully exposed, the skies rained mortar fire. The ground trembled under the Marines' feet. In seconds, Wahlen heard cries from men up ahead. The corpsman crawled to a writhing Marine whose thigh pumped blood down his shin. After treating him, he tended another soldier whose leg had disappeared in an explosion. Wahlen applied a tourniquet to keep him from bleeding to death. Then he crawled to the next Marine a few feet away as enemy fire continued to hail down on them. Shrapnel had torn into the rifleman's body. Wahlen cleared sand from the raw flesh, applied a battle dressing, and moved on. Then Wahlen found Eddie Monjaras, a corpsman whose chest and stomach had been ripped open. Wahlen stopped the bleeding, gave him a shot of morphine, and left him for the stretcher bearers.

Only a half hour had passed since the barrage had started. During that time, Wahlen treated at least fourteen badly wounded Marines under relentless enemy bombardment. Exhausted, he finally inched his way out of the death zone. Moments later, the shattered platoon moved off the plateau toward its objective: Hill 362A. As shell-shocked Marines crept toward the hill, a grenade landed in the sand a few yards from Wahlen. Before he had time to react, shrapnel ripped into his face, blinding his right eye. Lying on the ground, Wahlen bandaged his own oozing facial wound. Then he crawled more than twenty yards under enemy fire to another injured Marine. Three more grenades exploded in rapid succession. They seemed to follow Wahlen as he treated one soldier after another. Shrapnel burrowed into his buttocks and legs. Soaked in sand-caked blood, Wahlen attended to Marines for an hour until he depleted his two pouches of medical supplies.

When another corpsman refused to make the dangerous run back to the command post for supplies, Wahlen volunteered. He refused treatment. He hauled the provisions back up to the remaining Marines in his platoon on the front line. By the time the sun set on the eighth day of the assault, George Wahlen had treated nearly half his platoon's casualties, had been wounded repeatedly, and yet stood his watch that night. His Marine division had gained only three hundred yards. The Japanese still held Hill 362A.

Two days later, the enemy remained on high ground. Rocky outcrops blocked every approach to Hill 362A. As dawn broke on February 28, American artillery, rockets, and carrier-based aircraft pounded the Japanese positions on the hill. At 0815, the Marines launched another assault.

Corpsman John Willis quickly had his hands full. Marines fell as they advanced across a two-hundred-yard stretch of sand at the base of the enemy stronghold. They were met with a fusillade of small-arms fire and incoming grenades. Willis ran from one crater to the next, patching wounded soldiers. Shrapnel hit him, so the corpsman retreated to an aid station. After receiving treatment, he ran back to his platoon, which was engaged in hand-to-hand combat with nearly one hundred Japanese who had launched a late-afternoon counterattack.

As he administered plasma to a wounded Marine, a grenade dropped onto the sand next to Willis. He lobbed it back toward the enemy. Then a second grenade landed, followed by a third, a fourth, and a fifth. Corpsman Willis picked up eight Japanese grenades and threw each out of the crater, protecting the two men he was treating. The ninth grenade detonated in his hand. The youngster from Tennessee and the two Marines he had fought to save died instantly.

It seemed nearly every Marine in the battle knew what Willis had done. They spread the word as they fought both exhaustion and the enemy. When night fell, the Americans remained at the base of Hill 362A. The brutal battle had produced a gain of only three hundred yards.

On March 2, after twelve days of fighting, the Marines finally took Hill 362A and controlled two thirds of Iwo Jima. That night, more than fifty Japanese sneaked behind American lines to take back the high ground. They nearly succeeded—as the combatants fought face-to-face with sabers, knives, pistols, grenades, and explosive satchels, some filled with picric acid.

In less than two weeks of battle, more than three thousand men died on Iwo Jima. More than twelve thousand were wounded. Casualties were five times more than those suffered by the Marines on Tarawa. But the battle was not over.

The exhausted Marines received new orders to assault Hill 362B about a mile away—elevated land gutted with enemy tunnels, dugouts, and foxholes—but first they had to cross a minefield. Jack Williams's regiment would strike from the western beaches but had to traverse rippled ridges and winding gorges filled with the enemy and booby traps.

On March 3, at 0745, Marines climbed out of their foxholes and advanced. By now they knew what to expect. The sudden downpour of artillery, rockets, and grenades no longer surprised them. As Williams treated one wounded soldier, he heard the cry of another lying in enemy territory and ran to him. He grabbed the Marine under his shoulders and pulled him into a pan depression in the sand. With his body, Williams shielded the injured man from enemy snipers. A millisecond later, three enemy rounds ripped into the corpsman's groin and belly. As blackish-red abdominal blood spread through his uniform, Williams finished treating his patient while the gunfire continued.

Waves of pain rolled through him as he patched his own belly and staunched the river of blood flowing from his groin. Once his bleeding had slowed, Williams crawled toward another hurt Marine. After dressing his second patient's wounds and giving him a shot of morphine, Williams crawled toward the rear for help. But a sniper's aim found Jack Williams. The youngster who had once dreamed of owning a farm died a short time later.

George Wahlen's shoulder ached. Part of it had been blasted away the day before. Wahlen had refused first aid despite some momentary paralysis. Instead, he had instructed a Marine how to clean the ash-filled sand out of his raw flesh and then apply a battle dressing.

Furious fighting marked their agonizing advance toward the hill. Nearly invisible caves erupted with sniper fire at exposed Marines. Wahlen's company had advanced another three hundred yards after five hours and consolidated with other units for the major assault up the hill late in the afternoon.

As they pushed forward, Wahlen heard screams for help. Three wounded Marines huddled together in the bottom of a crater. At first, Wahlen couldn't see them through clouds of exploding sand and the smoke of detonating ordnance. As the Marines yelled directions to Wahlen, an explosion cut them off mid-word. An enemy artillery shell had found them.

Wahlen peered over the lip of the crater. One Marine had dissolved into a splattered mass of tissue, organs, and bone fragments. The other two had lost arms and legs. When Wahlen stood to scramble down into the crater, his legs buckled, pitching him into the hole. Part of his right foot had been torn away by a sniper's bullet. Ignoring his wound, he cinched a tourniquet at the base of one of the Marine's stumps. It was only when other corpsmen arrived and took the surviving Marines to an aid station that Wahlen treated his own wound. Once alone again, he heard the cry of another wounded man. Even though Wahlen had given himself a shot of morphine, he climbed out of the crater and crawled nearly fifty yards under enemy fire toward the injured soldier. Both of the

Marine's legs were broken. Wahlen pulled him into a crater and stayed with him until others arrived to evacuate them both.

The most seriously wounded on Iwo Jima would require treatment hundreds of miles away at permanent military hospitals. On the same day that Wahlen and others were wounded, a new type of military medicine specialist arrived in the Far East: nurses and corpsmen trained specifically for aeromedical evacuation.

On March 3, Jane Kendeigh became the first flight nurse to land on a battlefield when her plane touched down on a captured Iwo Jima airstrip. In early 1945, the Navy graduated its first class of flight nurses after training them to treat patients at high altitude. These nurses could swim a mile, tow or push a victim two hundred yards in the water, and swim four hundred forty yards in less than ten minutes. Kendeigh landed under enemy mortar fire aboard a Douglas C-47 Skytrain aircraft, filled its twenty-four litters with gravely wounded men, and took off on a fifteen-hour flight to a medical facility in Guam.

Two years earlier, the Army also had begun using flight nurses to evacuate badly wounded soldiers during the Tunisian campaign in Africa. The nurses had been trained in ocean, jungle, and desert survival. They cared for the seriously injured aboard C-46 aircraft, nicknamed "flying coffins" for the tragic tendency of faulty heaters to explode.

Medical evacuation by air shortened the time it took to deliver a gravely wounded soldier to sophisticated medical care. Trained inflight medical specialists augmented a military medical corps that was stretched dangerously thin on the ground in Europe and the Far East.

Some Marines became psychiatric casualties after weeks of continuous fighting on Iwo Jima. Corpsmen started seeing dramatic cases of what they called "combat fatigue." Some men fell into a semiconscious, catatonic state, while others became manic and irrational. Still others lost control of their bowels. The best that corpsmen could do at the bottom of a foxhole was to tag the soldier and call for a stretcher team to take the casualty to the rear.

It had been called "shell shock" in World War I, when soldiers endured relentless enemy attacks and the constant threat of death, disease, wretched living conditions, borderline malnutrition, and loneliness. Military psychiatrists developed the concept of "forward psychiatry" and a treatment regimen called PIES (proximity, immediacy, expectancy, and simplicity). Psychiatric casualties received treatment close to the front as quickly and directly as possible and were told that they would return to combat duty.

But many of the lessons of World War I had been forgotten by the outset of World War II. American military psychiatrists believed that young men with a propensity for becoming psychiatric casualties could be identified by their childhood experiences. Approximately 1.6 million inductees were deemed unfit for military duty based on an experimental screening program. The disqualification rate for World War II inductees was more than seven times that for World War I.

The military relied on the screening program to such an extent that no psychiatrists were assigned to combat battalions at the start of the war and no provisions were made for psychiatric facilities in the rear. Yet psychiatric casualties began appearing in some of World War II's early battles.

On March 15, at sunrise, 5th Division Marines again engaged the enemy. When a corpsman and two of the four stretcher bearers carrying two wounded Marines were injured, Francis Pierce, Jr., ran to their aid. As he neared Japanese snipers, he pulled the wounded corpsman and stretcher bearers into a sheltered position so he could treat them. The two hurt Marines whose medical evacuation to the rear had been cut short would have to wait.

Pierce stood up in the enemy's line of fire. He discharged his weapon from left to right, directing a second rescue party toward his position.

Once the wounded corpsman and two stretcher bearers had been carried to the rear, Pierce dropped to his knees to treat the two Marines still waiting to be evacuated. A Japanese sniper came out of his cave only twenty yards away and shot one of the Marines a second time. With the last of his ammunition, Pierce killed the sniper as he approached.

Pierce shouldered the first Marine, pushed hard into the island sand to stand up, and carried him two hundred yards to safety. He returned for the second Marine, retrieving him as enemy bullets pinged off rocks a few feet away. Pierce successfully dragged the semiconscious soldier behind friendly lines before falling to his knees in exhaustion. He had saved the lives of five Marines.

By the following day, the infantry's ranks had been depleted so seriously that corpsmen became riflemen. On March 16, Pierce led a combat patrol toward a sniper nest. When he stopped to treat an injured Marine, he was seriously wounded, but he refused first aid. Instead he acted as a spotter, directing fire at the enemy while others evacuated the hurt Marine. Only then did Pierce allow another corpsman to take care of his wounds.

Word spread from foxhole to foxhole.

The corpsman who had first impressed his buddies in boot camp with his marksmanship became a legend on March 16 on Iwo Jima, the same day senior military officials publicly proclaimed that the island had been secured. It had taken twenty-six days and nine hours of some of the most brutal fighting Marines and their corpsmen had ever faced.

The Marines discharged Francis Pierce on December 9, 1945. After a year in the Michigan National Guard, he settled in Grand Rapids and joined the police force as a patrolman. Three years passed before he learned he would receive the Medal of Honor. In June 1948, he reported to the Truman Presidential Library for a brief ceremony. Pierce returned to Grand Rapids and a career in law enforcement.

One of George Wahlen's orders before his discharge from the Navy on December 19, 1945, was to report to Naval Barracks in Washington, D.C., at 0830 on October 3. He and thirteen other Marines and sailors were to receive the Medal of Honor.

Terror gripped Wahlen when he arrived at the White House for the ceremony. He immediately spotted Generals George Patton and George Marshall. Not far away stood Admiral Chester Nimitz. Secretary of Defense James Forrestal sat nearby.

When George Wahlen heard his name called, he stood and walked forward, stiff with nervousness. He stopped two paces short of the president, and stood at attention while staring at the ground. After a moment's pause, President Harry Truman took a half step forward and reached out for Wahlen's hand to draw him closer. Wahlen smiled sheepishly when the president told him it was "good to see a pill pusher here in the middle of all these Marines."[55]

Daughty Williams had no interest in going to Washington for a Medal of Honor ceremony. So the Navy came to Harrison, Arkansas, a year and four days after her only son had been killed and buried on Iwo Jima. The delegation was far less impressive than the officials who attended the ceremony at the White House. A Navy captain, public information officer, photographer's mate, and recruiter stood on the stoop of the Williams house on the morning of March 8, 1946.

Only five members of Jack Williams's family attended the ceremony in the modest, five-room house: his parents, both grandmothers, and a sister. Captain Arthur Agerton read the award citation before he placed the medal around Daughty's neck.

"Heroism was commonplace on Iwo Jima," he told her. "The heroism of your son stood out in such company."[56]

Young Johnny Willis wasn't impressed with Secretary of Defense James Forrestal's office on a crisp, cold morning in early December 1945. Oblivious to the strangers in the room, he looked up and smiled at his mother, Winfrey. Johnny and Winfrey Willis had come to Washington to formally receive the Medal of Honor that John Harlan Willis had earned on Iwo Jima. Winfrey and John had been married for less than a year when he sacrificed his life for wounded Marines. Secretary Forrestal carefully pinned the Medal of Honor on Johnny's shirt. He had been born two months after his father collapsed on the sand of Iwo Jima.

John Willis was among the more than one hundred ninety other corpsmen who died on Iwo Jima. He was buried in one of hundreds of broad trenches in a cemetery surrounded by a white picket fence at the foot of Mt. Suribachi. A simple white wooden cross with his name and the corpsman's crest marked his location.

More than two dozen Medals of Honor were awarded for extraordinary acts of bravery and heroism on Iwo Jima, more than for any single battle. Four were awarded to young corpsmen. Nearly 530 other corpsmen were wounded on Iwo Jima. On average, during the 36-day campaign, a corpsman fell wounded every 90 minutes. Almost 6,000 Marines died, and 16,000 others suffered battle wounds. Roughly a third of all Marine casualties in World War II occurred on Iwo Jima.

Many survived due to a number of advances in military medicine during World War II. Corpsmen and medics were confronted by wounded Marines suffering from multiple injuries. Enemy artillery simultaneously could produce flash burns, contact burns, and injuries from hot penetrating shrapnel. Increased weapon use of chemicals such as phosphorus added to the burn incidence rate. Although improvements in burn care were made, soldiers who suffered widespread burns faced a bleak outlook. About half of those who were burned on more than 40 percent of their body survived their wounds.

Aerial medical evacuation became a critical link in the chain of battlefield care. Navy flight nurses helped evacuate 17,700 Iwo Jima casualties by sea and air. Army flight nurses assisted in the evacuation of more than 1.1 million soldiers by air over the duration of World War II. Only forty-six died in transport.

The military medical corps' most significant failure was its pre-induction psychiatric screening program. In 1943 on Guadalcanal, as many as 40 percent of the casualties in some units were psychiatric. It became evident that in some units in which leadership was poor, psychiatric casualties were widespread. In other cases, such as the Japanese-American 442nd battalion in Europe, soldiers endured a series of brutal missions with no reported cases of combat fatigue.

However, once the psychiatric lessons of World War I were reapplied, World War II marked some progress in military psychiatric care. The military medical corps learned that every soldier had a "breaking point;" that tests could not screen out those most susceptible; soldiers tended to fight for their buddies, units, and country rather than against an enemy; and that prompt treatment near the battlefield and a swift return to combat duty was more effective than shipping psychiatric cases home.

Yet for corpsmen like George Wahlen, the greatest medical tools may have been their courage, compassion, perseverance, and ingenuity. More than nine out of ten American soldiers and sailors survived World War II as a direct result.

Yet for some members of the medical corps, World War II did not produce personal or professional advancement in battlefield medicine. They were prisoners of war, trapped in a stench of despair while treating hundreds of desperately ill men.

Chapter 9
Medical Care Behind Bars

● ● ● ● ● ● ●

World War II: Philippines

Shock waves from the attack on Pearl Harbor on December 7, 1941, rolled across the Pacific to the Navy in the Philippines, an American colony since the United States emerged victorious from the Spanish-American War in 1898. The military medical corps braced for a Japanese attack on the Philippines. Officials at the U.S. Navy Hospital, Cañacao, knew their patients were at risk. The hospital was not far from the Cavite Navy Yard and the massive Navy complex on Manila Bay. If the Japanese attacked Cavite, bedridden patients could be killed by wayward bombing runs. The patients had to be evacuated. Ambulatory patients who could manage for themselves were discharged shortly after news of the Pearl Harbor attack, but dozens more still needed hospital care. As night fell on the first day of war, some Cañacao doctors prayed for a few days' peace so they could find a home for men too sick and weak to defend themselves.

On December 10, war reached Manila. Unopposed Japanese bombers destroyed Cavite Navy Yard. Truckloads of wounded sailors began arriving at Cañacao hospital. The medical staff treated their injuries through the night. The next day, they evacuated all remaining patients to Philippine Union College in Balintawak, not far from Manila. Abandoned dorms became patient wards, where doctors and corpsmen hoped to hide their patients from the advancing Japanese.

By Christmas Day, 1941, Balintawak stood in the path of the enemy's march on Manila. Once again the medical staff evacuated their patients, this time to Santa Scholastica College in Manila, hoping to avoid the primary assault. It bought only a week. On January 2, 1942, two dozen doctors, 5 pharmacists, 12 nurses, and 53 hospital corpsmen watched Japanese soldiers arrive at the gate of Santa Scholastica. The soldiers erected a machine-gun nest shielded by stacks of sand-filled gunny sacks. The machine gun pointed directly at the front door of the hospital to keep medical personnel and patients from escaping. Navy doctors and corpsmen stayed at their posts, knowing they risked capture by the enemy.

That afternoon of the second of January we awaited coming events, not without considerable trepidation. Our gates of iron, eight feet high, remained closed. An unarmed pharmacist's mate stood guard on the inside. In the Japanese concentration camp across the street the inmates were idly lolling about and superficially exhibited no special excitement or concern. The Filipino guards had disappeared in the night.

About six o'clock of that fateful evening we heard the first rumble of tanks approaching from the southeast ... The vanguard of the Japanese forces had just passed, and in its wake was a steady

process of command cars, loaded troop trucks, and more trucks …
We did not know at what moment our gates might be battered down.
Virtually we were already in the grip of the enemy. Only the
formality of capture remained.

—diary excerpt,

William Silliphant, U.S. Navy doctor

Bilibid Prison, Manila, 1942

Silliphant and dozens of Navy doctors and corpsmen spent the first few months of captivity in jungle work camps after the Japanese had taken them prisoner in early January. Brutal working conditions coupled with sweltering tropical heat and beatings by Japanese guards killed men daily. A few doctors and a handful of corpsmen, armed with little more than first aid kits, were powerless against jungle rot and the spread of gangrene. One surgeon wrote that:

"When it looked like some healing might occur, the patient suddenly would begin to get rigors, vomiting, and a rapid, sometimes irregular pulse. Within a few days, the inflammation completely burst the stump. At best, the inflammation and ulceration would eventually expose the bone, which might eventually slough, leaving the patient with a conical stump. In most cases, the patient would quickly die from the infection or linger until some larger arteries were eroded, and he would bleed to death."[57]

Dr. Josep Trueta had developed a more effective treatment to prevent wound infection during the Spanish Civil War in the 1930s. Rather than immediately amputate a mangled limb, he aggressively cleaned it, cut away the damaged and dead tissue, packed it with gauze, and left the wound open. He wrapped plaster-soaked lengths of flannel around the wound. The idea of sealing the limb in a cast was revolutionary. A clean environment under a cast substantially reduced the incidence of gangrenous infection. A horrible smell that built up under the cast came to be recognized as a sign of healing. Wound infections during World War I that ran as high as 90 percent in 1916 later declined by more than half twenty years later.

As a result, during World War II, surgeons and doctors possessed a greater understanding of how to give soldiers' and sailors' badly injured arms and legs a chance to heal. That, however, didn't help the poorly equipped doctors and corpsmen held as prisoners of war. They faced emaciated and badly injured prisoners in work camps and prisons with none of the basic supplies necessary to fight gangrene.

The prisoners in work camps such as Tayabas, San Fernando, Cabanatuan, Tarlac, and O'Donnell took comfort in the knowledge that no matter how dire their condition, at least they hadn't been sent to the worst prisoner-of-war camp, Bilibid Prison in downtown Manila. Conditions were so bad that prisoners transferred from Bilibid to the jungle camps were openly called liars when they described what it was like inside the ninety-seven-year-old prison. On May 29, Silliphant learned that he and others would be transferred to Bilibid. "We felt sure we were being sent to the most undesirable, the filthiest and most degrading prison in which it was possible for the Japanese to place us," he later wrote.

On Memorial Day weekend of 1942, truck convoys from several work camps drove through Manila toward Bilibid Prison. Filipinos lined the streets. When Japanese guards weren't looking, some flashed a "V" with their fingers at the American prisoners as they passed.

My first glimpse within its walls was about noon on the day of our transfer. It was one of those hot sultry days in the month of May which can be imagined only by someone who has lived in Manila during one of the hot seasons of the year. As each truck reached the massive [Bilibid] gates, it ground to an abrupt stop in order that the Jap guards could check each prisoner in ... The patients had come on the earlier trucks and they had already been moved inside to one of the large prison barracks which was to serve later as the main medical ward.

A few prisoners who had been with us at Pasay and had been transferred some days earlier were on hand to greet us. Seeing that they had survived the surrounding squalor seemed to lighten our spirits a little. They led us to the space in the old hospital to which we were assigned by the Japs. Before we entered, however, they cautioned us never to fail to salute the Japanese guard who was sitting just inside the door, as we passed by him going in or out. Failure to do that might result in a face-slapping or worse.

—William Silliphant[58]

The prison spanned about six acres, bordered by 15-foot-high concrete walls that formed a square compound with a towering iron gate at the midpoint of the south wall. An interior wall bisected the Bilibid compound. A round guard tower sat atop the interior wall's midpoint, giving guards a 360-degree view of Bilibid's interior. Ten barracks, each about 125 feet long and 25 feet wide, extended from the central guard tower, like the spokes of a wheel. A concrete building near one exterior wall housed the execution chamber. Inside, the stubs of 2,000-volt wires coming out of a concrete pad were surrounded by scuff marks left by the electric chair.

A stench of despair draped every building. Dozens of patients who had arrived earlier sprawled under the few trees offering shade. Legions of flies crawled over the bare bodies of men too weak with dysentery to swat them away. Some of the sickest were thrown inside the execution chamber, where they evacuated their bowels on the barren concrete. Others were so ill that they didn't recognize the arrival of the captured Navy medical personnel.

Twelve doctors, 7 dentists, and 125 corpsmen organized a hospital inside a prison that held more than 2,500 prisoners of war. Hundreds more arrived daily, most barely able to stand and some close to death. Corpsmen scavenged the prison grounds for anything that might be useful in the makeshift patient wards. They scrubbed floors and walls so that patients could be brought out of the tropical sun, even if it meant lying on concrete. Corpsmen propped up those suffering from dysentery under a shower they constructed and washed them from head to foot before taking them inside. The sickest patients were placed on canvas stretchers.

Today I begin my duties as chief of surgery. There is a lot to be done here. Within these dingy prison barracks are crowded all human flotsam and jetsam from Bataan and Corregidor. Filipino and American alike, side by side on the concrete deck. The mattresses they lie on are filthy, stinking, and vermin-ridden. Emaciated carcasses look up with staring eyeballs sunk deep in bony sockets. Their broken bodies, starved and bloated, hover near death. Some show anguish and apprehension, some are pleading, some even have hope; but most of them are past manifesting anything—or even caring.

My walk through the wards is one of the most depressing and heart-rending sights imaginable. The mixed smells of dirty bodies, rotting tissue, dried blood and excrement are repulsive to every filament of the esthetic senses. The conglomerate horror of it all beats upon my sensibilities as an outrageous defiance against all the principles of civilization, and dispels any delusion I may have had of human progress.

Our job here is to do all we can with the pitiful little available to us. But even badly needed surgery will not help. These starved, tissue-dead, zombie-like creatures can't stand surgery. At best, many will die. In this prison the war has just begun.

—POW diary excerpt,
Thomas Hayes, U.S. Navy doctor
Bilibid Prison, Manila, July 1942[59]

Commander Thomas Hayes arrived as part of a medical unit that had been captured on Corregidor, the island that guarded the entrance to Manila Bay, nearly two months earlier. When the Japanese moved the medical personnel from Corregidor, doctors were given only two hours to pack hospital supplies. They salvaged little, and most of that had been damaged in transit. Jungle work camps in the interim had failed to prepare Hayes for Bilibid's squalor and the inadequacy of provisions.

The promised deliveries of medical supplies failed to appear at Bilibid. When the Japanese allowed a truckload of medicine into the prison, it contained Carter's Little Liver Pills, talcum powder, and Lydia Pinkham's Vegetable Compound. Corpsmen suspected the Japanese guards had stolen the most useful medicines from the shipment. With the exception of a few doctors and corpsmen in jungle work camps, the region's entire Navy medical corps had been sent to Bilibid.

Deepening hunger defined life as a prisoner. Prisoners were fed very poor rice that had rocks, dirt, or worms in it. Many prisoners grew used to the grit in their rice. Men regularly swept the ground where it was unloaded in search of a few extra grains. Corpsmen scrounged for dirty rice for their bedridden patients. Prisoners, medical staff, and patients also were given watery, polished rice for breakfast, called *lugao*. The white rice contained almost no nutritional value. Worms sometimes floated on the surface, an additional source of nourishment that most prisoners learned to choke down. One day, an American doctor found a fully-grown mouse in his soup. He tossed the stiff rodent aside, reboiled his rice for ten minutes on a homemade hotplate, and ate it.

Sometimes guards served a half a cup of thin soup, made with a bitter swamp grass similar to bamboo. Shoots a half-inch thick could be chewed only by new prisoners whose teeth and gums had not yet rotted. As bitter as the gruel was, most prisoners preferred it to the shovelsful of minnows sometimes dumped into the noontime soup. The entire prison reeked of rotting fish when buckets of minnows were boiled for lunch.

Prisoners passed the time by reminiscing about childhood holiday meals. Some lost their desire for food, while others developed a starvation phobia, eating themselves sick for fear each might be their last meal. Corpsmen guarded small caches of rice and other food for their starving patients.

Survival sometimes rested on ingenuity. The Japanese allowed Manila merchants to sell food to those prisoners whose money hadn't been confiscated by their captors. Corpsmen and prisoners developed a variety of ways to cook the additional scraps they had purchased. Discarded pots, pans, buckets, or pails became cooking vessels. Rain-warped lumber was highly prized as firewood. The mung bean saved many lives. The size of a small shotgun pellet, it was rich in vitamin B-1 and tasted faintly of lentils. Prisoners wrapped the beans in a wet towel, placed them in the sun, and in a few days the germinated beans flavored the food provided by the Japanese.

Disease was epidemic inside Bilibid. Two types of dysentery ravaged thousands of men. Unsanitary prison conditions, rotten food, and rancid water made it inevitable. Sometimes a man recovered through sheer will, perseverance, and luck. Often, however, doctors and corpsmen were equipped only with their compassion to treat patients.

Corpsman T. F. Brannon took care of Malin Malloy, who had arrived from Tayabas, a jungle work camp notorious for dysentery. The parasitic condition had robbed his body of nearly all its fluid. He suffered from chronic diarrhea, fever, vomiting, and abdominal tenderness, which led Brannon to think the parasite may have infected Malloy's liver. If it reached his bloodstream, infection of his lungs and brain could be next. Without antiparasitic medication, Brannon had no means to stop its spread. Malloy was one of one hundred fifty dysentery cases in Bilibid on the day he died.

Corpsman L. F. Tyree spent extra time with Reginald Decker. The lack of thiamine, or vitamin B-1, in Decker's diet had led to a severe case of beriberi. Fatigue and irritation had given way to loss of memory and fitful sleep. One morning, a tremendous burning sensation enveloped Decker's feet. His calf museles cramped in pain. Later, his leg muscles atrophied as portions of his spinal cord disintegrated. Without massive doses of thiamine, Decker had little hope for survival.

Corpsman W. N. Thompson regularly checked on Jerrold Powell. A bright red rash on Powell's face had thickened and deepened in color, and large patches of skin were sloughing off. Powell's mouth and tongue had reddened and swelled as his diarrhea intensified and his memory faded. Powell had pellagra, a disease caused by an absence of niacin, or vitamin B-3, in his diet. Thompson knew the final symptoms would include stiffness of arms and legs, confusion, depression, and hallucinations.

Corpsman H. L. Kirby attended to Dan Foley, who had been complaining of blurry vision, a sensation that something was in his eye, and an unnatural sensitivity to light. Foley had exophthalmia, a condition in which eyes bulge out of their orbits and are consequently always dry. Nearly all Bilibid prisoners suffered from some degree of sight impairment. Dozens of patients developed ulcers on their corneas, a serious and common complication from prolonged vitamin A deficiency. A corneal ulcer could penetrate the eye, spread infection, and cause permanent blindness.

Corpsman J. T. Istock tried to ease the agony of a patient, simply listed as "Westbrook" in the prison records, who writhed and scratched his leg furiously. He knew the patient had contracted rabies from a dog bite in a jungle work camp. The Japanese guards had given him an out-of-date vaccine. The patient suffered from chills, fever, muscle aches, and irritability. By the fifth day, he could hardly swallow between hallucinations and convulsions. He died slowly, fully aware of every nightmare, every spasm.

Istock had given part of his food ration to Westbrook to keep him alive. He walked over to a corner of the ward and pulled a half-rotted rice gunny sack from the pile saved for death shrouds. The corpsman wrapped Westbrook's body in the sack that once contained the rancid rice. The dead man's belongings—a pair of handmade shoes, a threadbare shirt, and a worn toothbrush—were given to the neediest prisoners. Burial might have been delayed because rain often clogged Bilibid's sewer system, flooding the prison grounds with raw sewage.

I had been in my bunk for about an hour last night trying to fall asleep; when I suddenly heard someone in the shadow of the building next to mine whisper my name. I failed to recognize the voice and waited. Momentarily a man stepped out into the open. He was holding a small package. I eased out of my bunk and stood in the dark of the doorway. The parcel was pushed into my hands and the stranger disappeared in the darkness. I stowed the package under my bedding, then strolled quietly over to the barred window that looks out over the "sacred circle" and guardhouse. The sentries were seated around a table—nothing unusual astir.

I carried the box into the toilet and opened it under the light. It contained a sack of sweet smelling coffee and a box of cigars. Not that the coffee wasn't welcome, but I decided to try the tobacco first. The Japanese drink coffee, but they don't smoke "stogies." I wasn't the only one who knew that. Underneath the cigars was a message. (I can't write down how this contact was made, but will remember it.)

This was a dummy run that St. M. [a courier who smuggled messages into Bilibid] had tried and it worked to perfection. Her note mentioned that she doesn't intend to use this method again, but outlined other plans for contact after the first of September.

—POW diary excerpt,
Thomas Hayes[60]

Dr. Thomas Hayes was an American spy. The Philadelphia native was forty-four years old when the Japanese captured him on Corregidor. A graduate of George Washington University medical school, he spoke several languages. He joined the Navy in 1924 and was recruited by the intelligence corps. In 1940, he arrived in the Philippines aboard the USS *Milwaukee*.

On October 1, 1943, Hayes replaced Lea Sartin as Bilibid's senior medical officer, and imposed greater military discipline in the prison hospital. He also ran a network of spies. His informants included prisoners in work parties that were assigned duties outside the prison.

Shortly after taking command, Hayes determined which sick prisoners would receive rations of medicines or vitamins. "Light sick" patients who were mildly ill had priority for treatment. If a patient received vitamins at the onset of his condition, he stood a better chance of keeping his eyesight or surviving. There simply weren't enough medical provisions to treat the hundreds of modestly sick and seriously ill patients.

In early 1944, Bilibid prisoners faced the prospect of being shipped to work camps in Japan. They viewed transfer as a death sentence. Rumors of the brutal conditions aboard the Japanese "hell ships" rivaled those that awaited prisoners once they reached Japan. A patient's only real chance for survival depended on whether the Bilibid medical staff deemed him too sick for transport. But a reprieve might last only a few weeks. Weak, shrunken, and half-blind men were marched out of Bilibid, down to the wharf, and onto unmarked Japanese ships at anchor.

On September 21, 1944, Bilibid prisoners saw two Japanese planes overhead, towing targets for antiaircraft gunnery practice. More planes appeared in the distance, converging on Manila from three directions. They watched as American fighter aircraft rolled out of formation and attacked Nichols Airfield and the target-towing planes. As a Japanese aircraft nosedived into a Manila suburb, Bilibid prisoners cheered at the echoes of bombs destroying the airfield. Air-raid sirens shrieked across Manila for the next two days. Prisoner spirits soared at the prospect of rescue before being shipped to Japan.

Two months later, the American raids stopped. The halt was welcomed by more than one thousand prisoners who were bound for Japan on the next cargo ship. American aircraft had been attacking Japanese shipping. Some of the ships sunk had been unmarked vessels filled with American prisoners of war who had survived more than a year of captivity in Bilibid.

On December 12, when Bilibid's medical staff lined up for the daily roll call at 1800 hours, the dreaded order was issued: Commander Thomas Hayes and the majority of his two hundred fifty-man medical unit would leave the next day on Japanese transport ships. That night, prisoners ignored the 2000 hours curfew. No one slept, as prisoners cooked the last of their hoarded caches of food.

The next morning, more than sixteen hundred American prisoners, patients, chaplains, and medical staff marched to the waterfront. Guards divided the prisoners into three groups and took them aboard the *Oryoku Maru*, an aging cargo-passenger ship. It bore no markings designating it as a POW transport. Hayes and his medical unit were pushed into Hold Number Two, which had carried horses on a recent voyage. The stench and heat sucked the breath out of the men. At 1700, the *Oryoku Maru* hoisted anchor and joined a four-ship convoy headed for Formosa.

Panic swept the prisoners during their first night at sea. They were crowded so densely that few could sit down. On the verge of dehydration, men gagged at the smell of putrid horse urine. Japanese guards handed out a few canteens of muddy water. The water ration amounted to one canteen per forty-five men, about three teaspoons apiece. Prisoners passed food pails of watery rice and slop buckets around for men to relieve themselves in the dark. Men couldn't tell one bucket from the other until they ladled their share with a spoon. Soon the deck was covered with human excrement. Men who had been on the verge of death for months snapped. Fights broke out for space to breathe more easily. Paranoia followed. By morning, fifty men had died. The survivors stacked them in a corner like kindling.

As guards handed morning rations of watery rice to the prisoners, American aircraft suddenly appeared in the sky and dove toward the convoy. The prisoner transport shuddered with each hit. The Americans completed their bombing runs, turned around, and strafed each ship lengthwise. They left the convoy almost dead in the water. Hayes and his medical team climbed topside to treat the wounded Japanese crew. When they were finished, Japanese guards beat the prisoners as revenge for the attack that had badly damaged the *Oryoku Maru*. That night, the transport headed toward Subic Bay, which was only about sixty miles northwest of Manila Bay. Just before midnight, it ran aground three hundred yards offshore.

The following day, the Japanese crew abandoned ship, leaving the medical personnel to help injured and sick prisoners out of the holds and into the water. To their horror, American aircraft appeared as the prisoners paddled for shore. The water churned white from the initial strafing runs, killing corpsmen and their patients. When the American pilots saw white-skinned swimmers in the water, they pulled out of their strafing runs. As the exhausted swimmers reached the beach and a nearby seawall, sand erupted with gunfire. Hidden Japanese machine gunners pummeled the shore, pinning the POWs against the seawall to keep them from escaping inland. Hayes and a few corpsmen established a first-aid station. Over the next two hours, doctors and corpsmen used filthy shirts and beach flotsam to slow the blood from fresh wounds.

Finally, when all the prisoners who had not been shot dead in the water reached the beach, the Japanese herded two hundred fifty of them inland to a fenced tennis court. Hayes and his corpsmen set up another aid station in one section of the court. Under a baking sun, the prisoners went without food that day. By sunset, several had died of heatstroke.

On the second day ashore, each man received two tablespoons of rice. Corpsmen made their rounds. On the third day, still locked in the tennis court, more prisoners died. Equipped only with small knives and razor blades, Hayes and other doctors performed emergency operations on the wounded. They performed amputations without anesthesia. Corpsmen encircled them, trying to provide shade.

On December 27, trucks carried the survivors down to the wharf to another Japanese transport that reeked of livestock dung. Guards shoved and kicked those too weak to walk aboard the *Enoura Maru*. Clouds of horse flies greeted the prisoners as they were pushed into dank, steaming cargo holds.

On the first day of 1945, the *Enoura Maru* docked at Takao, Formosa. Despite crowding so severe that few men could sit, another two hundred American POWs were loaded into the cargo holds on January 6. It had been twenty-four days since the Bilibid POWs had left Manila Bay. Corpsmen and doctors fought to maintain a semblance of order and to stem raging infections from old and new wounds. On January 9, 1945, a squadron of American aircraft attacked the *Enoura Maru* and a Japanese destroyer that was tied up alongside.

More than one thousand POWs listened to the battle above them. Machine-gun fire ricocheted off metal and through portholes. Shrapnel spun through the air and sliced into Japanese sailors. Concussive waves from bombs exploding nearby rolled through the hull. Some prisoners cheered each detonation. Others prayed. Trapped in the hold, none knew when or whether the next bomb would spell their end.

It didn't take long for one of the American fighter planes to hit the *Enoura Maru*. The first bomb exploded just outside the rear cargo hold, tearing through the hull and the bodies below. It obliterated the eye of a man standing to one side of a corpsman and decapitated a prisoner on his other side. The second bomb detonated directly above the forward cargo hold, which held most of Bilibid's two hundred fifty-man hospital unit. Shrapnel and shredded pieces of the hull struck nearly every man, including commander Thomas Hayes.

After treating thousands of American POWs during the course of more than two years, while living on the edge of starvation, dozens of young corpsmen died in a darkened hole that reeked of manure. They died at the hands of unknowing American aviators they had once prayed would bomb the gates of Bilibid into oblivion.

Three days later, a crane lifted their mangled, bloated bodies out of the hold. Stiff, bloodied arms and legs protruded through the netting at grotesque angles. The corpses were dumped in a heap on a barge. Once the barge reached shore, many of the surviving nine hundred POWs tied ropes to the bodies' feet and dragged them inland for incineration.

William Silliphant and a few corpsmen remained in what had become a ghost town. Only a few hundred prisoners remained at Bilibid on January 10, 1945. They found a Japanese newspaper in a garbage can reporting that an American invasion force was approaching Manila. The article did not mention the bombing of the *Enoura Maru* the day before. Silliphant and the others waited. With food supplies almost gone, they wondered if they could keep their patients alive until help arrived.

On Sunday, February 4, 1945, a small American plane circled the prison several times; the pilot waved to the prisoners below. Shortly after it left, the Japanese guards lined up in formation near the gate. None looked at the American POWs. A Japanese officer stepped forward and handed a piece of paper to the prisoners. The crumpled paper was dated almost a month earlier. In part, it read:

> 1. *The Japanese is now going to releave [sic] all the prisoners of war and internees here on its own accord.*
> 2. *We are assigned to another duty and shall be here no more.*
> 3. *You are at liberty to act and live as free persons, but you must be aware of probable danger if you go out.*
> *We shall leave here foodstuffs, medicines, and other necessities of which you may avail yourselves for the time being.*
> 4. *We have arranged to put up a signboard at the front gate bearing the following context: "Lawfully release prisoners of war and internees are quartered here. Please do not molest them unless they make positive resistance."*

Without ceremony, the Japanese guards marched out of Bilibid, closing the gate behind them. The American prisoners remained inside, waiting and wondering. At sunset, a corpsman flinched at the sound of a rifle butt slamming against a shuttered window in the prison wall. He heard American voices outside the wall. Another jab, then another, as the wood splintered and fell away. The nose of a machine gun slowly protruded into the prison as American soldiers gathered outside the Bilibid Prison wall, only a few feet from prisoners.

"Hey, you guys, where are the Japs?"

"There are no Japs in here," answered a prisoner. "Who are you?"

"We're Yanks. We've come to rescue you. I'm Sergeant Anderson. I'm here with American soldiers. They are all around you. You've got nothing to worry about."[61]

A door in the wall came crashing down. Horribly emaciated men, most of them weighing around ninety pounds, started crying.

American soldiers walked into the compound as prisoners slumped to the ground in disbelieving relief. Shocked at the grotesque condition of the POWs, the rescuers opened cans of pork and beans for the prisoners. Many took a single spoonful and passed the cans around, making sure that everyone got some. The first Americans to reach Bilibid were the 148th Regiment of the 37th Buckeye Division from Ohio.

The prisoners and medical staff remained in Bilibid for another week, as fires sparked by battle raged in downtown Manila. As one fire approached, the last American prisoners were evacuated. Those who were still ambulatory insisted on walking out of the prison. For William Silliphant and many corpsmen, it was the first time they had been outside Bilibid's walls in more than three years.

Although advances in medical science during World War II were unprecedented, battlefield medicine often was hampered by a lack of available medical provisions. Dynamic combat situations, inconsistent shipments of supplies, and insufficient coordination made the practice of battlefield medicine reliant on ingenuity and resourcefulness. Sometimes doctors and corpsmen had only the most basic supplies with which to treat the wounded. In many cases, kindness and compassion were all that they could offer. Some medical personnel accepted capture by the enemy so they could treat their fellow soldiers.

More than three hundred members of the Navy's hospital corps became prisoners during World War II. Many had refused to leave their patients' sides as the Japanese army closed in. Some were fortunate to survive. Among them was William Silliphant, who later was promoted to rear admiral. He passed away in 1967.

All told, the Navy lost 1,170 corpsmen in World War II. One hundred thirty-two died from disease as well as enemy and friendly fire in jungle camps, prisons, and prisoner transport ships.

Seven corpsmen earned the Medal of Honor for their courage under fire during World War II. Nearly half of all Medals of Honor awarded to Navy personnel were received by corpsmen. In addition, Navy corpsmen earned 1,513 Navy Crosses, Silver Stars, and Bronze Stars for valor.

"Out of every 100 men of the U.S. Navy and Marine Corps who were wounded in World War II, 97 recovered. That is a record not equaled anywhere, anytime ... You corpsmen performed foxhole surgery while shell fragments clipped your clothing, shattered the plasma bottles from which you poured new life into the wounded, and sniper's bullets were aimed at the brassards on your arms ... Whatever their duty, wherever they were, the men and women of the Hospital Corps served the Navy and served humanity with exemplary courage, sagacity and effort ... Well done."

—Navy commendation excerpt
by James Forrestal, Secretary of the Navy
1944–47

Chapter 10

Medicine on the Fly

● ● ● ● ● ● ●

Korean War

The mailman's boots crushed the sidewalk grit, remnants of a Massachusetts winter warming into a 1953 spring of budding maple trees and resurgent daffodils in matted flower beds. As he climbed the stoop, Claire Keenan opened the front door.

"Here you are, ma'am," said the mailman. The ragged envelope he handed her had traveled a third of the way around the world. She stepped inside and read the letter.

Well we caught a lot of close mortar rounds today. The Goonies have their summer troops up in front of us now and they are hot for combat. We'll be off the lines in a couple of days and I'll be glad to get in the rear for awhile, and no more patrols at night. We expect

*to get hit before we leave here 'cause the Goonies overran Dog
Company's outpost and hit the rest of them except us.*

*I hope you all have a nice Easter and tell the kids I was asking
for them.*

*I have to close now on account of I volunteered to help dig outposts
on the trench line tonight where the rain and shell fire cave them in.*

Your son,

Joe[62]

Claire opened a bureau drawer in which she kept letters. She reread
another from the boy everyone called Joey:

Dear Mother & Father,

*… Everything that happens here usually happens at night and
it's rough on the nerves. Once every two weeks they pull a daylight
raid to get "Luke the Gook" worried. The hill had 1,000 rounds of
bombs and heavy artillery shells and mortar and rockets dropped on
it for eight minutes before zero hour, yet when the Marines got close
to the top, Goonies were all over the place. Some just stayed in their
holes and just threw grenade after grenade over the top without
hardly showing themselves at all.*

*They asked for a volunteer corpsman to go up to evac some
patients. I said I'd go but didn't realize what I said until after I was
in the halftrack. Then I got scared …*[63]

Corpsman Joe Keenan had arrived in Korea on Friday, February 13,
1953, and joked it was a good thing he wasn't superstitious. He had
joined a war that had begun when communist North Korea invaded
South Korea, an American ally, on June 25, 1950, in an attempt to reunify
the Korean peninsula. The North Koreans had gained control of a major
portion of South Korea by the time the Americans had reinforced their

military presence there and halted the advance. When Keenan arrived, the Korean War resembled World War I.

Early-war invasions and counterattacks across Korea had settled into stagnant battles of attrition. American forces faced troops from North Korea and its ally, communist China, along largely stationary front lines called Main Lines of Resistance. As far as a mile in front of the lines, the Americans established hilltop outposts that provided advance warning of attacks. Each was usually manned by forty Marines and a corpsman. Duty in an isolated outpost almost completely surrounded by the enemy was exhausting. Marines and corpsmen rotated between outpost duty, a few days' respite in the rear as part of a reserve force, and going out on patrols from the MLR.

For reasons unexplained to Keenan and most Marines, each type of patrol was named after an automobile. "Chevrolet" was code for combat patrol. These patrols in the middle of the night, sometimes to scout enemy positions and on other occasions to attack, were grueling, especially for the corpsmen who accompanied every patrol. The Marines typically went out on combat patrols every other night. Corpsmen, though, frequently strung together several night patrols in a row.

Within a month of his arrival in Korea, Keenan completed five consecutive night patrols. He prepared for patrols into enemy territory by piling his personal belongings on an open poncho. If he was killed, that would make it easier to ship his personal effects home to Dorchester, Massachusetts. His unit reviewed the expected engagement with the enemy before heading out shortly after midnight. Some patrols were intended to engage the enemy; others were reconnaissance missions. They typically returned to the MLR just before sunrise. In between patrols, Keenan made sure there were adequate medical supplies. The nightly series of raids added to the war's daytime casualty rate. On average in 1953, corpsmen treated seventy-one wounded soldiers each day, of whom seventeen would die.

Joe Keenan was a handsome, dark-haired Irish boy who had grown up in a Boston neighborhood of small houses, community parks, narrow streets, and clapboard "three deckers" with a different family on each floor. It was a working-class area rooted in family life.

As a boy, Joe Keenan's easygoing manner had sparked many friendships and quickly put strangers at ease. His heavy-lidded, wide-set eyes nearly disappeared when he broke into his characteristic wide, dimpled grin. He was as quick to ride his bike with its handlebar wicker basket to the drugstore to pick up medicine for a sick brother as he was to jump into a scuffle.

Joe had worked as a boy, first carrying groceries home for neighbors and later stocking shelves at Kennedy's Department Store. Occasionally, he brought clothes home for his brothers and sister. On Saturdays, Joe and a brother sometimes explored the backwaters of Boston Harbor, using a well-worn fishing line wrapped around a stick smoothed by use.

In Dorchester, sons followed in the footsteps of their grandfathers, fathers, and older brothers: finish high school and go to work or enlist in the military. Joe upheld the Keenan family tradition and joined the Navy in June 1951, leaving behind his sweetheart, Anne Grayken. When he enlisted, Joe had hoped to become an aerial tail gunner. Instead, the Navy sent him to corpsman school.

In the years following World War II, the Navy had closed 47 of 83 hospitals, and its medical ranks had shrunk from 170,000 to only 21,000. The military was in such drastic need of doctors that the Doctor Draft Law was enacted in 1950. It targeted physicians who had been educated at government expense during World War II but who had not served in the military.

The military medical corps also recognized the need for more qualified and better-trained frontline corpsmen and medics. The corps assigned men based on aptitude test scores. Some had been premed students, male nurses, or chiropractors. Training for Korea's corpsmen and medics was more comprehensive than it had been during World War II. Most completed a four-month premed curriculum that included anatomy, physiology, pharmacology, laboratory testing, and X-ray training. Classroom study was followed by two months of field training with the Marines and then a naval hospital internship. Keenan and others had nearly a year's worth of combat medical training before they landed in Korea.

Although training had gotten better, the life of corpsmen and medics had improved little from the previous war. Water was always in short supply. Clean clothes were available about once a month. When a corpsman changed his underwear each week, a thorough spray of DDT killed ever-present body lice. Early in the Korean War, winter battles had produced thousands of cases of frostbite in conditions so brutal that aid stations' plasma bottles froze solid and shattered. Hunkering down inside a bunker only six feet long and three feet wide was dry but claustrophobic.

Forward aid stations often struggled to maintain adequate morphine and plasma supplies. Ingenuity became a corpsman's most effective tool. One corpsman treated a soldier whose shattered bone and teeth blocked his airway by using a scalpel and the hollow bottom half of a ballpoint pen to perform a tracheotomy, saving the soldier's life. The same corpsman devised a way to seal a sucking chest wound using the cellophane wrapper from a pack of cigarettes.

March 26, 1953, was a pleasantly warm day. Keenan was a member of Fox Company of the 1st Marine Division, assigned to thirty-three miles of the MLR that spanned the main enemy invasion route to Seoul, the South Korean capital. Three combat outposts had been established on separate hills within enemy territory. They were named Carson, Reno, and Vegas. Reno was in the middle, about a mile forward of the nearest American reinforcements. Carson and Vegas were on either side, about a half mile in front of the MLR. The Marines assigned to them joked about how surviving duty in any of the "Nevada Cities" was a crapshoot. Fighting on the side of their fellow Communists, the Chinese had established similar outposts near each in elevated locations with superior firing positions.

At 1900 hours, explosions rocked the three outposts as the Chinese launched a massive attack. Detonations, cracking timbers, and screams fractured the elevated voices of radiomen choking on dust as they reported the unexpected assault. Artillery and mortar shells pounded the outposts at the rate of almost three shells per second. This was followed fifteen minutes later by small arms fire. A group of 120 Marines and three corpsmen at Carson, Reno, and Vegas faced an onslaught of more than 3,500 Chinese soldiers. The Americans defended themselves by calling for "box-me-in" artillery aimed at the enemy on all four sides of each outpost. Over the next eight hours, the Chinese launched 14,000 artillery rounds into three bands of exposed Marines. It was impossible to know whose shells were falling on which troops.

Fox Company was ordered to reinforce the outposts under attack. Keenan opened his green canvas medicine kit and counted the morphine Syrettes and small battle dressings. He mentally inventoried the rest of the contents: scissors, wire cutter, hemostats, needle holders, needles, and thread, plus a wide assortment of bandages and antiseptic. He cinched the kit around his waist before hiking into combat.

His unit moved out from the MLR toward an unfortified position fifteen hundred yards ahead of the front line. Their destination was the Reno outpost at the center of the Chinese attack.

The Chinese had reached Carson on one flank. The Marines who had survived the original artillery barrage engaged the Chinese in hand-to-hand combat, but the attackers prevailed and took control of Carson. Minutes later, Vegas fell to the enemy as well.

Reno was next. The relentless bombardment battered the outpost as hundreds of enemy soldiers moved in. Shrapnel and debris rained down on the remaining Marines who had sought shelter in trenches. When Chinese soldiers jumped into the trenches, the Americans fought with everything close to hand: rifle butts, knives, and shovels. Pistol shots reverberated. As more Chinese closed in, the few Marines still alive retreated into the Reno bunker. Explosive satchels collapsed the bunker, trapping the men inside.

The overwhelming Chinese forces devastated the first group of reinforcements sent to Reno. Several hundred yards behind them, Keenan's unit moved up the hill toward multiple casualties. As Keenan neared Reno he heard the hollow "thunking" of Chinese mortars firing. He guessed how far the enemy mortar was from him, counted a few seconds, and then hit the ground an instant before the shell's impact nearby.

At midnight, Joe Keenan entered the battlefield. Men writhed on the ground screaming in pain. Others lay at impossible angles. Blood soaked the ground, and body parts lay scattered among the corpses. They glowed ghostly white from the exploding phosphorus rounds.

Keenan sprinted from one wounded Marine to the next as the night sky brightened with exploding shells. A piece of shrapnel shredded his right wrist. "Don't worry about me!" Keenan yelled to another corpsman, William Jones, who had begun moving toward him. As Jones turned away to help other Marines, he died in the sudden cloud of a mortar shell.

Ignoring his bleeding wrist, Keenan kept treating wounded Marines who lay exposed to enemy fire. The artillery barrage seemed endless. Explosions were followed by the whrrrr of shrapnel spinning through the air, and slicing through stomachs, legs, and faces. Another piece found Keenan, this time wounding him in the head. Corpsman Everett Jones was less than ten feet away.

"Here, take my supplies," Keenan yelled over the explosions. "I've got an awful headache. I'm going down to the aid station."[64] He tossed his medical bags to Jones and headed down the hill. Jones lost sight of Keenan in the exploding dirt and billowing dust.

By 0100 hours, Keenan's head and wrist wounds had been dressed at the aid station, and he headed back up the hill into the heart of the battle. Meanwhile, fellow corpsmen near Reno treated horrific casualties. Paul Polley and Francis Hammond established an aid station in the middle of the artillery barrage. Polley continued treating the wounded after he had been injured in the chest and blinded. Not far away, Hammond, who had arrived in Korea within days of Keenan, dragged his badly injured leg across open terrain to treat as many wounded men as he could. Keenan joined them at about 0130, moving under enemy fire from one casualty to the next.

Joe Keenan was wounded a third time when a shell exploded next to him, driving dirt and debris into his eyes and partially blinding him. He refused care and would not retreat to the safety of the battalion aid station in the rear. Wounded Marines looked up at two partially blind corpsmen treating them under withering fire as another soldier acted as their eyes.

"Boy, this is a bad night for corpsmen!" said one of the wounded.[65]

Once Keenan finished treating an injured man, four stretcher bearers loaded him onto a stretcher, hunched over, and ran down the hill from Reno, trying to keep from dropping the stretcher or getting knocked off their feet by artillery blasts. Unarmed, sometimes they stopped to pick up a dead man's rifle or canteen if it had water left in it. Exhaustion threatened many who repeatedly climbed into enemy fire and then clambered down the hill, carrying one of Keenan's patients. They were the first link in battlefield evacuation that had undergone significant changes since the end of World War II.

Korea's rugged terrain posed daunting challenges to evacuating the wounded from the battlefield. The first documented use of a helicopter in combat was in 1944, when the Army rescued four aviators who had crashed in Burma. Two years later, the U.S. Navy tested the viability of helicopters for at-sea rescue. During Operation Frostbite off the coast of Greenland, a helicopter rescued USS *Midway* pilots who had crashed in the midwinter sub-Arctic. Sometimes the rescued aviators were dropped accidentally several feet onto the flight deck as helicopter pilots and the flight deck crew fine-tuned new search-and-rescue procedures.

In 1951, within six months of the outbreak of the Korean War, helicopters became critical in a country of poor roads and interminable mountain ranges. The H13 helicopter, called the "grasshopper" for its bubble canopy and lattice-like tail, proved effective but vulnerable. Its practical speed of seventy miles per hour, nonsealing gas tanks, and exposed gear boxes made it an easy target for small arms fire. Wounded soldiers strapped to the outside landing skids were exposed to enemy fire. The helicopter's center of gravity was so delicate that pilots brought along large rocks as ballast when they carried a wounded soldier on one side. In winter, some injured soldiers froze to death while strapped to the helicopters. Modifications were made to deflect manifold heat onto the exposed stretchers. Pilots learned to secure plasma bottles inside the warmed cockpits with tubes snaking outside and into the arms of the wounded.

Given their slow speed, low altitude, and vulnerability to enemy fire, medical evacuation (medevac) helicopters most commonly were called in when the enemy or terrain eliminated other evacuation options. Corpsmen learned to call for a helicopter only for the most critically wounded and to mark a landing zone with colored smoke. Pilots often refueled and loaded patients without shutting down their engines for fear the weak batteries wouldn't restart. The helicopters were limited to daytime operations.

Some of the wounded were flown directly to offshore U.S. Navy hospital ships that had been retrofitted with helicopter landing pads. For the first time, Navy hospital ships provided comprehensive care for the wounded rather than ferried casualties to land-based hospitals as they had done during World War II.

If Keenan and the stretcher bearers could get the wounded out of the immediate battle zone, their patients stood a good chance of surviving. In Korea, battalion aid station doctors had whole blood for transfusions to ward off shock. In World War II, whole blood's twenty-one-day shelf life had limited its viability in the battle zone, but by the early 1950s, faster air transport enabled whole blood from America to reach Korea in a few days. Battalion aid doctors also had an arsenal of antibiotics unknown in World War II. In addition to penicillin, new systemic and topical antibiotics including Aureomycin, Chloromycetin, and Terramycin were available for postop infections not controlled by penicillin.

Many of the wounded owed their lives to another advancement in battlefield care: mobile army surgical hospitals. MASH units had been developed during World War II as the battle lines swept across Europe. The closer doctors were to the front, the better were a wounded soldier's chances of survival. On August 23, 1945, the Army formally established mobile army surgical hospitals. Six doctors, twelve nurses, and ninety-six medics, corpsmen, and aides staffed a typical MASH. Although the military had no MASH units in the Far East at the start of the Korean War, they quickly became part of the Korean battlefield.

At first, MASH units kept pace with advances and retreats. Later, they became more permanent facilities, typically situated about ten to twenty-five miles from the front. By the outbreak of the Nevada Cities Battle in 1953, three out of four wounded soldiers were being treated at a MASH unit, often on the same day they were wounded due to evacuation by helicopter.

The Nevada Cities Battle stretched into the predawn hours of March 27. Two of Keenan's friends, infantrymen Daniel Holl and Floyd Caton, discovered the corpsman in a shallow gully, treating Marines through eyes filled with dirt.

"Joe, get the fuck outta here, you crazy son of a bitch. You're going to get killed," said Holl as Keenan bent over a wounded Marine.

"Go fuck yourself. I got a job to do and I'm gonna do it."

"Joe, stay with my fire team!" said Holl.

"Fuck no," said Keenan. "I ain't staying with your fire team. I got a job to do."[66]

Holl flushed Keenan's eyes with water and moved out with Caton. The three outposts had been lost. Holl and Caton needed to find a safe evacuation route for the Marines' retreat. Keenan stayed behind, high on the hill and alone in a shallow ditch, squinting in the dark to see the wounded men he treated.

At 0245, two companies of reinforcement Marines retreated toward the MLR. A rear-guard unit passed through the gully where Keenan had been treating the wounded. He wasn't there. Four days of counterattacks by the Marines followed before tensions finally eased. By that time, 156 Marines had been killed, 801 were wounded, and the Chinese had taken 19 prisoners.

The telegram arrived at the Keenan home on April 3, 1953.

BA175 MA257
M. WA203 LONG GOVT RX PD-WUX WASHINGTON DC
MR AND MRS THOMAS FRANCIS KEENAN
43 MATHER ST DORCHESTER MASS

IT IS WITH DEEP REGRET THAT I OFFICIALLY REPORT THE DEATH OF YOUR SON JOSEPH FRANCIS KEENAN HOSPITAL CORPSMAN THIRD CLASS US NAVY WHICH OCCURRED ON 26 MARCH 1953 AS A RESULT OF ACTION IN THE KOREAN AREA. WHEN FURTHER DETAILS INCLUDING INFORMATION AS TO THE DISPOSITION OF THE REMAINS ARE RECEIVED YOU

*WILL BE INFORMED. YOUR SON DIED WHILE
SERVING HIS COUNTRY AND I EXTEND TO YOU MY
SINCEREST SYMPATHY IN YOUR GREAT LOSS.*

*VICE ADMIRAL J L HOLLOWAY JR
CHIEF OF NAVAL PERSONNEL*[67]

The Keenans had read newspaper articles about the Nevada Cities Battle and knew it had taken place close to where Joe had been assigned. Like hundreds of other parents, they had anxiously awaited word of the fate of their son, hoping for a letter from him and dreading the arrival of a telegram.

The rest of the family and others would have to be told immediately. Anne Grayken left the subway station for the short walk home and found one of Joe's brothers at her front door. When he described the telegram, her world froze. As she stepped inside her home, her eyes fell on two unopened letters from Joe. She hadn't yet read them, but she knew neither would answer her questions nor make sense of a life without him.

Other letters, so confusing that they bordered on cruelty, soon arrived at the Keenan home.

Dear Mrs. Keenan,

This is just a short note to let you know about your son Joe. He got hit slightly in the arm by a mortar last night while on a raid with our company. He was with my firing team when we started the attack on the hill (Reno) and during most of the raid. He done the job of a platoon of men before he got hit and quite a while after. He also refused medical aid from anyone until he was sure everyone else was properly cared for. Your son is and will always be one of the most well liked guys in our company. I became good friends with him shortly after he arrived in Fox Co. We seen him leave the hill and I also checked in the aid station to see if he was alright. He got quite a bit of dust in his eyes but it didn't bother his vision after they were cleaned.

Joe's friend,

Dan Holl

P.S. Joe is in fine hands and there is no serious wounds.[68]

Dear Mrs. Keenan,

Just a few lines to let you know I was on the raid last night when Joe got hit, he never got hit bad so don't worry about Joe. He got hit in the wrist and also got a little sand in his eyes but not enough to hurt them. He was with our fireteam when it happened. So believe me Mrs. Keenan when I tell you Joe will be alright. When we were out there Joe was doing a wonderful job taking care of the wounded when the corpsman came over to take care of Joe when he got hit. Joe said to go help the other guys who need care more than I do.

Mrs. Keenan I haven't known Joe too long but in my book he's tops, he's one of the finest guys I've ever met. Well there isn't much more I can tell you about Joe. But Mrs. Keenan don't worry about Joe. He will be fine in a couple of days. I will close for now.

A very dear friend of Joe's

Floyd W. Caton[69]

The two letters had been delivered a few days after the telegram's arrival. Was it possible the telegram was wrong and that someone had made a horrible mistake? These two boys seemed so sure that Joe was all right. Was it possible?

Joe's father, Tom, asked Boston Congressman John McCormick for help. He called everyone he thought might have influence. Inquiries were made through official and unofficial channels. A few days later, the family received a second telegram, again from Vice Admiral Holloway Jr.

"AGAIN MY SINCEREST SYMPATHY IS EXTENDED TO YOU,"[70] it concluded, after explaining that Holl and Caton had seen Joe earlier in the battle and didn't know he had returned to action. Keenan had been killed sometime between 0200 and 0500 hours on March 27, 1953. A letter from then-Senator John F. Kennedy confirmed a second time that Joe Keenan had died in battle.

A letter from Keenan's battalion surgeon, William Beaven, provided scant solace when he declared:

> *"I can honestly say he was one of the most courageous and professionally capable corpsmen we had on the line. The amount of work he accomplished on his last night was an inspiration to every officer and man that came under his responsibility."[71]*

Almost thirty years later, Mike Keenan received his dead brother's war letters. Only thirteen years old when Joe was killed, Mike read each letter, over and over. A nagging feeling unsettled him. How could Holl and Caton report Keenan was injured twice, believe he had survived, and yet the Navy confirmed Keenan had died on the same battlefield? What had happened between Joe's nonthreatening injuries and his death? There had to be more to the story.

The questions nagged at Mike as he walked through the Boston Public Library one day while looking for a book for his daughter's school project. His eyes settled on *Medic* by Eloise Engle. He picked it up and found a passage about Francis Hammond, the corpsman who had been awarded the Medal of Honor for his courage in treating wounded Marines near Reno. Keenan contacted the author, who indicated Joe Keenan had treated injured Marines practically alongside Hammond, one of the most famous corpsmen of the Korean War. Bloodied and blinded, Keenan had helped save the lives of wounded men in indescribable conditions together with another corpsman who received the Medal of Honor. Why hadn't Keenan been honored for his courage and compassion?

Mike Keenan contacted the same Dr. Beaven who had written the family decades earlier about their son's valor. In 1983, Beaven, who worked at a military hospital in Saudi Arabia, wrote that he was certain he had recommended the Medal of Honor for Joe Keenan. Military officials could not explain what had happened to the nomination. Perhaps it had been lost when the Marines experienced a huge infusion of new personnel in the aftermath of the Nevada Cities losses, coupled with the usual rate of transfers.

Undaunted and encouraged by his discovery of Marines who had fought alongside Joe, Mike Keenan compiled one fact after another about his brother's final hours. Largely on the strength of Beaven's recollection, Keenan contacted various military officials. Surely they would be interested in rectifying an omission of posthumous recognition of more than thirty years' standing. But in the absence of original documentation, few showed interest in Keenan's pleas. Although hope had dimmed that the Joe Keenan case file would be reopened, Mike persisted. One day the Keenan family received another letter.

The Navy had completed an exhaustive six-month investigation and decided to posthumously award the Navy Cross to Joseph Francis Keenan. Researchers had compared Keenan's actions with those of other corpsmen on what became a night of unmatched corpsman bravery in the Korean War. Along with Hammond, corpsman William Charette received the Medal of Honor for his courage in the campaign to retake outpost Vegas. Keenan joined corpsmen Paul Polley, Thomas Waddill, and James McVean as recipients of the Navy Cross. Corpsmen Jay Guiver, Henry Minter, and Eldon Ralston received Silver Stars.

The Marine Corps color guard stood ramrod straight on the parade ground. A gray afternoon sky hung over the rectangular, grassy park at the Marines' Washington, D.C., barracks on May 12, 1999. Motionless, they faced two rows of blue-and-white folding chairs at the foot of a low-slung grandstand of a dozen metal rows. More than fifty members of the Keenan family, who had made the trip from Boston for the ceremony, filled the seats and benches.

At the far end of the parade ground, "The President's Own" Marine Corps Band began the national anthem, drums and horns echoing off the brick buildings that surrounded the ceremonial field established by President Thomas Jefferson in 1801. A half-beat after the anthem's end, a deep, unseen voice read an award citation over the public address system—a recitation of exploits by a young man who nearly fifty years earlier had repeatedly climbed into enemy fire to save the lives of wounded men.

General Charles Krulak lifted a medal out of the box and presented it to Mike Keenan, who gazed at it through misted eyes. The general stepped away to shake hands with each Keenan brother as applause rolled across the field. He turned and faced the crowd. As military aides escorted the Keenan brothers to their seats at the foot of the grandstand, Krulak looked up at the crowd.

"We few, we precious few, we band of brothers. For he who sheds his blood with me shall be my brother," said Krulak, a short man with a bearing and voice that filled the parade ground.[72]

Joe Keenan was "a very special, special man. He fought with the 2nd Battalion, 5th Marines," said Krulak. "He gave his life protecting the members of the 2/5. My father was the commanding officer of the 5th Marine Regiment, so this has a very special meaning for me."[73] Krulak had requested that he present the Navy Cross when he had learned the recipient had served under the command of his father, General Victor "Brute" Krulak. Keenan's family listened on as Krulak continued:

"For the children here, you'll never have a greater role model than this great, caring, sacrificing man, Joseph Keenan. There is no greater gift that a man has than to lay down his life for his fellow man. That's what Joseph Keenan did. He sacrificed himself for his fellow man."[74]

As thousands of corpsmen and medics were discharged from the military following the end of the Korean War, career medical officers assessed what had been learned during three years of combat. Beginning on April 19, 1954, top-ranking Army medical officers and doctors met for nearly two weeks at Walter Reed Army Medical Center.

They assessed nearly every factor of battlefield care in Korea. They devoted one afternoon to the medical aspects of body armor, experimental wound ballistics, and postoperative care of battle casualties. They spent a morning on a critical analysis of rectum wound treatment, new vascular surgery techniques, urinary tract wounds, and the treatment of eye casualties. They identified problems as well as achievements.

Mobile hospitals and helicopter evacuation were the principal advancements in battlefield medicine in Korea. Helicopters evacuated more than 21,700 wounded soldiers. Only 2.4 percent of the wounded died after reaching a hospital, a mortality rate half that of World War II.

The Korean War also validated a fundamental shift in thinking about combat care. During World War II, "shortest litter time" to an aid station was deemed paramount. In Korea, the effectiveness of helicopter evacuation proved that "the smoothest litter time" was more effective. Even if it took a few hours longer, a wounded soldier who hadn't been tossed about on the hood of a jeep was in better shape to withstand surgery. Smooth, seamless transport from the battlefield to a MASH unit became the standard for military medicine on the battlefield.

Despite suffering through brutally cold winters and sweltering summers, MASH surgeons pioneered other advancements. Once the war bogged down and MASH units became fixed, surgeons developed new surgical techniques. Two new vascular clamps as well as arterial and vein grafts enabled surgeons to save many limbs from amputation.

For the first time, penicillin and other antibiotics became widely available in war, providing a broad spectrum of efficacy against infection.

It also became clear that corpsmen and medics needed more training in the use of plasma in battle. Too many corpsmen assumed there had been no need for a plasma transfusion in the absence of overt symptoms of shock. Even soldiers bleeding from a severed leg sometimes didn't receive plasma until they reached an aid station. Postwar analysis highlighted the need for revised battlefield medicine training that would teach corpsmen and medics the value of using plasma transfusions before shock set in.

A decade would pass before the new treatments and expanded frontline training would be tested, before the lessons of medevac protocols under fire forged in the mountains of Korea would be refined for the jungles of Vietnam.

Chapter 11

Helos and Hospitals

● ● ● ● ● ● ●

Vietnam War

Invisible night prowlers ruffled the jungle's underbrush as the Marine patrol approached the bamboo stand silhouetted against the star-filled sky. Men soaked in sweat stepped single file out of a rice paddy filled with water and onto a game trail. The newcomers to Delta Company, 3rd Battalion, 5th Marines jumped at every sound. Veterans who had survived earlier South Vietnam night patrols scanned the vegetation for unnatural shapes and lines that might betray the enemy only yards away.

The war between South Vietnam and communist North Vietnam began in 1959. The United States began advising South Vietnam in the early 1960s and sent combat troops in 1965. In 1967, skirmishes between American soldiers and North Vietnamese Army troops intensified throughout the Que Son Valley. Two fresh NVA enemy regiments had moved into the area located south of Da Nang and midway between the coast and Laos. Repeated multibattalion sweeps by the Americans had failed to roust an increasingly entrenched enemy. U.S. intelligence officers speculated that the increased NVA presence was a precursor to attacks intended to disrupt South Vietnamese elections scheduled for September.

As the Marines continued their night patrol, less than fifty yards ahead, a tree line exploded in a blinding staccato of enemy gunfire. The string of Marines evaporated as mortar shells exploded. Startled Marines yelled for help or orders as Captain Robert Morgan consolidated his men into a defensive position. Just before sunrise on September 4, 1967, the Marines' weapons turned blister-hot as they shot at intensifying flashes of enemy weapons firing from the dense brush surrounding them. The enemy began infiltrating Delta Company's perimeter as the Americans reached into their pockets and satchels for the last of their ammo.

When they activated a strobe light to guide reinforcement helicopters, enemy fire grew mercilessly accurate. As the American air strikes forced the NVA to temporarily disengage, Bravo Company was ordered to hike two miles to reinforce the beleaguered Delta Company. When Bravo reached the battlefield at about 0820 hours, it, too, came under heavy fire. Huey helicopters dropped more than four hundred pounds of tear gas on the Vietnamese and forced them to disengage anew. It was clear to those at the regimental command post several miles away that Delta and Bravo companies were nearly surrounded by a superior force. The enemy had preempted an upcoming Marine operation, codenamed Operation Swift, with a carefully planned attack in a killing zone of its choosing.

"Mounting casualties! We're getting low on ammo! Request immediate support!"[75]

Officers huddled around the radios at headquarters. They noted the frantic voices, crackling with fear and confusion. When the radios fell silent, the officers debated how to rescue Delta and Bravo. A few grabbed clipboards and gathered around a map pinned to a bulletin board. Battalion chaplain Vincent Capodanno sat quietly to the side, taking notes. Others stood by, knowing the situation was dire, especially for the wounded.

"Dust-off" was the tactical call sign that meant wounded soldiers needed to be evacuated. By 1967, medical evacuation by helicopters had become a defining characteristic of battlefield care in Vietnam. The first Army air ambulance detachment arrived in 1964, flying UH-1 Hueys.

These rescue missions proved extremely dangerous. The Hueys were practically defenseless. Sometimes the pilot, copilot, crew chief, and medic were accompanied by a single rifleman or machine gunner to suppress enemy fire. The modified helicopters were equipped with a hoist-and-cable mechanism that lowered an empty stretcher to the ground at the rate of one hundred fifty feet per minute and retracted the wounded soldier slightly more slowly. When the helicopters hovered just above the tree line, they were extremely vulnerable to small-arms and rocket fire. Several dust-off pilots became famous for their willingness to fly into intense firefights to rescue wounded soldiers. In one famous instance, Chief Warrant Officer Michael Novosel flew into intense enemy fire fifteen times despite being wounded. He evacuated twenty-nine men who had been wounded or pinned down by the enemy and later received the Medal of Honor for his bravery.

At 0925 hours, the Marines decided to send two more companies, Mike and Kilo, as reinforcements. They would be flown to a landing zone about two miles away from the combat zone and would hike to the Marines' rescue before time and ammo ran out. Corpsmen would have to establish a medical aid station near the battlefield. Chaplain Capodanno decided to fly out with the companies.

Vincent Capodanno, a square-jawed Staten Island native, had a gruff voice that belied a gentle demeanor. His commanding presence led Marines to unconsciously lower their voices in his presence. The thirty-eight-year-old priest's career began when he entered the Maryknoll Missionary Seminary in 1949. As the war in Vietnam intensified, Capodanno decided to become a Navy chaplain. In 1966, after graduating from officer candidate school, he was assigned to the 5th Marine Division in Vietnam. He voluntarily extended his tour of combat duty.

While some chaplains seemed to disappear when fighting erupted, Capodanno frequently joined a medical unit in the field to be closer to the stricken. He refused to share a gas mask with a man in combat, saying the soldier needed it more than he did. The dozens of St. Christopher medals he distributed became the prized possessions of young Marines.

The corpsman tent quieted at the announcement from Armando Leal that the Marines were taking serious casualties in the field. The corpsman had grown up on the south side of San Antonio near Kelly Air Force Base, where his father worked as an expediting clerk. Leal loved basketball, although his short and slight stature made it a sport with a finite future. He often spent his free time in the recreation center at Southcross Junior High School. During high school, Leal played chess, joined a number of clubs, and played on the football team. In 1966, he enlisted in the Navy. His father beamed with pride, eager to share the news with coworkers. He started thinking about a transfer to a civilian job in Vietnam so he could be near his son if Leal was sent to war.

Leal met Nory Trevino within a day of arriving at the Navy's Great Lakes boot camp. He was as homesick as any recruit at Great Lakes, but Leal worried more than most about his parents, brothers, and sisters. Responsibility to his family was everything. His job was to set an example for his younger siblings and to make his family proud. Becoming a corpsman in the United States Navy seemed a good way to do that.

The daily corpsman training regimen at Great Lakes began with 0600 reveille, followed by medical classes from 0800 to 1500. After dinner, Leal and Trevino studied together to prepare for weekly Friday tests. They fired questions back and forth:

"Protein deficiency can result in which of the following conditions?"

"A corpsman may administer morphine to which of the following patients?"

"Which of the following is/are a recommended step(s) in treating deep frostbite?"

"Signs and symptoms of heat exhaustion include a weak rapid pulse, nausea, headache and ————?"

"After applying a splint to a fractured forearm, you notice the fingers develop a bluish tinge and are cool to the touch. What should you do?"[76]

Everyone knew that many advanced corpsman school graduates would be sent to Vietnam. Some of Leal's classmates intentionally failed classes to avoid the war in Southeast Asia. Others, like Leal and Trevino, stayed the course, while talking late into the night about what it would be like in a war. Leal worried about how his mother would cope if he were sent to Vietnam.

Almost a year later, Leal jogged toward the rescue helicopter's roiling dust cloud. He scanned his bag of medical supplies one last time before tossing it aboard. Seconds later his stomach sank as the helo lifted, nosed over to the left, and leveled on its way to a jungle clearing where wounded men were waiting.

In another helicopter sat Craig Sullivan, a muscled Southerner whose cap sat low and shaded a moustache that curled upward at each end. He was a sergeant in Mike Company's first platoon and had arrived in Vietnam only a month earlier. When Sullivan was eight years old, his father had taken him to a theater in Tallahasee, Florida, to see John Wayne in *Sands of Iwo Jima*. By the time the credits rolled, Sullivan knew he wanted to be a Marine.

Sullivan had been struck immediately by Leal's easygoing nature. The corpsman enjoyed sharing stories and playing cards. Sullivan also had grown to respect Leal's eye for detail, especially out in the field. "You need a salt tablet," Leal told a sweat-soaked Marine slumped under a tree, whose shirt and fly were open in search of every imaginary wisp of air in the tropical heat. "How's your feet? Socks dry?"[77] Leal usually carried extra socks for the troops because wet socks produced crippling blisters. He frequently asked each man if he had brushed his teeth recently.

The thundering noise of the helicopters swallowed conversation as the rescuers approached a landing zone near Dinh An. The trees surrounding the clearing shuddered as the helos touched down at 1245 Hours. Leal, Chaplain Capodanno, and the Marines jumped out, hauled their gear clear, and prepared for a four-kilometer march to a battle in the jungle. Capodanno approached Sullivan and a group of Marines.

"Sir, would you mind if I said a prayer for your men?" he asked. Sullivan, a Baptist, agreed. Over the whump of the helicopters, Capodanno led a brief prayer that ended with "May you go with God."[78] Mike Company began its march toward the sound of gunfire.

Sweat rolled down their spines as they slogged through rice paddies and followed game trails through stands of eucalyptus trees and hedgerows of dense brush. They walked under a cloudless sky in sweltering heat, jumping at every sound, praying the next step didn't trigger a land mine. Every few minutes they heard "*pop, pop … brrrrrrrpt … brrrrrrrrrpt*" in the distance as enemy snipers and machine gunners took aim at the trapped Marines ahead.

About two hours after landing, Mike Company reached a small plateau approximately twenty-five feet high. The top was bare, save for a few knee-high shrubs, bomb craters of varying sizes, and a handful of large black rocks. The lead platoon was exposed on all four sides as it crossed the plateau. Marines surveyed left and right as they descended toward a rice paddy that was almost two hundred meters wide. Delta was still an hour's hike away.

"Sergeant, a tree just moved," said a Marine named Bill Vandegrift. "If it moves again, shoot the son of the bitch," Sullivan replied.[79]

Moments later the camouflaged enemy flinched and was shot by Vandegrift. Before the shot's echo had subsided, hundreds of NVA soldiers opened fire and mortar crews zeroed in on the exposed Marines.

The enemy had caught both the first and second platoons of Mike Company in the open. The NVA had the advantages of position, crossing fields of fire, clear lines of sight, and camouflage. The Americans were stranded, with no immediate prospect of reinforcement. A dire situation faced by two companies of Marines in the morning became potentially catastrophic for three by early afternoon.

Mortar rounds pounded the ground around Larry Nunez. The one-time high school crosscountry star had turned down college scholarships to join the Marines and fight in Vietnam. It had taken two years, but he had finally received orders for Southeast Asia and arrived in February. As the enemy fire intensified, Corporal Nunez heard Bill Young scream with pain. Nunez ran to him, and dropped to the ground.

"Doc!"

Leal sprinted toward the two Marines, crouching low and lugging his aid kit. He slid to a stop as enemy bullets kicked up dirt into his eyes and mouth.

Leal looked Young over but couldn't find any blood. The air buzzed with shrapnel from exploding mortars only yards away as the corpsman gently rolled Young over. He found two small bullet holes in Young's pelvis and quickly applied a battle dressing.

"That's all I can do for him,"[80] Leal told Nunez. He straightened to scan the battlefield. A few yards away, a prone Marine's blood pooled on the dirt. Leal jumped to his feet and crab-walked toward him.

Meanwhile, squad leader Larry Peters assembled his men, who had not yet climbed onto the plateau. He needed firsthand intelligence before he could deploy them to face the enemy on the other side. Peters told them to stay put. He ran to the top of the plateau and into the field of fire. The sight of Marines writhing on the ground and huddling in shallow depressions as enemy rifles and machine guns flashed across the distant tree line shocked him. He watched Leal belly flop next to one man whose leg had been shredded to a bloody pulp. His squad crested the knoll and saw Marines lying everywhere.

Ray Harton had hit the ground among the screams and explosions. Bullets zinged inches away from their heads as the Marines returned fire. Peters ran past Harton, directly toward the enemy. He fell when a bullet tore through his leg. Harton and two other Marines started to crawl toward Peters when an NVA gunner opened fire, killing the two and hitting Harton in the arm, severing an artery. Harton screamed as he attempted to stem the flow of blood. He tried to remain still, knowing NVA machine-gun fire riddled any injured Marine who moved.

Meanwhile, Peters was hit again with mortar shrapnel, this time in the face. Twice wounded, he struggled to his feet to draw enemy fire and expose their position to the few Marines still able to return fire. Peters was shot twice in the chest.

Lying motionless on the ground, Harton slowly turned his head to look across the plateau. He spotted Armando Leal, bloodied by shrapnel and waving off an approaching corpsman. Leal kept moving across the battlefield. Every few minutes his head popped up from behind a shrub or rock to identify who needed help. Each time, Leal made direct eye contact with Harton, who lay only about twenty yards away. He knew Harton needed help, but so did many others. Leal had to make instant diagnoses from afar, deciding which Marine most critically needed his triage. Sometimes a bleeding Marine managed to crawl into a shallow crater. The depression gave no protection to Leal, who often placed himself between the wounded soldier and the enemy to give his patient a marginally better chance at survival.

Capodanno had seen Peters's chest explode in crimson. As Capodanno ran toward him, a mortar shell detonated only fifty feet away. Shrapnel hit the priest's shoulder and obliterated part of his right hand. He stumbled to Peters, lay down next to him, and ministered the last rites as bullets flew overhead.

Capodanno next ran to Howard Manfra, who had been wounded and was stranded by enemy crossfire. Although other Marines had tried to rescue Manfra, only Capodanno reached him and dragged him into a small depression. As he did, Capodanno and Leal locked eyes a few yards away from each other before Leal turned toward another screaming Marine.

The battle had stretched to more than ten hours. As the afternoon light faded, the enemy grew bolder. Alert Marines spotted "walking bushes" as the camouflaged enemy crept closer, sometimes to within yards of the Americans before opening fire. The entire battle raged in an area smaller than the size of two football fields. Only a few miles away, the medical staff at a sophisticated military hospital waited for the battle to stabilize enough for the Army's medevac helicopters to begin delivering the wounded.

Vietnam posed new challenges and opportunities to the military hospital corps. Unlike Korea, MASH units did not follow advances and then pull back alongside retreats. The Vietnam War was a guerilla war fought largely in place. The static nature of guerilla warfare in the jungle enabled the military to establish fully equipped hospitals on the fringe of combat. Some patient wards were inflatable and air conditioned. Most had complete surgical teams, a variety of specialists, and comprehensive recovery facilities. Field hospitals in Vietnam functioned at the level of a four-hundred-bed general hospital in the United States.

Still stranded on the plateau, Harton prepared for death at the point of an enemy bayonet. Someone touched his shoulder. Inches away, the grimy, haggard face of Father Vincent Capodanno melted into a smile. The priest's condition shocked Harton. He was covered in dried blood. Rivulets of sweat flowed from the corners of his eyes, down his cheeks, and along a prominent jaw. A bloodied hand had been quickly bandaged but still oozed.

"Stay calm, Marine," Capodanno said. "God's with all of us today. Someone will be here in a minute to take care of you."[81] Perhaps the chaplain was thinking of Leal. He had seen the young corpsman darting from Marine to Marine for hours. A gasping, high-pitched scream only twenty feet away cut Capodanno short.

"My leg! My leg!"[82]

It was Armando Leal. The corpsman sat upright, his uniform now soaked in blood and dirt, both hands clutching his thigh just above the knee as if he had pulled a hamstring. He gently rocked back and forth in pain, chin down, his eyes glassy with shock. Capodanno quickly blessed Harton with his good hand before running to Leal. He put an arm around Leal and leaned closer to whisper into the young corpsman's ear. After treating wounds for hours under fire, Leal was white with shock.

"Watch out! There's a Viet Cong with a machine gun!" Frederick Tancke yelled at Capodanno.[83] Tancke had spotted the enemy setting up his machine gun only about fifteen yards away. The enemy heard Tancke and laughed as he squatted to take aim at the priest and the corpsman. As Capodanno spoke to Leal, two bursts of machine-gun fire ripped into them. They fell as one, side by side.

The battle continued as dusk deepened. Dozens of Marines still stranded in the open huddled together in shallow craters across the plateau. Darkness would bring an enemy advance. The Viet Cong would infiltrate the perimeter and then storm the exhausted Marines. Soon the enemy would be shooting point-blank at Marines who were nearly out of ammunition.

Second platoon leader Ed Blecksmith surveyed his troops. Blecksmith had grown up in Los Angeles. A gifted athlete, he had played receiver and safety at the University of Southern California before following his father and two uncles into the Marine Corps.

Blecksmith pulled wounded Marines into bomb craters, some of which were only a few feet across and shallow, not nearly large enough for a soldier to get out of the line of fire. Others were fifteen feet across and nearly five feet deep. These were the only possible refuges if the Marines of Mike Company hoped to survive the night.

Blecksmith and others pulled several wounded men into one of the largest bomb craters. Some still writhed in agony, but most had gone into shock after lying in the afternoon sun, bleeding. Many were alive because, hours earlier, Leal had applied a battle dressing to slow the flow of blood. The crusted wounds of others who had gone unattended were scraped open as they were dragged into craters, sometimes on top of other wounded men who screamed in pain.

At the battle's outset, the Marines had been yelling to one another, usually asking for orders or reporting enemy movement. That night, a man called out for Blecksmith. It sounded as though he were only a few yards from the crater where Blecksmith and others huddled.

"That's not any of our guys calling you, sergeant," said one Marine as Blecksmith prepared to climb out.[84] It grew quiet in the crater as they listened to the repeated pleas. Just barely, they could hear an accent. It was the enemy. No one moved. The jungle quieted.

The Marines called for night air support. When the spotter aircraft arrived overhead, it fired a white star cluster that turned night into day. The pilots in the following attack aircraft looked down at the dimpled plateau, each depression filled with prone Marines. They lined up to bomb the surrounding tree lines and hedgerows. As the ground shuddered from the explosions, the Marines climbed out of the craters and dragged as many of the wounded as they could to the other side of the plateau, where Mike Company had established its command post.

Someone rolled Harton over. "Doc, this one's alive!" he yelled.[85] Unseen hands placed Harton onto a poncho and dragged him into a shell hole. A Marine lit a cigarette for him. Another stuck a needle in his arm. As the morphine took effect, Harton grew drowsy, but he kept peering out of the crater, as American aircraft blasted enemy positions. When the bombing stopped, quiet returned, and the enemy disappeared into the safety of the jungle.

The next morning, Harton awoke under a blinding sun. Waiting for a helicopter, he walked across the hill, now littered with ponchos covering dead Marines, including Leal and Capodanno. The corpsman had been hit in the neck and throat, while the chaplain had taken nearly two dozen rounds in his chest. Most men die with an expression of shock. The Marine covering Capodanno marveled at the serene look on his face. Leal was curled up nearby. Dead NVA soldiers lay within a few yards of the two. Once the surviving Marines regrouped, they were ordered to pursue the retreating enemy.

A proud Armando Leal, Sr. had pulled some strings to get transferred to a rapid area supply support team in Vietnam so he could be close to his son, the corpsman. He had waited a month for the transfer to a civilian supply team near Da Nang that distributed jet engines. As he was flying over the Pacific, an enemy machine gunner killed his son. He arrived in time to identify his son's body. Later, at the funeral in Texas, the closed casket was opened only for the father to say goodbye.

"I lost my son and my world," he often said.[86] The patriarch of the Leal family never completely recovered from the loss of a son who died in battle just two weeks short of his twenty-first birthday.

September 4, 1967, marked the start of Operation Swift, the series of Marine missions to rid the Que Son Valley of North Vietnamese troops. That day sixteen Americans died and thirty-one were wounded. Eighty-five enemy soldiers lay dead. That day also became known as one of the most remarkable concentrations of bravery in the Vietnam War.

Armando Leal received the Navy Cross for his courage and compassion. Father Vincent Capodanno and Sergeant Larry Peters both became Medal of Honor recipients. The Navy Cross also was awarded to Mike Company's commanding officer, Captain John Murray, as well as to Lance Corporal Thomas Fisher. Sergeant Howard Manfra received the Silver Star, while 2nd Lieutenant Ed Combs and Sergeant Craig Sullivan both received the Bronze Star. Their citations provided only vague clues for families anxious to understand the horror they had faced.

The day after the ambush, a letter arrived at regimental headquarters:

"I am due to go home in late November or early December. I humbly request that I stay over Christmas and New Year's Eve with my men. I am willing to relinquish my 30 days' leave."

It had been written by Father Capodanno the day before Operation Swift.

A community movement in San Antonio organized a successful campaign to rename Southcross Junior High School as Leal Middle School. In 1973, it became the first school in San Antonio to be named after a Vietnam veteran. Every day, teachers, students, and parents pass the glass-encased tribute to a quiet young man who grew up only a few blocks away. His eulogy in the display case is Leal's Navy Cross citation:

"... During Operation Swift, the Second Platoon was providing security for the Battalion Command Group when the platoon came under heavy enemy fire. Petty Officer (then Hospitalman) Leal ran through the fire-swept area, and began administering first aid to several casualties who were directly exposed to grazing fire. Although constantly exposed to heavy fire, and painfully wounded himself, he

rendered aid for two hours to wounded Marines who were located between friendly and enemy lines. He refused to be evacuated in order that he might continue his mission of mercy. While treating his comrades and moving them to protected areas, Petty Officer Leal was severely wounded a second time and, despite being immobilized, calmly continued to aid his wounded comrades. A Marine tried to drag him to a covered position, but was shot in the hand and, at that time, Petty Officer Leal received a third wound. Petty Officer Leal pushed the Marine and told him to take cover from the assaulting enemy whom they both could see. Suddenly a North Vietnamese soldier fired a machine gun from close range, mortally wounding Petty Officer Leal.

Through his swift actions and professional skill in aiding and protecting the wounded, he significantly eased the suffering and undoubtedly saved the lives of several of his comrades. His exceptional courage and unfaltering dedication to duty in the face of great personal risk were in keeping with the highest traditions of the United States Naval Service."

America's longest war abroad to that point produced numerous acts of medical corps valor as well as several military medicine advancements. Army medical rescue helicopter missions had evacuated three hundred thousand wounded soldiers to aid stations and hospitals. By the end of war, it took only nine minutes for an evacuation helicopter to launch from the time a request was received from the battlefield. On average a wounded soldier was treated within an hour of being shot, compared with four to six hours in Korea.

But Army medevac teams and Navy corpsmen paid a steep price for near-immediate treatment and evacuation of the wounded in battle. Two hundred eight pilots and crew were killed, 545 were wounded, and 199 medevac helicopters were shot down. That amounted to about one in three helicopter crewmen who were wounded or killed in Vietnam.

All told, 638 corpsmen were killed and 4,563 were wounded. The Army and Navy medical corps earned 21 Medals of Honor. Navy corpsmen were awarded 30 Navy Crosses, 127 Silver Stars, and 290 Bronze Stars for valor.

Another major milestone was the widespread availability of whole blood transfusions for the first time in war. The Military Blood Program established in the Far East produced as many as thirty-eight thousand units of whole blood per month.

Rapid evacuation and battlefield transfusions were key to warding off shock and delivering more critically wounded soldiers alive to military hospitals than in past wars. The hospital mortality rate in Vietnam was 2.6 percent, slightly higher than in Korea even though soldier wounds in Vietnam often were far more extensive and life threatening. The injury rate from land mines in Vietnam, for example, was three times as high as in Korea.

The permanent nature of many military hospitals in Vietnam also led to medical advances. Neurosurgeons developed techniques to tunnel through tissue surrounding a wound and install temporary blood vessel grafts to keep a limb viable until the wound healed and a permanent vascular graft could be inserted. Hospital personnel also tested new respiratory equipment that minimized the risk of bacterial infections in combat conditions. And the Army experimented with an aerosol-based antibiotic treatment that its medics used on the battlefield.

As a result of these advancements, of 3.4 million men and women who served in Vietnam, 47,000 were killed in combat, a mortality rate of 1.4 percent.

Sometimes in war, sailors and soldiers become involuntary corpsmen and medics for a few hours or days when the mass casualties are overwhelming. One day off the coast of Vietnam, an aircraft carrier's bakers, boiler tenders, electricians, dentists, signalmen, and supply clerks were threatened by a catastrophe that swallowed nearly the entire flight deck crew. The survival of hundreds aboard the USS *Forrestal* depended upon a ship full of heroes.

Chapter 12

Mass Casualties

•••••••

Vietnam War

By mid-1967, more than 450,000 American troops were in Vietnam. As the war escalated, senior military officers asked President Lyndon Johnson to authorize an additional 200,000. On June 6, the aircraft carrier USS *Forrestal* departed Norfolk, Virginia, bound for Vietnam.

Combat operations required a well-trained and cohesive crew. Sailors new to the ship had to learn the layout of about two thousand compartments and a bewildering array of departments and activities. There was a newspaper, radio station, television station, convenience stores, and dry cleaning aboard. Church services, basketball tournaments, and movies broke up the monotonous routine of life at sea. Yet most sailors never saw more than 20 percent of the ship. If a sailor had no business in a particular department, he had no business being there, including the flight deck. Much of the crew often went a week or more without seeing daylight. They lived on a twenty-four-hour clock, and no one took weekends off at sea.

The ship quieted at night when *Forrestal's* lights were dimmed. The steady hum of exhaust fans and intake vents sounded as though the carrier was breathing. The rhythmic vibration from the power plant and the massive propellers pulsed through the steel decks.

For weeks the crew conducted drills as the aircraft carrier approached the coast of Vietnam. As the first day of combat neared, anxiety grew. Personnel in the medical department, called "sick bay" by most of the crew, reacted in different ways to the imminence of war. Some corpsmen fidgeted. Others found reasons to recheck their supplies or return to their bunks for an overlooked item. Most of the men on board were new to war.

Early on July 25, *Forrestal* launched its first air strikes against North Vietnam. More than five thousand sailors waited and wondered if all the pilots and their aircraft would return intact. Corpsmen assigned to sick bay and the flight deck emergency crew stood by nervously as the carrier launched multiple air strikes almost daily.

Forrestal was commanded by Captain John Beling. Short and thin, Beling flew bombers in World War II and studied nuclear physics at MIT. One of the largest departments on the ship was engineering, which was headed by Merv Rowland. Engineering was responsible for the massive power plant, the ship's maintenance, and emergency response, called damage control.

More than sixty corpsmen and four doctors, including Medical Officer Gary Kirchner, comprised the medical department. Kirchner was working at the Mayo Clinic when he was drafted into the military in 1967. He came aboard *Forrestal* shortly before it left Norfolk. He tended to be gruff and was called "Cranky" by some of the corpsmen.

Kirchner had a difficult time adjusting to the realities of *Forrestal's* medical department after his experience at the Mayo Clinic. Most of the corpsmen had been drafted into the military, and few had any interest in making healthcare a career. Many had graduated from high school only a few years earlier. "I'm at sea with a bunch of sixth graders," Kirchner complained to his wife.[87]

He was unimpressed particularly with *Forrestal*'s capability for at-sea surgery. He didn't have the surgical specialists he was accustomed to. His corpsmen had about twelve weeks of basic training, and some had an additional year's worth of specialty training, such as pharmacy or laboratory. But a single specialty aboard an aircraft carrier was a luxury. Each corpsman on board *Forrestal* underwent long hours of on-the-job crosstraining in other specialties so he could serve as a back-up assistant.

Kirchner also thought *Forrestal*'s surgical equipment was inadequate. He noted that sick bay was comprised of forty beds stacked two high, making it difficult to closely monitor a critically ill or injured sailor in the top bunk. He quickly devised a plan to stabilize seriously wounded sailors and fly them to a hospital ashore for advanced surgery.

Chief petty officers, usually fifteen- or twenty-year Navy veterans, directly supervised the corpsmen. Sam Walker was typical. The World War II veteran had a square jaw and faded tattoos on both arms. He ran the pharmacy and told corpsmen that if he could grab their hair, it was too long.

Most days at sea were filled with routine. Corpsmen ate breakfast at 0600 hours and then prepared for the day's activities. Starting at 0900, they administered the first of two daily sick call sessions. They gave vaccinations, saw sailors who had health complaints, took vital signs, and notified a doctor when necessary. Following sick call, they conducted weekly galley and barbershop inspections, administered hearing tests, checked for radiation, and scrutinized sleeping quarters. Every fourth day, a corpsman was on call as part of the emergency medical response team. Comprised of four corpsmen and a physician's assistant, the team stood ready to respond to trauma incidents. Its job was to assess injured sailors and prepare them for transport on stretchers down ladders and bomb elevators to sick bay.

Privacy was practically unknown on *Forrestal*. Corpsmen slept in compartments filled with bunks, not far from sick bay. In some places on the ship, more than one hundred bunks were housed in a single compartment, three high, and separated by three-foot-wide passageways. Corpsmen with the least seniority typically were assigned a bottom bunk just off the deck at the compartment's entrance, where it was the noisiest and most difficult to sleep.

The dental offices were next to sick bay. Both were located nearly in the center of the ship with multiple access routes in case of an emergency or mass casualties. One of the dentists was Samuel Mowad. He was a quiet man with a long, thin face accented by thick, heavy eyebrows. Born in Philadelphia, Mowad graduated from Seton Hall University in New Jersey and was on his first cruise in the Navy. He had three sons under the age of four back home.

Nearly everyone participated in drills. Each corpsman was assigned to a specific battle dressing station or repair locker in an emergency when "general quarters" was announced. They were joined by dental technicians and dentists at battle dressing stations located throughout the aircraft carrier, which was more than three football fields long. Corpsmen would triage injured sailors first before they were taken to sick bay or the flight deck for evacuation.

Some questioned the authenticity of the drills. Others resented standing around for what seemed like hours after they reached their emergency gear. Yet most knew an emergency could happen at any moment. A year earlier, the USS *Oriskany* was operating off Vietnam when a sailor mistakenly placed a lit magnesium flare into a flare locker. He closed the hatch tightly, thinking the flare would burn out. He was wrong. The flair ignited five hundred others. It became so hot that the steel hatches were welded shut just before the locker exploded. More than forty sailors were killed, most from the fireball that rolled through nearby sleeping quarters and sucked out the oxygen.

By July 29, combat flight operations on *Forrestal* were routine. Every sixty seconds beginning at 0700, an attack jet thundered off the bow in the first launch of the day. Three hours later, flight deck activity increased as crews reorganized, took their positions, and prepared for the second launch at 1100. Pilots checked their gear one last time as they left their squadron ready rooms and climbed into their aircraft. By then, the tropical heat and humidity were intense.

Nearly thirty jets were designated for an air strike on a rail line north of Hanoi. Facing inward toward the carrier's centerline, the planes were parked wing tip to wing tip along the edge of the flight deck, from just behind the island back to and across the stern and then forward along the port side edge. The large semicircle of aircraft were fueled and loaded with seventy bombs plus rockets, missiles, and ammunition as *Forrestal* turned into the wind for launch. About one hundred flight deck, ordnance, fuel, launch, safety, emergency, flight deck control, and aircraft readiness specialists focused on preparing the aircraft and staging them for launch off the bow. Four corpsmen were stationed at a battle dressing station just off the flight deck, and two others were on the flight deck.

When pilot Jim Bangert started his aircraft and switched from an auxiliary power unit to internal power at 1052, a Zuni rocket on his aircraft accidentally fired. It streaked across the flight deck and through a sailor's shoulder, severing his arm. The rocket punctured the fuel tank of Lieutenant Commander John McCain's jet without exploding and continued into the ocean. A moment's shock was replaced with alarm and fear. McCain's jet began leaking fuel that pooled on the flight deck. When burning embers from the rocket fell into the jet fuel, a giant fireball erupted on the flight deck. McCain scrambled out of the cockpit, jumped off the nose of his plane, and escaped unharmed. Sailors standing nearby were swallowed by flames.

"Fire! Fire! Fire on the flight deck aft!" blared the 1MC public-address system, followed by the sixteen-bell code for general quarters. Captain Beling ordered "emergency full back" to immediately put the carrier into reverse. That reduced the thirty-knot wind down the flight deck that threatened to spread the fire faster than it could be contained.

The day before, *Forrestal* had taken aboard several tons of ordnance from the supply ship USS *Diamond Head*. Some of the bombs were more than thirty years old because the Navy faced a critical shortage at that time. The old "Comb B" bombs were unstable and known to detonate from heat or vibrations. Despite this, they were loaded onto an aircraft carrier sailing in the tropics only eighteen degrees north of the equator.

About ninety seconds after the rocket misfired, a bomb exploded on *Forrestal*'s flight deck almost directly above sick bay. The blast incinerated *Forrestal*'s primary firefighting team in a split second. Pilots who remained in their aircraft were burned alive. Blackened body parts littered the flight deck. Some men were blown as far as fifty feet away as shrapnel tore into their abdomens, legs, and arms. Sailors' faces were shaved off; others were beheaded. Some were thrown off the aircraft carrier and fell sixty feet into the sea.

Ten seconds later, a second bomb exploded. Below deck, momentary speculation that the first explosion might have been from a plane crash evaporated. JP5 jet fuel cascaded through two gaping holes in the flight deck into sleeping quarters filled with sailors who had worked the night before.

At the sound of general quarters, corpsmen scrambled around each other in the tight compartments, grabbing supplies and preparing for the casualties they knew would be coming. Some corpsmen and dental technicians ran out of sick bay to their assigned battle dressing stations.

Forrestal's medical department faced a mass casualty situation that threatened to overwhelm its capacity.

Mowad raced onto the flight deck to see how he could help. Dozens of others did the same, at first ignoring their assigned emergency stations in an instinctive desire to help at the scene of the disaster. A blast pelted Mowad with shrapnel, but he was far enough away that it only dented his helmet. He retreated to his station along with two corpsmen. The compartment was too small to accommodate a stretcher, making it useless for emergency treatment. Mowad received permission to move his battle dressing station to the fo'c'sle ("forecastle") just below the bow where the ship's anchoring mechanism was operated.

Portions of the flight deck became so hot from uncontrolled fires that sailors' shoes melted. Several men volunteered to string the fire hoses across their shoulders to keep them from melting. Many were not trained as firefighters and were not assigned to the flight deck. Strangers stood shoulder to shoulder hosing down the raging flames.

About thirty minutes after the first two blasts, Chief Engineer Rowland became alarmed at damage control reports of temperatures in many compartments, including the weapons magazines. The bulkheads in the compartments that stored liquid oxygen became so hot that sailors devised a way to connect a garden hose to the oxygen tanks and drain more than five hundred gallons of the combustible material over the side.

Meanwhile, corpsmen had established a triage station near the island on the flight deck. As the intense heat detonated more bombs, fired ammunition, and triggered ejection seats, sailors with blackened faces and exposed craniums were being helped to the island. Some sucked air through a hole where their lips had melted away. One had lost his face, was missing an arm, and had a serious abdominal wound. His pants were smoldering.

The flight deck was slick with fuel, foam, and blood. Some of the injured were conscious. A few screamed and writhed. Others were as still as statues, staring up into the sky. Sailors tried to help the corpsmen. They packed open wounds with brown paper or their shirts because medical supplies were exhausted quickly. Some sat next to mangled sailors apparently unaware they were already dead.

Corpsmen and doctors had about thirty seconds to triage each patient. They used colored tags to mark the state and fate of the wounded. Category 1 patients (black tags) were likely to die. Pain control was all that mattered. Kirchner set aside one of the compartments in sick bay for Category 1 patients. A lone corpsman stayed with them, comforting them as best he could and administering morphine. Kirchner knew the patients screaming were fighting death. It seemed the quiet ones somehow knew they would die. Either way, Kirchner thought it was important that injured sailors who might survive be separated from those who had almost no chance. Category 2s (red tags) were the injured who required varying degrees of immediate care; Category 3s (green tags) were sailors with minor wounds who could wait for treatment.

After a quick assessment, the seriously injured were brought down to the mess deck where the crew normally ate their meals. Corpsmen could hear sailors screaming in pain as they were helped or carried down the passageways toward the mess deck and sick bay. Sometimes a sailor carried a wounded man's severed arm or leg, in case it could be reattached.

Bloodied and burned men sat or lay on the deck near sick bay, waiting for a doctor. Some were being held by a friend or stranger who didn't know how else to help. Others screamed "Doc!" because they had been deafened by the explosions. The clothing on several still smoldered, while some had airplane parts sticking out of their bodies. The first patient who entered sick bay had serious facial wounds and couldn't breathe. A tracheotomy was performed immediately.

Seriously burned victims needed the most immediate and intensive care. The priorities were always the same—ABC: check the airway, monitor the breathing, and assess the quality of the pulse. Corpsmen paid careful attention to the airway. Singed nose hair or eyebrows often meant the patient had inhaled smoke, heat, and gases. A burned airway could become life threatening within hours. Corpsmen cleared the nose and throat of soot, started an IV, and inserted a tube, so a respirator could help the sailor breathe. *Forrestal*, though, had a limited number of respirators, and there weren't enough corpsmen to manually help patients breathe.

Corpsmen next attended to a variety of burns. Treatment in the first hour was crucial. They removed sheets of burned skin, applied silver nitrate to raw flesh, and loosely wrapped burn sites. Facial burns were gruesome. Eyelids and lips tended to swell. A sailor with a burned penis required catheterization due to inflammation. Chest burns were critical. Traumatized internal organs could swell against a sailor's burned chest, which if untreated, became rigid. Corpsmen kept each burned chest as pliable as possible with ointment to allow the lungs to expand. Burn treatment for a single patient could be extremely time-consuming.

Sailors with other serious physical injuries were not always given the same intensive, immediate care as burn victims. A sailor with a lacerated abdomen could be temporarily patched and be given an IV and morphine. He could wait for evacuation off *Forrestal*. If he developed a raging thirst, it could be a sign of internal bleeding.

Meanwhile in the fo'c'sle, Mowad faced a stream of wounded men. Just before *Forrestal* left Norfolk, he had taken a one-week class in triage. Other than that, the dentist relied on first-year medical school classes in gross anatomy and pharmacology. In less than half an hour, he performed two tracheotomies, the second on a man who was in critical condition.

"Doc, why are you doing that?" asked a corpsman. "It's not going to help him."

"Maybe, but I know it's going to help you, and it's going to help me because we're trying, and the patient's going to feel better seeing us try," Mowad replied.[88]

Minutes later another sailor was carried into the fo'c'sle. A single sliver of tendon connected a foot to a knee. The rest of the man's calf had been blown away. With one snip, the dentist performed his first amputation. A nearby chief petty officer fainted on the spot.

Several Navy ships turned and headed toward the black smoke that billowed from *Forrestal*. Although the hospital ship USS *Repose* was a day away, the USS *Bon Homme Richard*, USS *MacKenzie*, USS *Rupertus*, USS *Tucker*, and USS *Oriskany* ceased operations and turned to assist *Forrestal*. Within fifteen minutes the *Rupertus* began picking up sailors who had been blown overboard. Medical evacuation helicopter landing areas were designated on *Forrestal*'s undamaged bow. The helicopters carried firefighting equipment. As they were being unloaded, corpsmen accompanied the most seriously injured on stretchers and onto the flight deck. The wash of the helicopters almost knocked some over as they approached while monitoring their patients' vital signs. They watched for a change in the color of the inside of a man's mouth or his fingernails that might indicate a sudden deterioration. If a patient worsened, a corpsman called sick bay for instructions.

"Don't get on that helicopter with your patient," Kirchner told them. "No matter what, stay aboard."[89] He didn't want any corpsmen suddenly deciding it was prudent to accompany a patient off *Forrestal*. None did.

Soon *Oriskany*'s sick bay overflowed with *Forrestal* patients. *Oriskany* sailors volunteered to sit with the injured and burned men. Even though most of them had a large "M" written with a grease pencil on their foreheads for the morphine they had been given, they lay in pain. Some were burned so completely there wasn't any place for an "M."

A fog of burning rubber, fuel, and other combustibles filled the hangar deck on *Forrestal*. Sparks periodically showered down from transformers bolted to bulkheads. By mid-afternoon, the majority of the wounded had been treated, and the dead were laid out in body bags on the hangar deck. Some were bizarre shapes because bodies had contorted into freakish positions and carbonized. Others corpses fell apart when sailors placed them in a body bag. Dazed men, faces streaked with tears and sweat, stepped over the dead, gently pulling back blankets and opening bags in search of their buddies. After a while, the Marines who provided security on *Forrestal* created a morgue by rigging some pipe with blue curtains around the dead and standing watch to keep sailors from looking through them.

Mowad and another dentist checked the pockets of the dead for clues to their identities if their dog tags had melted or been blown away. They also looked for names stenciled on sailors' shirts if they hadn't been burned. Sometimes a tattoo was enough to identify a man.

Holes were cut through the solid steel flight deck so that makeshift firefighting teams could reach the compartments where fires continued to burn more than four hours after the first bomb had detonated.

Captain Beling read a prayer over the 1MC that night:

"Our heavenly Father, we see this day as one minute and yet a lifetime for all of us. We thank you for the courage of those that gave their lives in saving their shipmates today. We humbly ask you to grant them peace. And to their loved ones, the conciliation and strength to bear their loss. Help us to renew the faith we have in you. We thank you for our own lives. May we remember you as you have remembered us today. From our hearts we turn to you now, knowing that you have been at our sides in every minute of this day. Heavenly Father, help us to rebuild and re-man our ship so that our brothers who died today may have not made a fruitless sacrifice. Amen."[90]

Forrestal was a shaken ship. Many sailors slept up in the fo'c'sle or on the catwalks next to the flight deck. The last fire was extinguished at 0400 the following morning. It had burned for seventeen hours, but the danger wasn't over. Later that day, three sailors entered a battery locker to search for anyone who may have been trapped. All three suffocated when acid from broken batteries mixed with seawater to create chlorine gas.

Mowad flew by helicopter over to *Repose* with parachute bags filled with dental X-rays. He used them to identify the burned bodies that had been transferred to the hospital ship. He and two dental technicians worked in a walk-in cold storage unit, trying to match the burned bodies on the tables with more than four hundred sets of X-rays. In one case, Mowad didn't need the X-rays. He recognized the three fillings he had put in the sailor's mouth just two days before.

On July 29, 1967, the USS *Forrestal* endured more direct hits from bombs than any aircraft carrier since World War II. The accident resulted in the deaths of 134 sailors. That dwarfed the typical mass casualty on an aircraft carrier when fewer than 20 sailors might be injured in a particularly bad plane crash. Medical personnel treated more than 150 injured men. Scores more were assessed for minor shrapnel wounds, sprained shoulders, or twisted knees. Kirchner estimated sick bay saw more than 300 patients in 24 hours.

In the week after the disaster, sailors on *Forrestal* continued to discover the bodies of men who had been listed as missing. Some were found in inaccessible spaces that required extensive cutting to reach the corpses. In early August, the heavily damaged aircraft carrier off-loaded more than fifty bodies at the Navy's Subic Bay base in the Philippines. After temporary repairs were made, *Forrestal* returned to Norfolk thirty-four days later. The carrier had lost twenty-one aircraft. Forty others had been damaged. Two years of comprehensive repairs cost $72 million (roughly $475 million in 2010 dollars).

The investigation into the tragedy started before the smoke had fully cleared from *Forrestal*'s compartments. It became evident that two shortcuts taken by flight deck personnel made the disaster possible. One group of sailors pulled the safety pins on rockets before the aircraft reached the catapult. Although that saved time on the launch cycle, they were supposed to pull the safety pins after the planes had reached the catapult. Another flight deck crew prematurely connected rockets to the jets' electrical firing systems. That, too, saved time when the plan of the day called for multiple air strikes.

If a rocket was connected to the firing system, it was secure if the safety pin stayed in place. Similarly, if the safety pin was removed but the rocket wasn't connected to the electrical system, it could not be fired. But two crews independently violated safety procedures. When the jet was started, a stray jolt of electricity fired the live Zuni rocket across the flight deck.

In addition to these procedural lapses, investigators were critical of the inadequate training of the firefighting and damage control crews, as well as the lack of respirators available on board.

Captain John Beling was reprimanded for poor judgment. After a stint at the Pentagon, he was transferred to a post in Iceland. Dr. Gary Kirchner left the Navy and became a county coroner in Pennsylvania. Sam Mowad, the dentist, made the Navy his career. So did chief petty officer Sam Walker, who ran the pharmacy. He was proud of the sick bays on his ships and the young corpsmen who answered to him. Lieutenant Commander John McCain later was shot down and became a prisoner of war in Vietnam. After leaving the Navy, he was elected to the U.S. Senate and was the Republican presidential nominee in 2008. Most of the corpsmen on *Forrestal* left the Navy when they fulfilled their military service obligation. Some went to college, and many reentered civilian life at a time when public opposition to Vietnam was mounting. Few outside the Navy acknowledged the ship of heroes.

More than half of the burn injuries sustained during the Vietnam War were accidental. Combat burns from an artillery round exploding inside a bunker, armored personnel carrier, or ship's compartment were particularly horrific and could lead to dehydration and shock. Often they were compounded by penetration wounds from shrapnel and other serious complications such as smoke and flame inhalation. A trachea badly burned by heat could become swollen and cut off oxygen to the lungs. The complexity of serious burn injuries from enemy fire carried a 70 percent fatality rate.

If a soldier or sailor survived the first few hours, the new antibacterial cream Sulfamylon reduced burn infections by half. Developed by the Army's biological warfare medical researchers in the 1950s, Sulfamylon replaced the standard treatment of a copper sulfate solution that was found to be toxic.

Preventive medicine was far more effective during the Vietnam War than it had been in previous wars and military conflicts. A new policy of six weeks of acclimation upon arrival in Vietnam before transfer to a combat unit contributed to a decline in disease incidence. In addition, Dapsone, a drug known to be effective against leprosy, was used to reduce the incidence of malaria among troops. It was particularly effective in reducing the malaria recurrence rate from a high of 40 percent to 3 percent. Although disease still accounted for 70 percent of Army hospital admissions, the rate per 1,000 soldiers was 66 percent less than that of soldiers in Southeast Asia during World War II and 40 percent less than the disease rate during the Korean War.

Casualty care underwent several changes in the Vietnam War. Most doctors were trained to rely heavily on X-rays, laboratory results, and consultation with other doctors. That was possible only at a permanent hospital. In Vietnam, the priority became expedited battlefield evacuation to hospitals both in the rear and offshore. Highly efficient helicopter medical evacuation to permanent Army hospitals led the Army to assign fewer medical officers to combat battalions. Instead, the wounded were brought to the doctors at hospitals by helicopters with crews that received increased training in resuscitative care.

The Navy's deployment of the World War II-era USS *Repose* and USS *Sanctuary* as hospital ships improved the chances of survival for many patients. Both vessels were modified with helicopter pads to accommodate the steady stream of medevac arrivals. The hospital ship fleet employed state-of-the-art trauma medicine equal to that in the most sophisticated trauma centers in the United States.

In many respects, the defining medical advances of the Vietnam War were in logistics, communications, coordination, and transportation of wounded soldiers and sailors, supplies, and equipment more advanced than that which had been available in the Korean War.

In the three decades following Vietnam, increasingly sophisticated technology was developed and incorporated into military medicine. Corpsmen and medic training was expanded. Battlefield medics who were called "aidmen" during World War II for their first aid training would become highly trained emergency medical technicians under fire.

Chapter 13
Battlefield ER

• • • • • • •

Iraq

He looked impossibly young and serene lying on the desert sand. His weapon lay a few feet away, and one of his boots had disappeared. Dust hanging in the darkened air blurred the view of the nearby Iraqi city. Blood pumped out of his thigh. The odor of a slashed belly mixed with those of explosives and burned flesh and hair. The medic knelt as he studied the casualty. He pulled what looked like cat litter from his kit. He sprinkled it into the gaping chest wound, and the blood clotted in seconds. He turned his attention to the bleeding abdomen. A choking sound gurgled up from the chest. Two quick blinks. A gasp. Another. Stillness. Death had beaten the medic.

Unseen lights overhead were turned on as the medic pushed himself up on his feet. He first should have checked under the body armor.

The shrapnel that had buried itself in the chest cavity would have been impossible to miss. He'd remember that tomorrow when his turn came again in the simulation chamber at a military medical training center at Fort Drum, New York.

Combat medicine in World War I had been little more than first aid: slow the bleeding and get the soldier onto a stretcher bound for a hospital in the rear. World War II medicine in the bottom of bomb craters had been similar, though modestly trained corpsmen and medics were armed with antibiotics and a better understanding of how to ward off infection and shock. By the time America waged war in the Middle East in 1991 and again in 2001, sophisticated training and technology turned corpsmen and medics into well-equipped battlefield emergency medical technicians and paramedics.

Realistic simulations converted the classroom into a war-like environment where corpsmen and medics practiced tracheotomies and inserted chest tubes under challenging conditions. Some training regimens were increased from ten to sixteen weeks and included far more technical instruction than corpsmen and medics had received for previous wars.

Soldiers also were taught "buddy aid." When they patrolled in Iraqi neighborhoods in 2003, many carried one-handed tourniquets and an antibiotic coagulant that looked like cat litter. They had been shown how to provide immediate care for themselves and other soldiers within minutes of being wounded. That training was developed after a 1993 military mission in Somalia had gone awry and eighteen Marines had died. One stranded Marine had bled to death only a mile away from a military hospital. Guerilla warfare had demonstrated to the military that greater medical training for all soldiers in combat was crucial to survival.

The Iraqi desert heat made sleep impossible for the Marines scheduled for a predawn patrol "outside the wire" into neighborhoods controlled by the enemy. Land mines were buried in dirt roads, snipers were posted atop cinder-block buildings, and caches of ammunition and artillery shells were hidden in backyards and vacant lots.

As sunrise brightened Ar Ramadi on October 4, 2005, the Marines prepared to leave their base of operations, Camp Snake Pit. Located in the northwest corner of the city at the junction of a major canal and the Euphrates River, the Pit was the Marines' 3rd Battalion headquarters. It was also home to Lima Company, which had arrived from Twentynine Palms, California, in September.

Chaos reigned in Ar Ramadi, a city of nearly 400,000 inhabitants. The police force had vanished when the United States invaded two years earlier. Warring Sunnis and Shiites held sway over individual neighborhoods. The northern half of the city, with its commercial districts and paved streets, retained some semblance of order. The south, the Marines' patrol area at dawn, teemed with insurgents, spies, improvised explosive devices, and promised deadly crossfire ambushes.

Ar Ramadi was the southwest corner of the Sunni Triangle, formed by Tikrit to the north and Baghdad to the east. The region was the epicenter of Muslim insurgents dedicated to driving the United States out of Iraq. Nearly 90 percent of Sunnis supported armed resistance against the Americans. The insurgents' war of attrition in and around Ar Ramadi grew increasingly deadly in late 2005. Twice as many Marines were killed in Ar Ramadi as in Baghdad, a city whose population was fifteen times greater.

Young soldiers, some still teenagers, prepared for their patrol mission. Lieutenants Brad Watson and Matt Hendricks, Corporals Andrew Bedard and Shawn Seeley, and corpsman Nathaniel Leoncio would patrol in one of the twenty-one Humvees assigned to the mission.

Captain Rory Quinn knew that nearly all of his Lima Company Marines faced battle for the first time. Most had less than a month's combat experience as part of a battalion that had a long and storied history dating back to World War II amphibious assaults on Peleliu and Okinawa and the brutal Battle of Chosin Reservoir in Korea. Marines in the battalion had earned fifteen Medals of Honor.

Quinn had studied World War II, Korea, and Vietnam combat tactics that dictated avoiding movement on obvious trails where the enemy lay in wait. But Iraq had become America's first "road war." Patrols were limited to asphalt and dirt streets. Few advances moved across open fields or through stands of timber. The Americans rarely caught the enemy by surprise in stark desert neighborhoods devoid of vegetation. The insurgents planted IEDs along expected Marine patrol routes. The IEDs often were preludes to deadly ambushes.

At twenty-four years of age, corpsman Nathaniel Randell Leoncio was older than most of the Marines who had joined Lima Company about a month before it deployed to Iraq. Short and slightly built, "Doc Leo" nonetheless radiated a commanding presence. His wide Filipino eyes narrowed almost to slits when he smiled, pushing dimples into his cheeks. The corpsman enjoyed jokes, pranks, and "talking smack." Leoncio also represented the increasing speed of combat care.

For more than sixty years, the distance between battle and definitive trauma care had been shortening. During World War II, mobile Army hospitals trailed soldiers across Europe. In Korea, helicopters ferried the wounded out of foxholes to MASH units a few hours away. In Vietnam, acute-care hospitals were established in the combat zone. By the time Operation Iraqi Freedom was launched in 2003, both the Army and Marines had established small, extremely mobile hospitals that practically accompanied the infantry on patrols. An Army Forward Surgical Team was comprised of twenty personnel, including four surgeons. The team used one tent and surgical supplies contained in a handful of specialized backpacks (intensive care unit, surgery, anesthesia, and orthopedics, among others). It traveled in six Humvees and in one hour could set up a few hundred yards from a planned mission.

Miniaturization made the FST's mobility possible. Sonogram machines were the size of cassette recorders, and laboratory blood analysis units were as small as PDAs.

Typically, a combat support hospital was located less than an hour away from the battle zone, with about two hundred beds that could be assembled in forty-eight hours. From there, the gravely wounded could be evacuated to Germany or the United States within days for even more comprehensive care.

Although the Marines had trained in California's high desert near Palm Springs for months, the heat felt different when they arrived in central Iraq. It drained the men who faced as many as three patrols a day. Even on days with no scheduled patrols, the Marines maintained "two-minute warning" status, ready to roll out on minimal notice.

Each type of patrol held a unique danger. Door-to-door searches were tediously slow. Other patrols required Marines to sprint from one sheltered location to the next. The precise positioning of a Marine's gear on his body was crucial. No one could afford to be distracted by raw blisters from a flak jacket, gloves, knee pads, signaling devices, helmet, or spare ammo when running to avoid snipers.

Corpsmen accompanied Marines on every mission. Chronically undermanned, Marines relied on corpsmen to jump the same walls, hit the ground, and scan the darkness with night-vision goggles, just as they did on patrol. Corpsmen often were tasked with calming a family or guarding detainees while soldiers completed a search. On occasion they used mirrors to search Iraqi women out of respect for the local culture. Most corpsmen in the battalion carried an M16 rifle or shotgun to blend in with the other Marines. Earlier in Iraq, some corpsmen carried only M9 pistols, which marked them as desirable targets for enemy snipers. To the enemy, an American soldier in the field carrying only a pistol was likely a corpsman or medic. Many corpsmen, though, carried other weapons in addition to their medical gear.

Corpsmen knew that despite their training, the element of the unknown made every mission and every casualty impossible to anticipate. Many adopted a combat mindset when they arrived in Iraq. Each expected to face enemy fire and multiple casualties, and each also understood it was entirely possible that he was replacing a corpsman who may have been wounded or killed. Some adopted a fatalistic approach to cope with the unknown, believing "those who were going to die, would die." Each knew the primary mission: combat triage. The goal was to keep the wounded alive until they could be evacuated.

If I do this first, how much time is it going to buy? Corpsmen made instant decisions with this question in mind. Buying time was critical because corpsmen could not always be sure when evacuation might be possible. It could range from a few hours to days due to enemy fire, dust storms, or sand storms. Speed and effectiveness were paramount. A wound that might require stitches in a hospital could be closed quickly with a safety pin on the battlefield. In a hospital, an injured soldier unable to breathe might have a tube inserted to assist him. On the battlefield, a corpsman more likely would cut a hole in the soldier's trachea to help him breathe, while taking care not to sever nearby arteries. Lifesaving decisions were made without the benefit of sophisticated equipment.

Corpsmen monitored their medical supplies in the field as closely as soldiers kept track of their ammunition. A corpsman frequently used the tourniquet or pressure dressings contained in the individual first aid kit carried by each soldier. Under dire battlefield circumstances, corpsmen sometimes reused bandages taken from soldiers who had died minutes before.

After spending about fifteen minutes with a wounded soldier, most experienced corpsmen knew whether or not he would survive. They called it "going intimate" with the wounded man, assessing and treating his most serious injuries, staying close to him, monitoring his condition, and watching for complications.

Doc Leo quickly learned that the most deadly enemy lay hidden under his feet: improvised explosive devices. Insurgents had looted the nation's armories of an estimated 250,000 tons of weapons and supplies when the United States invaded Iraq and overthrew Saddam Hussein. They tied two to five one-hundred-pound artillery shells together with a battery-powered detonator and buried these IEDs under unpaved roads. Sometimes they hid them under chunks of concrete or trash or inside the bellies of dead animals. They posted a lookout up to seventy-five yards away, and when a convoy of Marine Humvees passed over the IED, a garage door opener or cell phone triggered an explosion that shredded steel and bone. IEDs that included a gasoline-and-sugar mixture coated Marines with fuel that clung to their skin as it burned.

In past wars, artillery fired one or two ridges away from the target was not particularly precise. But in Iraq, artillery shells exploded directly underneath the Marines with deadly accuracy. More than seventy-five pounds of shrapnel in a hundred-pound shell the size of a small trash receptacle rocketed out of the ground at 23,000 feet per second. If two or three shells were wired together, the impact was far greater.

The Marines who had escaped sniper fire and IEDs on patrols returned to Camp Snake Pit drenched in sweat, their muscles burning with fatigue in the one-hundred-degree heat. But before they headed for a shower, dry clothes, a bottle of Gatorade, and something to eat, most stopped to clean, organize, and stow their equipment. "Weapon, gear, body—in that order," their drill instructors had screamed at them.

Corpsmen monitored the soldiers' health needs, distributing medication and treating heat rash inflicted by flak jackets. Constant quizzing between corpsmen about triage techniques and emergency care protocols often surprised the Marines who marveled at their corpsmen's continued dedication in the field. That diligence also reassured the combat Marines whose survival might depend upon their corpsmen.

Corpsmen maintained a subculture within the battalion that inspired heartfelt respect among the infantry who depended on them.

At 0300 hours on October 4, 2005, Lima Company received orders to mount a search patrol as part of a one-day neighborhood sweep codenamed Operation Bowie. Lima Company's 4th platoon Marines assembled their gear at daybreak. As "go hour" approached, each soldier prepared for the mission in his own way. Leoncio became quiet. He checked his medical bag and then checked it again. Some Marines smoked cigarettes or packed a pinch of Copenhagen inside their lower lip. Others closed their eyes, unaware that they rocked slightly. Corporal Neil Frustaglio listened to Metallica on his headset.

"We're clear. Roll," said Quinn, commanding officer of Lima Company.[91]

As they headed for their Humvee, Lieutenant Matt Hendricks said to Leoncio, "You're the angel on my shoulder."

"Yeah, you're mine, too, sir," Leoncio replied.[92]

Lima Company rolled out of Camp Snake Pit at 0700 and headed south on Central Avenue toward Ramadi's ramshackle Humara District. Through the night, advance patrols had destroyed seventeen IEDs along the four-lane boulevard, but once the 4th platoon reached the southern end of Central Avenue, they were on their own. Unsecured dirt roads, the lack of an American presence, and the absence of a functional Iraqi government structure made Humara an ideal staging area for insurgents intent on disrupting the national elections that were less than two weeks away.

Eleven Humvees in Lima Mobile One and ten Humvees in Lima Mobile Two encircled and slowly patrolled through a neighborhood looking for anything out of the ordinary: drums of flammable materials; a vehicle that seemed out of place; caches of ammunition, perhaps buried in open fields. It was an agonizingly slow and tedious patrol. The Marines knew that insurgents traced their movements by phoning each house on a street. When a home's occupants didn't answer, the insurgents knew the Marines were nearby.

Andrew Bedard, a young Marine from Montana, drove the lead Humvee of Mobile Two onto a dirt road that the Marines called Main Street. Matt Hendricks sat beside him, with Leoncio and Brad Watson, the executive officer of Lima Company, in the two back seats. Shawn Seeley was in the four-foot gun turret above them. Their Humvee had been reinforced with additional armor after the underbellies of earlier models had proven vulnerable to IEDs. Still, the five Marines knew that their Humvee was designed more for mobility than survivability or firepower.

Seconds later, the Humvee disappeared in a dusty white bloom of desert sand that instantly turned gray-black. The massive explosion was followed by another deafening detonation. The initial blast between the first and second Humvees left a sprawling roadbed crater. The second blew up under the lead Humvee, and launched the six-ton armored vehicle into a soaring back flip. Landing upside down in a five-foot-wide crater, the Humvee's rooftop gun turret was buried in the sand.

As the Humvee's cabin filled with smoke, dust, and heat, the Marines inside heard a loud ringing in their ears. Diesel fuel flowed into the compartment from a ruptured fuel tank.

We have got to get out of here before this starts to burn, thought Brad Watson as he crouched, dazed, on the roof's roll bar inside the upside down Humvee.[93] As the dust cleared, he saw the passenger door, unmarked. It opened to his touch, as if nothing had happened.

Only twenty-four minutes into the mission and less than twenty yards from the secured asphalt boulevard, commanding officer Rory Quinn instinctively knew he had lost Marines. He didn't know how many of his men had been injured or whether the enemy was about to ambush his crippled patrol.

"We have a KIA and need help," squawked the radio in Quinn's Humvee.[94]

Mobile Two Marines leaped out of their vehicles and raced toward the lead Humvee. Some swung their weapons at the cinderblock buildings along the dirt road, expecting to see snipers. The lead vehicle resembled a horribly gutted animal that had been left belly-up and half-buried in the desert sand. Fuel and oil pooled at the bottom of the crater and ran into the open turret that had been driven into the ground.

Neil Frustaglio spotted Brad Watson helping Matt Hendricks away from the lead vehicle. A chunk of muscle the size of a golf ball hung from Hendricks's thigh. Watson struggled under the weight as he carried the injured man to a nearby Humvee. He made sure the pistol on his right leg was free in case he needed it, believing the enemy might open fire on the bloodied Marines.

Frustaglio ran to the other side of the mangled Humvee, looking for the other Marines. He ran headlong into a bloodied corpsman. The massive Humvee pinned Leoncio's leg to the sand. Blood bubbled from his mouth. Shock gripped his ashen, dusty face.

"I can't get you out, Doc!" Frustaglio yelled at Leoncio. "Look, I'm going to pull up and you gotta pull yourself out. Okay? Ready? Let's go! Let's go! Let's go!"[95] Frustaglio didn't wait for an answer as he pulled up on the still-hot engine compartment. The burly Marine rocked the overturned Humvee a few inches to the side. Leoncio used his arms and elbows to pull himself out from under the armored vehicle.

"Oh, shit." Frustaglio looked down at the few strings of tendons that kept Leoncio's right foot attached to a shattered knee. Hot steel had peppered the corpsman's face. His belly had taken the brunt of a devastating concussion and a fistful of shrapnel. A thigh bone was badly broken. While Marines circled the wreckage, scanned the desert, and set a perimeter defense, Frustaglio knelt next to Leoncio. Somehow the corpsman ignored his own pain and focused on triage for everyone who had been injured.

"Okay, Frag," said Leoncio, calling him by his nickname. "Get out the tourniquet. That's it. Now slide it up to about here," said Leoncio, touching his grizzly thigh and gritting in pain. "That's it. Good. Now twist. Tighter. Tighter! Cinch … okay that's it. Now tie it off!"[96]

When Kurtis Bellmont—a Marine with emergency medical training as a combat lifesaver—arrived, Leoncio asked about the others in his vehicle. Bellmont knew the wounded corpsman would sacrifice his mangled leg trying to crawl to other wounded Marines to treat them if he knew any lay nearby.

"Right now, Doc, everybody's gone [to another Humvee for evacuation]. We need to get you out of here," said Bellmont.

"Am I going to be all right?" Leoncio asked.

"Yeah, but your foot's gone."

"Okay. I'm good to go." Only then did Leoncio allow his fellow Marines to gently pick him up and carry him back to the Humvee medevac where Watson had brought Hendricks. A second later, another Marine delicately lifted the remainder of Leoncio's leg into the Humvee.[97]

Meanwhile, Quinn had reached the lead vehicle within two minutes of the IED explosions. Where were the other Marines who had been inside? The driver, Andrew Bedard, lay in the desert about twenty feet away. He had been blown clear and killed instantly, the blast severing both feet. Blistering heat had cauterized the amputation wounds, leaving almost no trace of blood. Fine desert talc covered his strangely placid face. He looked asleep. The three-hundred-pound driver's door rested a few feet away from Bedard.

Gunner Shawn Seeley was nowhere to be seen. But his strangled, muffled voice could be heard—barely—from the overturned Humvee. Seeley was crammed inside the half-buried turret. Somehow he had survived a 180-degree flip from a massive detonation while careening from one side of the steel turret to the other. Once the Marines located Seeley, hopes rose that maybe they hadn't suffered a second death that morning.

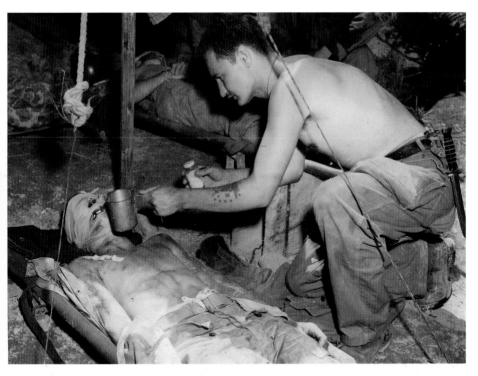

Corpsmen on Iwo Jima treated badly wounded soldiers who suffered multiple injuries from enemy artillery that included flash burns, contact burns, and internal injuries caused by hot, penetrating shrapnel. *(USMC)*

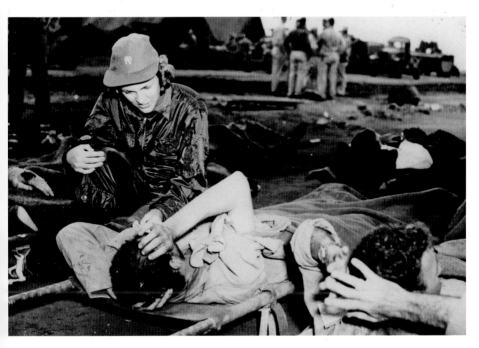

Trained flight nurses significantly improved the survival rate of severely wounded soldiers who were evacuated from remote Pacific islands aboard aircraft. Flight nurses not only received medical training, they also had to pass physical endurance tests. *(USMC)*

Iwo Jima corpsman Francis Pierce had been a Grand Rapids police officer for three years when President Harry Truman presented him the Medal of Honor. Like most heroic corpsmen and medics, Pierce lived the remainder of his life largely in anonymity. *(U.S. Navy, Bureau of Medicine & Surgery Archives)*

Prisoners of war, such as these marching to a jungle work camp in the Philippines during World War II, presented unique challenges for the military medical corps. *(U.S. Navy, Bureau of Medicine & Surgery Archives)*

Some medical corps personnel allowed themselves to be captured during World War II. They established a hospital ward for thousands of prisoners of war who fell ill while confined in a dilapidated prison in downtown Manila. *(U.S. Navy, Bureau of Medicine & Surgery Archives)*

Corpsmen like George Wahlen exhibited extraordinary poise and focus under horrific battle conditions. But when President Truman presented the Medal of Honor to Wahlen, the corpsman suffered stage fright, forcing the President to step forward to shake his hand. *(U.S. Navy, Bureau of Medicine & Surgery Archives)*

Above: Extended and extreme starvation suffered by American POWs in World War II led to epidemics of deadly disease. Medical personnel who also were prisoners had neither food nor medicine for most patients. *(U.S. Navy, Bureau of Medicine & Surgery Archives)*

Right: Corpsmen and medics in combat often are confronted with a shortage of medical supplies. Battlefield ingenuity has saved countless lives when medical supplies have been exhausted. *(USMC)*

Shock from loss of blood on the battlefield had always been a major cause of death in war. Improvements in air transport during the Korean War greatly improved the availability of whole blood for transfusions in the battle against shock. *(USMC)*

The development of mobile army surgical hospitals, or MASH units, in the Korean War enabled wounded soldiers to receive sophisticated medical care more quickly than they had during World War II. *(U.S. Army)*

Brutally cold weather in war can become as lethal as enemy fire. The Korean War became infamous for its harsh winters as it was fought well to the north of where much of the American fighting in World War II had taken place. *(U.S. Army)*

Wounded soldiers who were ambulatory sometimes faced a rugged hike to the nearest aid station. *(U.S. Army)*

Corpsman Joe Keenan (left) and a friend relax during a break in the fighting. Corpsmen rotated between front line assignments, reinforcement unit duty, and off-duty time away from the battlefield. *(Keenan Family)*

In Vietnam, special operations forces relied on their corpsmen deep in enemy territory with little or no prospect for additional medical assistance or emergency evacuation. *(U.S. Army)*

Field medical personnel in Vietnam knew that if they could keep a wounded soldier alive on the battlefield, he stood an excellent chance of survival due to increasingly efficient evacuation to sophisticated military hospitals nearby. *(USMC)*

Hundreds of casualties suffered in the USS *Forrestal* flight deck fire required nonmedical personnel to assist corpsmen and medical officers as others fought to save the ship. *(U.S. Navy)*

Thousands of soldiers wounded in Vietnam owed their lives to courageous helicopter pilots and medical personnel who routinely flew into enemy territory and firefights to evacuate the seriously injured. *(U.S. Army)*

Concealed IEDs utilizing artillery shells in Iraq and Afghanistan were detonated by remote control directly underneath patrol vehicles and produced multiple penetration and blast injuries. *(USMC)*

Survivability improved markedly in Iraq where sixteen soldiers were wounded for every soldier killed. Many, including corpsman Nathaniel Leoncio, lost a limb or suffered brain injuries from IEDs. Disability became the medical signature of the wars in Iraq and Afghanistan. *(USMC)*

Medic Monica Brown was in violation of Pentagon policy prohibiting women in combat when she was ordered to accompany a patrol mission in Afghanistan. *(U.S. Army)*

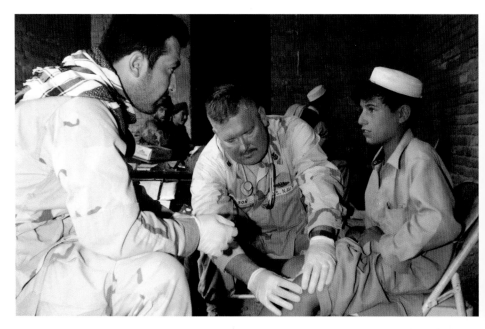

Providing medical care to civilians caught in war has always been part of the medic's mission. *(USMC)*

The universal truth among corpsmen: "You can lay there under fire and die, or you can get up and go. I decided the men needed me out there." *–Vietnam corpsman Robert Ingram, Medal of Honor recipient. (USMC)*

As the Marines waited for a boom wrecker to arrive and lift the destroyed Humvee off Seeley, Bellmont, and Watson sat on a side bench, anxious to get Leoncio and Hendricks to the hospital, which was less than ten miles away. Bellmont gestured toward Leoncio's destroyed leg. Watson looked, closed his eyes briefly, and nodded at Bellmont. Leoncio didn't know his leg lay next to him. Diesel fuel soaked his uniform, and his breathing became short and choppy.

"Corpsman up!" yelled Watson as he looked down at the two wounded Marines.

"What are you calling a corpsman for?" asked Leoncio. "You've got one right here."[98]

When Leoncio saw that Hendricks's thigh wound required a field dressing, the corpsman tried to roll over so Bellmont could reach his back pocket filled with medical supplies. Stunned, Watson and Bellmont steadied Leoncio, telling him to stay put as they pulled a bandage out for Hendricks. On the edge of consciousness, Leoncio called out treatment instructions. First, check Hendricks's breathing. Second, treat him for shock. Then Leoncio told Bellmont and Watson how to treat his own massive wounds. Finally, he closed his eyes and lay still. Periodically, he asked about Hendricks's condition as the Humvee rushed toward the military hospital. During the ride, Leoncio asked Bellmont for a sip of water and to hold his hand.

"I don't want to go into shock," said the corpsman. "How bad's my leg, sir? How bad's my leg? How much blood have I lost?" There was no panic in his questions. He remained cool and clinical, a corpsman assessing the patient's condition.

"You've lost some blood, Doc, but you're going to be okay. We're almost to Ramadi Med," said Watson, as the medevac Humvee sped along one of the most heavily mined roads in western Iraq. Leoncio smiled when Bellmont told the other wounded Marine that he knew Leoncio had to be a corpsman by the way he stayed so focused on others, despite his injuries.

When they reached the military hospital, at least ten U.S. Army medical personnel in their standard gray and green digital camouflage appeared at the back end of the Humvee.

"Amputated left leg," said one as Leoncio looked up at him.

"No, it's the other one," he said. Bellmont shook his head in amazement at the corpsman whose only priority while lying on the battlefield had been to take care of his Marines. Leoncio went straight into surgery. Watson and Bellmont would not see Doc Leo for another six months.

While Leoncio was being wheeled into the operating room, a boom wrecker gently lifted the shattered Humvee off Shawn Seeley. His heart barely fluttered; his breathing was shallow and strained. He had suffered a broken pelvis, two broken legs, a broken arm, a torn rotator cuff, a mangled right hand, and bruised lungs and spleen. His face had been sandblasted by the explosion. Looking down at Seeley, few Marines thought he would survive. His body had been torn open in several places. His brain and organs had been battered.

The prevalence of IEDs produced an unprecedented incidence of traumatic brain injury, the signature casualty in Iraq. When IEDs detonated underneath soldiers, the shock waves rocketed up through their skulls. The "secondary wind" hit a split-second later as air rushed to fill the void created by each shock wave. The damage from the double-fisted wave pounding their brains could be devastating. Many who survived the traumatic amputations and shrapnel injuries faced a wide array of TBI symptoms: moodiness, anxiety, depression, impulsiveness, and antisocial behavior. Others suffered from headaches and hypersensitivity to sound and light. Cognitive abilities to make decisions, pay attention, and react to others were adversely affected as well.

From the outset of combat in Iraq, military hospitals saw extraordinary numbers of wounded soldiers suffering from TBI. After three years of war, nearly two thousand soldiers had been diagnosed with TBI. For the first time in military history, the medical corps treated more brain injuries than chest and abdomen wounds. Vastly improved body armor protected soldiers against penetrating injuries. In Vietnam, about 12 percent of all injuries had involved the brain, and more than 70 percent of those were fatal. In Iraq, about 20 percent of soldiers treated in a military hospital in the first four years of combat suffered from TBI, often complicated by other injuries.

Brad Watson sat on a cot in the military hospital. He had been treated for minor wounds: a few lacerations, a right hand burn probably from hot motor oil, and some bruises. Nothing serious. He kept thinking about Leoncio in surgery:

> *"When Doc Leo was lying in the Humvee, he could have allowed himself to go into shock. Maybe pass out. I've never seen wounds that bad. But he didn't! He seemed to make a conscious decision to render aid, no matter what. Doc Leo refused medical aid until he was sure Hendricks had been taken care of. And he was ready to be our corpsman for the others, even with a mouth and belly full of blood, his leg lying on the bed of the Humvee. God, I've never seen courage like that. That was unbelievably brave."*[99]

Watson pulled out his write-in-the-rain notebook from a cargo pocket and retrieved a pen from his flak jacket. He wrote "For heroism ..." It would be up to others to decide whether Leoncio deserved a medal for bravery.

Meanwhile, the remaining Marines reassembled in their Humvees and continued their house-to-house search mission. They returned to base that night, fourteen hours after the mission had begun.

Eleven days later, a bright fall sun warmed the shoulders of mourners at St. Mary's Cemetery in Missoula, Montana. Andrew Bedard's flag-draped casket had been carried to his grave, not far from his rifle, which had been planted bayonet down in the grass, his helmet balanced on the rifle butt with his combat boots nearby. A Celtic bagpipe group played "Amazing Grace," followed by Taps.

Corpsman Leoncio and gunner Seeley underwent months of emergency and reconstructive surgery, complications, and agonizing physical rehabilitation. Both were flown to the National Naval Medical Center in Bethesda, Maryland, where they were joined by Matt Hendricks. Leoncio was transferred from Bethesda to the Brooke Army Medical Center in San Antonio, Texas, for intense postoperative care and physical therapy. He underwent an abdomen reconstruction. Shawn Seeley was transferred from Bethesda to St. Joseph Medical Center in Tacoma, Washington, following a series of surgeries, fears of a hole in his gall bladder, crippling pain, and casts for both legs and both arms. Only Lima Company executive officer Brad Watson had escaped hospitalization. Within an hour of reaching the military hospital in Ar Ramadi with Leoncio, he had written a medal nomination for the corpsman.

Neil Frustaglio endured a nightmare of his own. On December 7, 2005, two months after the IED that had shattered Seeley, Leoncio, and Hendricks, an IED destroyed Frustaglio's Humvee. Corporal Joseph Bier was killed instantly. The three other Marines in the Humvee, including Frustaglio, each lost both legs. After emergency care in Germany, Frustaglio began rehabilitation, which led to a reunion with his wounded buddies.

On March 31, 2006, the Marines completed their six-month deployment and returned to the Marine Corps Air Ground Combat Center at Twentynine Palms, a live-fire training complex less than one hundred miles from Palm Springs. Leoncio, Seeley, and Frustaglio were there to greet them. The grins, hugs, and tears were a welcome relief.

A week after the reunion, Captain Rory Quinn paused as he looked down from the podium at corpsman Leoncio and his family. Some of

Doc Leo's relatives had flown from the Philippines for the April 6 ceremony at Naval Hospital Camp Pendleton, the Marines' sprawling training base in California. On either side of Quinn, forty-five corpsmen in their dress whites stood in formation. Others in the nearby hospital leaned out of second-story windows.

Quinn's throat thickened with emotion as he took nearly fifteen minutes to describe the initial moments after the blast. For many of Leoncio's relatives, it was the first time they had heard the specifics of what happened.

"He won't brag on himself, so I have to do it for him," said Quinn:

"We had to lie to Doc and tell him that all the Marines had been taken off the battlefield before he would allow himself to be moved. Doc, you are an inspiration to Lima Company. You are a hero, Doc."[100]

Leoncio made his way to the podium to receive his Bronze Star and Purple Heart.

Tears welled up in Quinn's eyes as he hugged his corpsman. Neither heard the applause.

"When you look at this brave warrior standing beside me, evil is in for a rough ride," said Lieutenant General John Sattler as he pinned the awards on Leoncio.

On May 30, 2006, Lance Corporal Shawn Seeley walked across sodden grass at the Tahoma National Cemetery in Kent, Washington, to attend a Memorial Day Ceremony. Missing a thumb and with a face webbed with scars, the nineteen-year-old was eager to rejoin the Marines.

After the hole in his thigh had healed, Matt Hendricks became a teacher in Virginia. Lima Company's executive officer, Brad Watson, escaped the blast with minor injuries and left the Marines, destined for

Chicago. Meanwhile, Neil Frustaglio rebuilt an uncertain life in Wisconsin.

Within a year of his amputation, Leoncio joined the Paralympics training program. He ran-walked the Army Ten-Miler a year after losing his leg. In early 2007, he snowboarded on Mammoth Mountain in California's Sierras on a specialized prosthetic leg outfitted with a mountain bike shock absorber. Six months later, he was surfing.

In some ways, Leoncio was typical of soldiers wounded in a war marked by increased survivability and disability. In Vietnam, one in four wounded soldiers died. In the first three years of the war in Iraq, one in ten wounded soldiers died. By the fourth year, the wounded-to-killed ratio improved to 16 to 1.

Many factors contributed to increased survivability. Corpsman and medic training became more sophisticated. All Army combat medics took the National Registry of Emergency Technicians course, which included life-support and prehospital trauma care training. They had to validate their critical-care skills every six months.

Well-equipped mobile military hospitals usually were situated less than one hour from the battlefield. Advances in medical transport by air enabled a soldier gravely injured in Iraq to receive state-of-the-art treatment en route and arrive in the United States within four days. In Vietnam it had taken the seriously wounded an average of forty-five days to reach a U.S. military hospital.

Improved body armor also contributed to survivability. Guerilla warfare in Iraq was one of detonation rather than gunfire. Nearly 70 percent of soldier injuries in the first three years of Operation Iraqi Freedom were the result of explosions, while only 16 percent were from gunshot wounds. Body armor protected soldiers' chests and abdomens but left arms and legs exposed. As a result, the ratio of killed to wounded in Operation Iraqi Freedom was 1:7, compared to World War II when almost as many soldiers were killed as wounded (1:1.7).

Increased survivability has produced greater disability with postbattle medical care sometimes failing to keep pace. Only about half of the veterans who lost an arm or hand used prosthetics because they were heavy, difficult to manipulate, and broke easily. They differed little from the prosthetics that were available to World War II veterans. In 2005, the Department of Defense unveiled a $35 million research program to improve arm and hand prosthetics.

Improved body armor, more rapid treatment, and increased use of explosives by the enemy have resulted in traumatic brain injury becoming the most common injury on the battlefield. Various military reports estimate more than 130,000 American soldiers have returned home from Iraq and Afghanistan with traumatic brain injuries. Research has shown TBI is related to but not the same as post-traumatic stress disorder, resulting in an unprecedented generation of postbattle casualties that place a premium on mental health care.

The prevalence of disabled Iraq veterans has threatened to overwhelm the Veterans Administration. By 2007, the VA estimated that the Iraq war had produced 300,000 psychiatric injuries whose lifetime cost of care of $600 billion exceeded the cost of the Iraq war to that point. That same year, the Government Accountability Office reported that the VA was taking an average of 150 days to process a disability claim and that appeals were averaging 657 days. The claims backlog totaled 600,000, and the GAO predicted 638,000 new claims by 2012 at a cost of $70 billion to $150 billion.

On September 30, 2008, the VA received increased federal funding to hire two thousand additional claims processors and $1.6 billion to provide veterans with prosthetics that employed new biomedical technology.

Although advances in military medicine made war more survivable than at any time in history, they produced a generation of warriors whose wounds and disabilities have created new demands on military medicine off the battlefield.

Chapter 14
Invisible Scars

●●●●●●●

Afghanistan and Iraq

On April 25, 2007, as the setting sun neared the horizon, the Army patrol entered a dry riverbed in the Paktika province of eastern Afghanistan. The soldiers had been in the field for several days, looking for weapons in the small villages that dotted the region's rocky plain. It was similar to many missions that had lasted two or three days in the field. Soldiers returned to their outpost for a day or two to resupply and rest, then headed out again. The patrol also typified changes that were taking place in military medicine. The medic on the mission was a woman.

Monica Brown's patrol convoy consisted of four Humvees and one Afghan National Army pickup truck. As the convoy entered the riverbed, the last vehicle in the column disappeared in a deafening explosion. It had triggered an IED that detonated directly underneath the soldiers inside. At almost the same instant, the enemy opened fire on the convoy. The ambush threatened to pin down the soldiers, with little hope of rescuing anyone who might have survived the explosion.

Brown jumped out of her Humvee as enemy rifle and machine-gun fire ricocheted off the vehicle. It was her first firefight. She and platoon sergeant Jose Santos sprinted more than one hundred yards back to the burning Humvee, out of which four wounded soldiers had managed to climb. Some were rolling in the dirt, smothering their burning uniforms. Sergeant Zachary Tellier had pulled a fifth soldier, specialist Larry Spray, clear of the wreckage. Spray and another soldier, Stanson Smith, were seriously burned.

Gunfire intensified as Brown and two soldiers with relatively minor injuries moved the critically wounded into a depression a few yards away. When the enemy began launching mortars at the exposed patrol, the medic shielded Spray with her body. The situation became even more dire when mortar rounds, grenades, and fifty-caliber ammunition began exploding inside the burning Humvee. Shrapnel as large as softballs ripped through the air near Brown and the men she was treating.

Brown stabilized Spray and Smith, but she didn't have enough supplies to treat all their burns. Under enemy fire, other members of the patrol positioned another vehicle so the two men could be loaded into the back and evacuated to a safer location about five hundred yards away. Again Brown protected the wounded, positioning herself between them and the enemy. She monitored their condition and gave instructions so accompanying soldiers could assist her. Nearly two hours after the attack began, Spray and Smith were evacuated by helicopter. The enemy disengaged, and the battered patrol returned to its outpost.

Two years earlier, Brown had accompanied her brother to a Texas gulf coast Army recruiting office. Raised by a grandmother, she had attended nine different schools because her grandmother's work forced the fractured family to move frequently. Brown didn't meet her father, who was serving a prison sentence for drug use and distribution, until she was thirteen years old. Her mother was estranged from the family. At seventeen years of age, Brown enlisted in the Army. She thought about being an X-ray technician, but decided to serve as a combat medic instead.

Her four months of training as a medic were difficult: she nearly vomited the first time she watched a surgical procedure on a patient's throat. But by 2007, she was assigned to the 782nd Brigade Support Battalion of the 82nd Airborne Division and was stationed at a large American military base in Khost, Afghanistan. A few months after she arrived, Brown was sent to a remote Army outpost in Paktika. It was a small collection of tents that included a forty-square-foot aid station.

Brown was one of thousands of women serving in Afghanistan and Iraq.

The military became an all-volunteer force in 1973 when the draft was abolished. That led to new opportunities for women in uniform. Although women have served as nurses and in other noncombat positions since the Civil War, their roles expanded following the Vietnam War. In 1994, women served aboard U.S. Navy battleships. Four years later, women flew combat missions over Iraq.

The war in Afghanistan began on October 7, 2001, when the United States launched Operation Enduring Freedom to support a new national government against the Taliban, which had ruled the country since 1996; capture the terrorist Osama bin Laden; and destroy his organization, Al-Qaeda, which was responsible for the September 11 attacks on the United States. Less than two years later, on March 20, 2003, the United States invaded Iraq. Operation Iraqi Freedom was intended to eliminate suspected weapons of mass destruction, overthrow Saddam Hussein, and establish a democratic government. By the end of 2008, women accounted for approximately 11 percent of the 1.6 million Americans who had been deployed to Afghanistan and Iraq.

Female corpsmen and medics not only treated wounded soldiers, they attended to civilians and refugees. They had some advantages over their male counterparts. Only female medics could provide care to women in homes and clinics in Afghanistan, where traditional culture prohibited treatment by a male medic or doctor without a male family member being present. In this deeply patriarchal society, female medics sometimes gathered tactical intelligence from women who otherwise would not speak to male soldiers or medical personnel.

They also operated with and treated Afghan National Army soldiers on joint missions. They slept on the ground, ate Afghan food, and gradually overcame initial Afghan male resistance to their presence on the battlefield. They faced the same risk of death, combat stress, and multiple tours of duty in war zones as their male counterparts.

The increasing presence of women on the battlefield notwithstanding, the belief persists among some in the military that war is best fought by men. Some objectors maintain that women are unable to perform some duties required of soldiers and the medical corps in combat. For example, some argue that a wounded, nonambulatory soldier lugging up to one hundred pounds of gear should not have to rely on a female corpsman or medic who may not be strong enough to carry him off the battlefield. In 1994, the Department of Defense issued a policy prohibiting women from being permanently assigned to or alongside ground combat troops. Women were limited to support roles such as analyzing intelligence, driving trucks, flying helicopters, and being corpsmen and medics confined to military base hospitals and clinics.

Despite the experience of guerilla warfare in Vietnam, the 1994 policy was issued at a time when the Pentagon still considered the battlefield to have identifiable forward combat zones and relatively safer rear areas. But the conflicts in Afghanistan and Iraq didn't conform to what had been the bulk of the American experience in war. There were no clearly defined battle lines. Nearly every patrol was a "bubble mission" in which U.S. troops potentially could become surrounded and ambushed by the enemy. Regardless of their official assignment, female corpsmen and medics in Afghanistan and Iraq were effectively an integral part of America's combat ground forces.

Although they have accounted for only 2 percent of combat deaths in Afghanistan and Iraq, women have been present on the battlefield. Nearly every outpost, hospital, and military base was within range of enemy fire. Clashes with insurgents took place in mountains, deserts, cities, towns, and villages. By 2007, more than 10,000 mothers had served in Iraq. Women in Afghanistan and Iraq have completed more than 170,000 tours of duty. By the end of 2008, nearly five times as many women had been killed in Afghanistan and Iraq than had been killed in World War II, Vietnam, and the Persian Gulf War combined. Many were mothers and more than half were under the age of twenty-five.

On March 21, 2008, Vice President Dick Cheney awarded Monica Brown the Silver Star. She was only the second woman in more than sixty years to receive it. Four nurses had received the award in World War II, and an Army policewoman in Iraq had been awarded the Silver Star in 2005. But by the time she received the award, Brown was no longer treating wounded soldiers in the field.

Within a week of the firefight, Brown was transferred back to the Army base at Khost. Her presence in the riverbed had violated the rule that banned women from the battlefield. Smith, one of the soldiers Brown treated under fire that day, agreed with the policy. Others, however, including several soldiers on patrol with Brown that day, said she performed as capably as any male medic.

Not everyone, though, believed Brown's actions merited the Silver Star. There were those, including men who belonged to Brown's unit, who believed she received the award in part because she was a young woman, only eighteen years of age. Some cited the actions of other medics who courageously saved the lives of wounded soldiers under intense enemy fire yet did not receive any recognition.

The ban on permanently assigning women to combat units remained, although in Afghanistan, Army officers continued to temporarily attach female medics to combat units as a way to circumvent the regulation. For some, it added to the combat stress that always has been a hallmark of war.

With each war, the military medical corps' perception and treatment of combat stress has evolved. During the Civil War, it was called soldier's heart. In World War I, it was referred to as shell shock. During World War II, it was identified as battle fatigue or hysteria. One Marine Corps report revealed that approximately 10 percent of troops were diagnosed and treated for battle fatigue in the war zone during World War II. In Vietnam, about 1.2 percent of the troops received care in the field for what generally was considered to be a weakness or personality disorder.

War traditionally has been viewed as a test of manhood. A soldier proved his worth to himself and to others on the battlefield. For more than thirty-five years following the elimination of the military draft, Americans have volunteered for military service. To become a psychiatric casualty after volunteering for combat has been seen by some as particularly damning. Psychological wounds that otherwise may be invisible have made acknowledgment shameful for many soldiers. In 1980, post-traumatic stress disorder became a diagnosable mental disorder recognized by the American Psychiatric Association. For many in the military, however, "some water and a good run" remained the best way to restore a soldier's mental health. Although PTSD is now more widely accepted, the stigma remains, effectively rendering these wounds somehow less honorable in some eyes than gunshot or shrapnel wounds.

Combat stress has always been used as a weapon of war. A stressed enemy is a less dangerous foe. For decades the United States has conducted psychological operations against enemies designed to weaken their will to fight. In Afghanistan and Iraq, heightened combat stress among American troops was one of the goals of insurgents who planted and detonated IEDs and conducted ambush missions in order to create uncertainty, shock, and devastation.

Today, the military medical corps acknowledges that nearly everyone deployed to a war zone is affected by combat and operational stress reaction. Medics and corpsmen constantly watch for emerging signs of COSR, which generally is considered to be an expected emotional reaction to combat stress, while PTSD is a more protracted psychological condition. A soldier who no longer makes eye contact, whose body language indicates a detachment from his surroundings, who appears numb, or has difficulty remembering details of a battle may have COSR. It typically surfaces shortly after an incident or series of events. With time and counseling, the symptoms usually abate without significant treatment or removal from the war zone.

Many stress factors can lead to COSR. In Iraq, corpsmen and medics endured desert heat that could exceed 120 degrees, made worse by modern combat and medical equipment. Their Kevlar helmets and body armor intensified body heat, making dehydration a constant threat. The fine, powdery grit of the desert sometimes created massive "brown out" clouds that resulted in respiratory issues, helicopter crashes, and more dangerous missions.

Noise, too, could wear down soldiers and medical personnel. Newcomers to the Middle East war zone often were unprepared for the sounds of battle. Enemy fire split the air, bullets ripped into the sand, and exploding mortar rounds produced a continuous roar and frequent sensory overload on the battlefield.

Yet most deployments of medical personnel were marked by long stretches of monotony and boredom punctuated by what many called the terror of patrols, missions, and firefights with the enemy.

A veteran corpsman or medic learned to appreciate the relative routine of base camp "barracks medicine" that meant distributing various medicines, conducting inspections, and monitoring troop hygiene and mental health.

In some cases, COSR developed into more severe PTSD. The soldier, corpsman, or medic frequently relived the traumatic events and became lost in memories vivid with the sights and sounds of the battlefield. Recurring memories left him in a continuously anxious state. He found it difficult to concentrate, suffered memory lapses, was unable to sleep, or became irritable. Hallucinations and paranoia sometimes followed, requiring significant treatment. Not only did corpsmen and medics watch for signs of combat stress among their troops, they maintained a level of self-awareness for the same symptoms.

Military operations that included medical personnel in Afghanistan and Iraq were based on training, teamwork, and trust. Corpsmen and medics were trained in hand-to-hand combat and weapons. They were expected to support mission objectives as well as treat fallen soldiers. In turn, most soldiers found it unimaginable to lose a corpsman or medic. Medical personnel provided a sense of security, a reassurance that somehow the soldier would return home even if he was wounded. Soldiers were more effective warriors when a trusted corpsman or medic was nearby. They would do anything for their corpsmen and medics on the battlefield, but often considered it almost impossible to forgive one who failed them. Corpsmen and medics knew they could not quit or offer excuses in battle.

Most corpsmen and medics were very young: many were under twenty-one years of age. Youth often led them to believe they were invincible, but they soon discovered that fallacy on the battlefield. They also bore a dual responsibility, apart from their fellow soldiers. Marines were deployed on the battlefield in tight, cohesive units. There was a clear chain of command, as well as support and complementary roles. Unit operational integrity was paramount. Corpsmen performed as Marines under the same structure. But an injured Marine instantly transformed a corpsman into an emergency medical professional. A man's life sometimes depended on how quickly and effectively a single corpsman could make that shift. The corpsman usually found himself alone, solely responsible for emergency care, often issuing commands to others.

These were responsibilities unique to combat corpsmen and medics. They demonstrated toughness on a par with their soldiers, learned to contain personal fears, and never revealed weakness. One way of coping was to find a friend in the field or back at base in whom they could confide. They trusted in the unwritten code that such conversations were never shared with anyone else.

It was during the relative quiet between missions that corpsmen and medics confronted their greatest fear: failing their troops under fire. They had to accept their inability to save the lives of fatally wounded soldiers and to acknowledge the fragility of life in combat. Unlike civilian paramedics, trauma doctors, and surgeons, most corpsmen and medics found it impossible to "depersonalize" in the war zone. The shared mission and kindred spirits forged on the battlefield prevented them from simply treating a chest wound. Every injured soldier was a brother fighting for a common cause who needed potentially lifesaving care. Failure to save their men could haunt corpsmen and medics long after they returned home. Guilt was the defining characteristic of corpsmen and medics who suffered from PTSD. The emotional toll on combat medical personnel could be severe.

On October 6, 2005, Joseph Dwyer's nightmares became too real to ignore. In his mind, Texas became Iraq. That night, the former Army medic repeatedly shot at an imagined enemy he thought had broken into his second-floor apartment in El Paso. Frightened neighbors called the police. A three-hour standoff ensued before Dwyer surrendered his pistol and was taken into custody.

Dwyer spent ninety-one days in Iraq two years earlier. He became famous on March 23, 2003, when a photograph of him carrying an Iraqi boy who had been hit by shrapnel to safety appeared in newspapers around the world. But when Dwyer returned home three months later, the medic was scarcely recognizable to his friends.

He had lost nearly thirty pounds and was tormented by nightmares. He began abusing alcohol, sniffed inhalants, and was sure that the enemy had followed him to Texas. He sat with his back to the wall in restaurants. He fortified his apartment against enemy attack, turned a closet into a bunker for protection against infiltrators, and answered the door with a pistol in his hand. One day Dwyer veered off an El Paso street to avoid what he thought was an IED and crashed into a street sign.

Dwyer entered several drug treatment and psychiatric programs following his return from Iraq. He admitted to therapists that he had denied suffering from PTSD when he returned to the United States because he wanted to become a policeman. The hallucinations continued. Dwyer was admitted to another treatment program several weeks after his confrontation with police.

In July 2007, Joseph Dwyer's wife obtained a restraining order to keep the former Army medic away from their two-year-old daughter. The breaking point came when he grew enraged after she took an AR-15 assault rifle away from him.

Dwyer was living on disability payments. His life had turned inside out. He slept during the day and at night patrolled the neighborhood against imagined enemies. He hid knives throughout the house in case he was attacked. Dwyer spent hours on the computer, looking at Iraq war photographs that were set to patriotic music. He was embarrassed by the photo taken of him carrying the injured boy to safety four years earlier. On July 27, 2007, Dwyer checked into another psychiatric inpatient program. He was discharged in March 2008, and returned home with twelve drug prescriptions. Within a week, the nightmares returned.

On June 28, 2008, Joseph Dwyer called a local taxi service in Pinehurst, North Carolina, where he had moved from Texas. When the driver arrived, Dwyer's front door was locked. Dwyer yelled that he could not get up to open the door, so a police officer who also had responded kicked it in. They found Dwyer lying in his urine and feces. He had been sniffing a refrigerant-based aerosol used to clean electrical equipment.

"Help me, please! I'm dying. Help me. I can't breathe," he told police.[101]

Thirty minutes later, Dwyer died from a drug overdose. He was thirty-one years old. In many ways, Dwyer was a combat casualty.

Combat injury in the early years of the twenty-first century has been studied more than at any time in our history. Research has shown that soldiers and military medical personnel suffer psychological injuries more than any other type of combat injury. These can come from experiencing a traumatic event, grief, fatigue, or inner conflict (incongruity between personal values or religious beliefs and the realities and demands of war).

Studies have revealed that there is little difference in combat stress, PTSD, and related disorders between men and women. Even though women technically were not assigned to combat units in Afghanistan and Iraq, they were as likely as men to know someone who was killed on the battlefield and to be exposed to enemy fire. One study linked the incidence of PTSD to the number of firefights in which a soldier, corpsman, or medic engaged. About 40 percent of PTSD cases were comprised of those who had participated in six or more firefights. Combat exposure, not gender, was the most direct predictor of modern war's most common and potentially long-lasting battlefield injury.

Yet psychological casualties remained one of the least likely to be treated on the battlefield. Many soldiers were hesitant to acknowledge PTSD or related symptoms in the war zone. Two thirds feared they would be perceived as weak or would be treated differently by other soldiers. A majority feared a loss of confidence by their fellow soldiers, and about 40 percent simply were too embarrassed to seek treatment.

The psychological impact of multiple deployments also affected the Navy's ability to supply the Marines with field corpsmen. Navy corpsman reenlistment rates declined 5 percent to less than 60 percent in 2006 among those who were six- to ten-year veterans. In 2008, the Navy reduced the reenlistment bonus for some basic corpsmen ratings and increased the bonus for more experienced corpsmen. It came at a time when the Navy needed approximately 2,500 new corpsmen annually to meet personnel needs, in part to supply the 4,500 corpsmen who were assigned to the Marines. Although the corpsman rating has been one of the most highly decorated in the Navy, it has not been recognized as a fast track to promotion. In addition, other nonmedical specialties offering higher reenlistment bonuses and better postmilitary service compensation prompted some corpsmen to apply for transfers.

Some psychological casualties became fatalities before a soldier returned home. Between 2001 and 2008, nearly six hundred active-duty Army soldiers committed suicide, the equivalent of a battalion. The Army active-duty suicide rate rose from 12.4 per 100,000 in 2003 to 18.1 in 2007, an increase of nearly 50 percent. In late 2008, the Army suicide rate was on pace to exceed that of 2007. Suicide was the fourth most common cause of death in the war zone, behind enemy fire, accidents, and disease. In early 2008, Veterans Administration officials acknowledged that 12,000 of the veterans seen at VA facilities attempted suicide annually, approximately one attempt every forty-two minutes.

Unlike other battle wounds, psychological casualties can take months or even years to identify. A 2004 study revealed a PTSD incidence rate of 6.2 percent among soldiers three months after they were sent to Afghanistan or Iraq. It increased to 16.6 percent one year after their deployment.[102] Today, the military conducts multiple postdeployment assessments to monitor their soldiers' mental health, and the reported incidence of PTSD has increased significantly.

In 2008, RAND Corporation released a study estimating that 300,000 of the 1.6 million men and women who served in Afghanistan and Iraq to that point suffered from PTSD, major depression, or related mental health issues. The one-in-five incidence rate increased to one in three when mental and emotional damage inflicted by traumatic brain injury was included. This 33 percent incidence rate was consistent with the findings of long-term studies of PTSD among Vietnam veterans.

The RAND study estimated the cost of treatment to be more than $6.2 billion in the near term, but that figure could be much higher due to associated unemployment, drug abuse, violence, and suicide if veterans did not receive care. Although veterans make up approximately 11 percent of the population, they account for 25 percent of America's homeless.

The physical, mental, and emotional casualties suffered in combat in Afghanistan and Iraq, coupled with veterans' long-term disabilities, threatened to overwhelm the VA. Veterans seeking VA services faced a gauntlet of bureaucratic approvals. In 2007, some veterans were required to complete as many as twenty-two documents to obtain care. An audit of the VA revealed sixteen information systems, many of which did not communicate with each other.

The Army's showcase medical facility, Walter Reed Army Medical Center, became a symbol of military medicine's struggle to adapt to the evolving needs of war's casualties. The facility provides state-of-the-art, life-saving surgical and medical care for thousands of critically wounded soldiers. It treats about 25 percent of all soldiers wounded in Afghanistan and Iraq, but has been ill equipped to meet the needs of outpatients. In 2007, there were seventeen outpatients for every hospital patient. Walter Reed's inadequate outpatient facilities and services became a national shame. Many of its five outpatient buildings were riddled with cockroaches, rats, mice, and mold. Wounded soldiers who had supervisory duties were responsible for as many as two hundred rooms. Basic services, such as hot water, were unreliable in facilities in which the average outpatient stay was ten months but could be as long as two years. The medical center's commanding officer acknowledged a reluctance to promptly discharge some outpatients who might leave the armed services at a time when some branches of the military were under pressure to meet recruitment quotas.

That same year, Congress appropriated $900 million to fund stress-related research projects, psychological health programs, and traumatic brain injury initiatives. The funding was made available within months of reports by a Department of Defense task force and the President's Commission on Care for America's Returning Wounded Warriors, which outlined shortcomings in the military's mental health care and the need for significantly increased research, diagnosis, and treatment programs.

Researchers across the country evaluated new techniques of treating PTSD and related mental disorders suffered by veterans. In 2008, the Army made $4 million available for clinical, evidence-based research projects that focused on alternative treatments for PTSD. Possible therapies included massage, art, dance/movement, acupuncture, and yoga.

Treatment programs involving virtual reality appear to hold significant promise. One simulation program, called "Virtual Iraq," was created by Albert Rizzo, a clinical psychologist at the University of Southern California. He modified an existing computer game, "Full Spectrum Warrior," to create two scenarios: an Iraqi market square and a military convoy of Humvees on a rural road. Rizzo's prototype program received a lukewarm response in 2004 when he sought funding for trials. That year, the first mental-health assessment of troops returning from Afghanistan and Iraq was published in the *New England Journal of*

Medicine. The study concluded that 17 percent of Iraq veterans and 11 percent of Afghanistan veterans were suffering from PTSD and related disorders. The magnitude of the problem surprised the military, and soon thereafter the Office of Naval Research offered to fund clinical trials using Rizzo's simulation program.

Four years later, the Veterans Administration and American Psychiatric Association endorsed two principal types of virtual reality use in continuing clinical trials. Using realistic computer simulations, head-mounted displays, sophisticated surround-sound systems, and vibrating platforms, they placed veterans suffering from PTSD in a realistic war environment. The therapy immersed the patient in conditions similar to what had triggered PTSD.

Long-exposure therapy utilized virtual reality sessions repeatedly until a patient learned to master his emotional response to what he had experienced. Cognitive-processing therapy also employed virtual reality simulations as therapists helped patients think through their experience and put it in the proper perspective. One approach was based on re-experiencing the traumatic event, while another helped patients analyze the event. Some researchers also used an old tuberculosis drug, D-cycloserine, which was found to inhibit the fear response in laboratory animals.

By the end of 2008, increasingly sophisticated virtual reality simulations enabled therapists to control the level of intensity by adjusting the sound, adding bomb blasts and gunfire, and incorporating the smell of sweat and smoke while monitoring their patients' vital signs. Virtual Iraq was being tested by the Department of Defense in six locations, including Naval Medical Center San Diego, one of the Navy's foremost medical treatment and research facilities. Navy psychologists reported that some veterans recovered in less than two months of virtual reality-based treatments that addressed their fundamental fears, tendencies to avoid associated personal issues, and pervasive anxiety.

Overall, clinical trials using prolonged virtual-reality treatments reduced PTSD symptoms in veterans in 65 percent of the cases, compared to a 40 percent success rate for behavioral therapy and 20 percent for patients using antidepressants.

Widespread recognition of the prevalence of psychiatric casualties not only led to new research, it spawned changes in how the military trained personnel for combat. Soldiers and medical personnel were instructed on what to expect in battle. They learned that experiencing tunnel vision, a temporary loss of hearing, and other involuntary reactions was not unusual. In some cases, virtual reality was incorporated into corpsman training, better preparing them for the battlefield.

In late 2008, Congress authorized a $41 billion annual budget for VA health programs, which were expected to serve 5.8 million veterans. The appropriation included $3.8 billion for mental health services, twice the funding level in 2001, and $584 million for substance abuse programs. Several veterans' organizations believed the funding levels for both were inadequate to meet growing demand. Congress also appropriated $5 billion for VA hospitals, a 14 percent increase over the previous year.

Meanwhile, the Navy took steps in 2008 to increase psychiatric care on the battlefield. Officials announced a plan to increase its deployable psychiatric teams from seven to twenty-three, one for each Marine Corps regimental combat team. A social worker was to be added to the existing four-person teams comprised of a psychiatrist or psychologist and three psychiatric technician corpsmen. The plan reflected the recognition that psychiatric specialists in the war zone would be able to build the relationships and trust necessary for more effective treatment and would eliminate soldiers' guilt over leaving their comrades to seek mental health treatment in the rear. The teams were expected to be fully deployed in 2011.

The Navy also established the Naval Center for Combat and Operational Stress Control, its first comprehensive program to include stress training during both pre- and postdeployment. The center's goals are to become a principal hub of data management, act as a catalyst of diverse stress research projects, and lead community outreach efforts within the military to reduce the stigma attached to PTSD and related disorders.

For more than two hundred years, America's military medical corps has raced to keep pace with the evolving realities of war, both on and off the battlefield. In the twenty-first century, the American way of war is premised upon mobility, speed, technology, precision, and warrior empowerment. We may never be completely without war, but for as long as men and women in uniform serve our nation's causes, equally heroic corpsmen and medics will carry on the proud tradition of risking their lives to save those who fall wounded on the battlefield.

Conclusion

• • • • • • •

Eight generations of Americans have confronted war. More than 1 million have died on battlefields that over two centuries have been transformed by industrialization, science, and technology.

As America has gone to war more frequently in our recent history, war's lethality has accelerated as well. Nearly ninety years passed between the Revolutionary War and the Civil War. Weapons evolved in size and speed and grew more deadly, but it was not until America entered World War I more than fifty years later that industrialization produced massive, mechanized weaponry capable of killing thousands in a day and hundreds of thousands in a single battle. World War II, the Korean War, and the Vietnam War each resulted in widespread death, increasingly complicated injuries, and new challenges for America's military medical corps.

Military medicine adapted to the unique realities of the battlefield in each war and pioneered medical advances that frequently redefined civilian health care. The modern ambulance system was developed during the Civil War when Union and Confederate armies and their doctors faced thousands of casualties for the first time in battle. The pavilion design adopted by hospitals for nearly a century was conceived by Civil War doctors who sought to improve the sanitary conditions in military hospitals in the mid-nineteenth century.

At the outset of World War I, military surgeons sewed a wounded soldier's basilic vein at the elbow to a donor's radial artery at the wrist for direct, unmatched blood transfer. The failure rate demonstrated the need to match donor and recipient blood types, which served as an impetus to the creation of a viable blood bank. Although at the time they lacked the technology to preserve blood, the military medical corps demonstrated the enormous potential of blood transfusions and blood banks. They also refined the practice of triage, the immediate assessment and staged treatment of injuries, which was originated by French doctors.

During World War II, corpsmen and medics helped establish antibiotics as a cornerstone of modern medicine. They were the first to use sulfa drugs on a widescale basis to control infections. By the end of the war, they also proved that the new drug penicillin was even more effective. That validation on the battlefield served as a harbinger of the development of dozens of other antibiotics in the postwar years.

Emergency helicopter transport, a service provided at most major metropolitan hospitals today, can be traced to the initial helicopter medical evacuations in the Korean War. Civilian medicine also has benefited enormously from the trauma care database created during the Vietnam War when six hundred military surgeons submitted reports on more than eight thousand vascular treatment cases. Meticulous medical corps recordkeeping has helped educate successive generations of doctors. The Vietnam records remain one of medicine's most valuable databases of specialized trauma treatment today. Increasingly sophisticated and computerized military medical care in Iraq and Afghanistan is expanding that knowledge base.

Military medicine has contributed to a higher standard of civilian care. Many soldiers first experienced the benefits of regular medical attention after they entered the military. Others who had known only their family doctor benefited from access to medical specialists in the armed forces. In World War II, nearly a third of the nation's doctors were pressed into the service to care for the 8 percent of the population that was in uniform. Those soldiers returned home with a greater understanding and expectation of medical care.

One of the greatest victories in the history of military medicine has been the defeat of disease on the battlefield. For thousands of years, disease was the deadliest enemy. Approximately 90 percent of deaths in the Revolutionary War were due to disease. It wasn't until the twentieth century that rifles, grenades, mortars, artillery, and bombs killed more combatants than malaria, yellow fever, dysentery, and typhus. Disease-related deaths declined to 60 percent of fatalities in the Civil War, 50 percent in World War I, and 25 percent in World War II. Preventive medicine has been one of the primary beneficiaries of military medicine.

New technology continues to play a significant role on the battlefield. In 2003, the U.S. military debuted an innovative stretcher that brought sophisticated care to the wounded. The Life Support for Trauma and Transport is a mobile, five-inch-thick platform that has a variety of devices built into it: vital signs monitor, blood chemistry analyzer, suction equipment, defibrillator, ventilator, and infusion pump. Twenty prototypes were sent to Marine ground forces and Navy amphibious ships that year. The two-hundred-pound platform proved too heavy for field use but was effective in stabilization and evacuation. Researchers continue to enhance its capability to become a fully mobile intensive care unit for each wounded soldier and to reduce its weight to closer to forty pounds.

Similarly, in 2008, an armored ambulance, the Mine Resistant Ambush Protected Vehicle, made its first appearance on the battlefield. Designed to counter the prevalence of IEDs in modern warfare, the massive, heavily modified Humvee ambulance can hold up to six patients and is equipped with oxygen, suction, and vital-sign-monitoring capability. In some respects, the tide of military medical advances has shifted to taking acute-care capability onto the battlefield as a precursor to battlefield evacuation.

War has never been more survivable. About 30 percent of all wounds in World War II were fatal. From the Korean War to the first Gulf War in 1991, the wound mortality rate remained at approximately 25 percent. Less than 3 percent died after reaching a hospital, so the vast majority of those killed in battle died within minutes of being hit. By 2007, the mortality rate of the wounded in Iraq dropped to 10 percent.

Warfare continues to evolve and pose new challenges for military medicine. Inaccurate fusillades of fire in past wars have been replaced by remote-controlled precision weaponry. The muskets of old are now fully automatic weapons with night scopes. Horse-drawn artillery has given way to laser-guided missiles and multiple-launch rocket vehicles that can fire up to a dozen rockets that reach a speed of Mach 3.5 in eight seconds and have a range of three hundred miles. Future weapons will become even more lethal.

Researchers are working on technology that will make firearms more reliable in harsh conditions and enable the military to operate them electronically. The technology will produce exponential increases in firepower: 16,000 rounds of 9mm bullets per second and 250,000 40mm grenades per minute. In addition, the Army is developing a target-seeking cannon that is lightweight, mobile, and fully automated. It can fire six one-hundred-pound artillery rounds in sixty seconds, timed to detonate simultaneously on a single target.

Warfare in the twenty-first century has become expeditionary, mobile, and remote. American military interventions since 1989 have ranged from Kosovo to Somalia to Sierra Leone. The increasingly isolated nature of modern war results in seriously wounded soldiers far from established medical facilities. Military medical research and development is focusing on new technology that insulates the soldier against injury, enables greater self-care, and provides automated evacuation and treatment.

For one project, researchers engineered transportable blood platelets that can be stored at room temperature for up to two years and retain their clotting capability. For another, they are studying how estrogen can help wounded soldiers withstand significant blood loss. A more futuristic model shows soldiers being injected with magnetic nanoparticles before entering battle. If they are wounded, a magnetic tourniquet or similar handheld device could be used to concentrate the nanoparticles at the wound site to enhance clotting. Scientists at the Defense Advanced Research Projects Agency are working on a mobile device for use in the field that uses ultrasound to locate and stop internal bleeding. All four projects would give corpsmen and medics in remote regions valuable new tools to reduce gravely wounded soldiers' vulnerability to shock from excessive blood loss.

Combat medical research also has focused on the speed of treatment. One goal is to increase by tenfold the ability of a soldier to treat his own wounds. Another is to enable pain control and treatment by a medic or by a wounded soldier himself within five minutes of being injured. In addition, DARPA researchers are seeking a fivefold increase in tissue repair efficiency, the ability to return a soldier to active duty within ninety-six hours of being wounded, and the reduction of medical logistical needs by at least half.

Military medical research may prove particularly useful in harsh desert and alpine combat environments. Some scientists are studying how mountain-climbing sherpas produce a natural hormone that enhances blood-oxygen exchange, enabling them to climb to the top of Mt. Everest without oxygen bottles. The hormone could help a wounded soldier survive when severe bleeding reduces his internal oxygen supply. Others are analyzing how a particular species of sea lion can keep blood flow away from vital organs in cold water. What they discover may help protect soldiers in subfreezing conditions. Still others are investigating a microorganism that produces an enzyme that deflects heat, which could prove useful in keeping soldiers in optimal condition during desert warfare.

Telemedicine technology based on wireless communication is being developed as well. The Telemedicine and Advanced Technology Research Center has worked on biosensors that could be woven into a soldier's uniform. These would enable corpsmen and medics to remotely monitor each soldier's condition, determine which casualty on the battlefield needs to be evacuated first, and prepare for incoming casualties.

Someday a remotely controlled Battlefield Extraction Assist Robot could be sent onto the battlefield to rescue the most seriously wounded. The humanoid BEAR is designed to enter the combat zone, pick up an injured soldier, and return to a sheltered position. The BEAR's lifting capacity is five hundred pounds. It would reduce the frequency with which corpsmen and medics run into enemy fire to rescue wounded soldiers.

Once the soldier is delivered to a safer location, the corpsman or medic might use medical supplies airdropped only minutes before. In Afghanistan today, unmanned aerial vehicles are in greater use. Researchers are working on a version that could deliver a twenty-pound canister of medical supplies into battle. In the future, they hope to increase that capacity to two hundred pounds.

After a wounded soldier is treated, someday corpsmen and medics may be able to enter vital information onto a radio-frequency wristband via a handheld device. The wristband, which is under development, would contain the soldier's personal information, medical history, and just-completed treatment and vital-sign data. This comprehensive medical file would accompany the injured soldier throughout the entire military medical care process.

Once the injured reach an aid station, surgery might be performed without a surgeon present. Robotic trauma pods are being developed, in which four operating tables extend out in four directions from a centralized console of remotely controlled surgical equipment. Surgeons would perform operations from another location. Trauma pods could reduce significantly the amount of time and distance between being wounded and receiving lifesaving surgical care.

Disease plays a significant role in any military force's readiness, and it comes from many sources. In guerilla warfare conditions, IEDs can blast septic residue from Humvee tires and axles into soldiers' bodies. In 2008, military vaccines were effective for only about eight of the forty-four pathogens known to exist in contemporary war zones. More than a dozen pathogens were identified during the past sixteen years. In order to keep pace with remote pathogen discovery, some researchers are working on methods to develop vaccines without access to the pathogens. The Defense Sciences Office at DARPA is working on techniques to produce as many as 3 million doses of vaccine in less than a month, using a transportable system.

Regenerative medicine is a priority of the military in an era when badly wounded soldiers are more likely to survive with permanently disfiguring injuries. In 2008, the Armed Forces Institute of Regenerative Medicine received $85 million for a variety of research projects. One project has focused on stem cells taken from the healthy skin of a burned soldier and spraying them onto the wound site to stimulate regrowth. Harvard and MIT scientists are developing biological scaffolds for destroyed noses and ears that can be implanted with a patient's skin cells.

The cells grow into a nose or ear that can be surgically attached to the wounded soldier.

The future of military medicine will continue to be a reflection of the environmental and physical hazards of the battlefield as well as the increasing lethality of weaponry.

During the past five hundred years, for every soldier killed outright by the enemy, four were wounded. About one third of those wounded warriors required significant medical treatment. That treatment often began on the field of combat at the hands of a corpsman or medic and continued along a chain of care that reflected the medical knowledge and social values of the day. In that, war has changed little.

There always will be a common denominator that links past battlefields with future war zones: the courageous and compassionate individuals who devote themselves to saving the lives of their brothers and sisters in uniform. Shorthanded, defenseless, and poorly equipped at the outset of nearly every major war, corpsmen and medics have proven to be innovative, independent, resourceful, creative, and motivated in the extreme. They often have emerged as the most decorated rank by each war's end. Ray Duffee, Armando Leal, Nathaniel Leoncio, Monica Brown, and hundreds of thousands of other Americans have overcome their fear of death and their dread of disability to care for the broken and bleeding under unfathomable conditions.

Therein lies the true essence of military medicine: the extraordinary and unwavering devotion to duty by frontline corpsmen, medics, nurses, doctors, and specialists. They are the real heroes of military medicine. Millions of Americans owe their lives to these battlefield angels.

CONCLUSION

A corpsman is the guy who, as bullets explode all around and are kicking dirt up into his face, must expose himself to enemy fire to run to the aid of a wounded Marine. Then, when he gets there, he has to concentrate on treating wounds, even though oftentimes hit himself, while calmly and confidently saying, "I'm here .... You'll be okay."

Paul Baviello, Corpsman
Vietnam[103]

Acknowledgments

· · · · · · ·

No author flies solo. The route to a completed book often becomes convoluted, full of side trips, delightful discoveries, and dead ends. Regardless, not a single minute of the four years of research into *Battlefield Angels* was wasted because individuals and organizations all over the country kindly helped keep me on track and headed toward my destination.

Other than my family, literary agent Scott Mendel perhaps was the first to believe in the vision and potential of *Battlefield Angels*. Both his counsel and perseverance were invaluable, and he was responsible for finding a home for the manuscript. Two editors, Casey Ebro and Kelli Christiansen, were enormously helpful by keeping the manuscript on course and focused. Their editing rarely was disputable as they polished the ragged edges. Both Vicki Gibbs and Mary Sekulovich provided excellent editing guidance on early drafts as well.

I also am indebted to many people who generously offered the time, expertise, and insights that led to this remarkable story. Jan Herman and Andre Sobocinski at the U.S. Navy's Bureau of Medicine and Surgery were as enthusiastic as they were helpful. They are unsung historians dedicated to preserving the legacy of naval medicine. Similarly, colleagues at the Naval Historical Center, National Museum of the Marine Corps, and National Archives supplied historical documents and public domain photography for use. Attorneys Christopher Neils and Barrett Marum played a key role in my quest to find a publisher.

My gratitude extends to many who wear our nation's uniform today. Captain Matt Brown, USN (ret.), and public affairs officer Sonja Hanson were as responsive as they were resourceful. Major Rory Quinn, USMC, was among those who opened doors, provided contacts, and marshaled troops to provide indispensable firsthand reports and experiences. Captain Paul Hammer, USN; Commander Scott Johnston, USN; and others enabled me to comprehend the incredibly demanding world of frontline medicine and the unique responsibilities of corpsmen and medics who not only volunteer to serve their country but also willingly risk death on the battlefield to saves the lives of others. Former corpsmen Martin Olmeda and HM2 JuanCarlos Montgomery, among others, helped me understand the life of a Navy corpsman as well.

On a more personal note, I must salute former corpsmen and medics who invited me into their living rooms and shared what were often painful memories. Midwesterners Ray and Helen Duffee were typical of families who allowed a stranger to enter their lives and ask questions that I suspect became more personal than they anticipated. Their candor, generosity, and hospitality led to new friendships I value deeply.

I reserve my deepest gratitude for my wife, Marjorie. She was extraordinarily supportive throughout countless writing sessions at dawn, interviews at all hours, and research trips from coast to coast. Her unwavering confidence and encouragement is perhaps my most cherished gift in life.

It's been an extraordinary journey and I thank all who made it possible.

Select Bibliography

•••••••

This is not a complete inventory of all sources and resources used in the development of this book. They represent the substance and range of research I conducted and are offered as a resource for those interested in pursuing individual study.

Books

Bayne-Jones, Stanhope. *The Evolution of Preventive Medicine in the U.S. Army 1607–1939*. U.S. Army, 1958.

Boardman, Robert. *Unforgettable Men in Unforgettable Times*. Mukilteo, WA: Winepress Publishing, 1998.

Bosworth, Allan R. *America's Concentration Camps*. New York: W.W. Norton & Co, 1967.

Burns, M.D., Stanley. *The Face of Mercy*. New York: Random House, 1993.

Condon-Rall, Mary Ellen. *Medical Service in the War Against Japan*. Washington, D.C.: Center of Military History, 1998.

Cooter, Roger. *Medicine and Modern Warfare*. Atlanta: Editions Rodopi B.V., 1999.

Cowdrey, Albert E. *Fighting for Life*. New York: Free Press, 1994.

Freeman, Gregory A. *Sailors to the End*. New York: HarperCollins, 2002.

Gabriel, Richard and Metz, Karen. *A History of Military Medicine*. Westport, CT: Greenwood Press, 1992.

Gillett, Mary C. *The Army Medical Department 1818–1865*. Washington, D.C.: Center of Military History, 1987.

Greenwood, John T. and Berry, F. Clifton. *Medics at War: Military Medicine from Colonial Times to the 21st Century*. Annapolis, MD: Naval Institute Press, 2005.

Hayes, Thomas. *FDR's Prisoner Spy: The POW Diary of CDR Thomas Hayes, USN*. Pacifica, CA: Pacifica Press, 1987.

Herman, Jan. *Battle Station Sick Bay*. Annapolis, MD: Naval Institute Press, 1997.

Langley, Harold D. *A History of Medicine in the Early U.S. Navy*. Baltimore, MD: Johns Hopkins Press, 1995.

Mode, Daniel L. *The Grunt Padre*. Oak Lawn, IL: CMJ Marian Publishers, 2000.

Neel, Major General Spurgeon. *Medical Support of the U.S. Army in Vietnam, 1965–70*. Department of the Army, 1991.

Oman, Charles M. *Doctors Aweigh*. Garden City, NY: Doubleday, Doran & Co., 1943.

Shaw, Henry. *Operations in World War II, Volume III, History of the U.S. Marine Corps*. Historical Branch, G-3 Division, Headquarters, U.S. Marine Corps, 1966.

Sledge, E. B. *With the Old Breed*. New York: Presidio Press, 1981.

Tateishi, John. *And Justice for All.* Seattle, WA: University of
Washington Press, 1984.

Toyn, Gary W. *The Quiet Hero.* Clearfield, UT: American Legacy
Media, 2006.

Tsokos, M.D., George. *Combat Medicine.* Totowa, NJ: Humana
Press, 2003.

Vedder, James S. *Surgeon on Iwo.* Novato, CA: Presidio Press, 1984.

Wilber, M.D., C. Keith. *Revolutionary Medicine.* Guilford, CT:
Globe Pequot Press, 1997.

Articles and Documents

_____. "Military Medicine During the Eighteenth and Nineteenth
Centuries." Maxwell-Gunter Air Force Base, n.d.

_____. "Military Medicine Through the Eighteenth Century."
Maxwell-Gunter Air Force Base, n.d.

_____. "Operation Swift: After-Action Report." 3rd Battalion,
5th Marines, USMC, October 13, 1967.

_____. "Rules and Regulations for (American) Prisoners of War
(in Bilibid)." Japanese Army, transcribed March 25, 1946.

_____. "USS *Seadragon* Patrol Reports." U.S. Navy, October 1942.

_____. "USS *Tang* War Patrol No. 5 Report." U.S. Navy,
October 1944.

Ayers, Leonard P. "The War with Germany: A Statistical Report."
Government Printing Office, August 1, 1919.

Bergeld, Carlos. "Caring for War's Casualties." *BusinessWeek,*
July 26, 2006.

Buchan, M.D., W. "Domestic Medicine." n.p., 1785.

Capodanno Medal of Honor Nomination Dossier. 3/5 Marines,
1st Marines, October 9, 1967.

Carter, Phillip. "Iraq 2004 Looks Like Vietnam 1966."
Washington Post, December 24, 2004.

Dixon, Bernard. "Sulfa's True Significance." *Microbe Magazine*, November 11, 2006.

Figg, Laurann. "Amputation in the Civil War: Physical and Social Dimensions." *Journal of Medicine*, Vol. 48, 1993.

Gawande, M.D., Atul. "Casualties of War: Military Care for the Wounded from Iraq and Afghanistan." *New England Journal of Medicine*, December 9, 2004.

Hacala, Mark T. "The U.S. Navy Hospital Corps: A Century of Tradition." *Navy Medicine*, May–June 1998.

Holcomb, M.D., John. "2004 Fitts Lecture: Current Perspective on Combat Casualty Care." *Journal of Trauma*, October 2005.

Keen, W.W. "Surgical Reminiscences of the Civil War." Jefferson Medical College, 1905.

Monitz, Dave. "Military to Fund Prosthetics Research." *USA Today*, October 6, 2005.

Owens, M.D., Brett. "Characterization of Extremity Wounds in Operation Iraqi Freedom and Operation Enduring Freedom." *Journal of Orthopaedic Trauma*, April 2007.

Peck, Michael. "Golden Hour Surgical Units Prove Worth." *Military Medical Technology*, August 9, 2003.

Pruitt, Jr., M.D., Basil. "Combat Casualty Care and Surgical Progress." *Annals of Surgery*, June 2006.

Pueschel, Matt. "Navy Corpsmen Training Enhanced." *U.S. Medicine Magazine*, April 2005.

Sartin, L.B. "World War II Diary." March 20, 1946.

Scott, M.D., Russell. "Care of the Battle Casualty in Advance of the Aid Station." U.S. Army Graduate School, Washington, D.C., 1954.

Silliphant, William. "World War II Diary." Personal diary transcribed 1968.

Stewart, Henry P. "Impact of the USS *Forrestal*'s 1967 Fire on United States Navy Shipboard Damage Control." U.S. Navy, 2004.

Strott, George. "Corpsman's Handbook." U.S. Navy, 1943.

Swift, Foster. "Report of a Surgeon of the Eighth." *New York Times*, August 18, 1861.

Weina, Peter. "From Atabrine in World War II to Mefloquine in Somalia." *Military Medicine Magazine*, September 1998.

Zbailey, Michael. "Sullivan Ballou." *Washington Post*, July 8, 2001.

Selected Interviews and Recorded Oral Histories

Arend, Bill. February 2005.

Barker, Francis. 2003.

Berley, Ferdinand. 1995.

Blecksmith, Ed. February 2005.

Bonacker, Beryl. 1995.

Bray, James. 1987.

DaSilva, Jesse. Undated.

Duffee, Raymond. November 2005.

Farren, Ann. March 2005.

Frustaglio, Neil. February 2007.

Hammer USN, Capt. Paul. January 2009.

Harton, Ray. March 2005.

Hauge, Anna. February 2005.

Hensley, Arlen. April 2005.

Herman, Jan. Multiple, 2005.

Hoskins, Franz. 1977.

Johnston, USN, Cdr. Scott. January 2009.

Jones, Everett. March 2005.

Keenan, Jim. March 2005.

Keenan, Mike. April 2005.

Keenan, Paul. March 2005.

Keenan, Richard. March 2005.

Kelliher, Kelly. January 2005.

Kennedy, Tom. March 2005.

Kirchner, Gary. January 2007.

Leal, Zulema. February 2005.

Lipes, Bruce. May 2005.

Lipes, Wheeler. 1986.

Montgomery, HM2 JuanCarlos. January 2009

Moorer, Thomas. 1993.

Mowad, Sam. January 2007.

Nunez, Larry. February 2005.

Olmeda, Martin. January 2007.

Quinn USMC, Major Rory, including group interviews with Kurtis
    Bellmont, USMC, and members of Lima Company, 3rd Battalion,
    7th Marine Regiment. January 2007.

Renner, Herbert. 2001.

Seeley, Shawn. 2007.

Smart, Harry. 2001.

Smith, Alfred. 1985.

Sobocinski, Andre. 2005.

Sullivan, Craig. January 2005.

Tapscott, Donald. 1998.

Trevino, Nory. January 2006.

Warren, Bob. March 2005.

Watson, Brad. 2007.

Notes

● ● ● ● ● ● ●

1. "Military Medical History," *United States Army Medical Department Center and School Correspondence Course*: 2–9.

2. "Surgical Memoirs of the War of the Rebellion v.2," *United States Sanitary Commission* (1871): 63.

3. Michael Zbailey, "Dispatch Delayed," *The Washington Post* (July 8, 2001): F–1.

4. John Billings, *John Shaw Billings A Memoir* (New York City: G.P. Putnam's Sons, 1915), p. 65.

5. Richard Wheeler, *Voices of the Civil War* (New York City: Crowell Company, 1976), p. 219.

6. Mary C. Gillett, *The Army Medical Department, 1818–1865* (Washington, D.C.: Center of Military History, U.S. Army, 1987), p. 279.

7. Zbailey, "Dispatch Delayed:" F–1.

8. Wheeler Lipes, multiple Bureau of Medicine & Surgery oral history interviews, 1986, 1993.

9. *Ibid.*

10. *Ibid.*

11. Albert Maisel, *Miracles of Military Medicine* (Freeport, NY: Books for Libraries Press, 1943), p. 236.

12. *Ibid.*

13. George Weller, "One Merchant Ship, One Oil Tanker And One Successful Appendectomy," *The Chicago Daily News* (December 14, 1942).

14. James Fife, Commander Submarine Squadron Two, *FC5-1/A16-3/SS194 Report* (October 20, 1942).

15. Admiral Thomas G. Walsh, SS188/A9-8 Submarine Squadron Two Memorandum (October 22, 1942).

16. Admiral C. A. Lockwood, Jr., *SSWP/P4-1/P15/MM Memorandum* (October 27, 1942).

17. Jan Herman, Bureau of Medicine & Surgery, interview with the author, May 10, 2005.

18. *Ibid.*

19. *Ibid.*

20. *Ibid.*

21. _____, "One Merchant Ship, One Oil Tanker, and One Successful Appendectomy," *U.S. Navy Medicine* (January–February 1987): 23.

22. Joseph H. Alexander, *Across the Reef: The Marine Assault of Tarawa* (Collingdale, PA: Diane Publishing, 1996), p. 1.

23. Ray Duffee, interview with author, March 2005.

24. Irving Werstein, *Tarawa, A Battle Report* (New York City: Crowell Publishing, 1965), p. 25.

25. *Ibid.*, p. 53.

26. *Ibid.*, p. 67.
27. John Costello, *The Pacific War 1941–45* (New York City: HarperCollins, 1982), p. 433.
28. *Ibid.*, p. 435.
29. Duffee interview, March 2005.
30. *Ibid.*
31. *Ibid.*
32. *Ibid.*
33. *Ibid.*
34. *Ibid.*
35. *Ibid.*
36. John Costello, *The Pacific War 1941–1945*, p. 437.
37. Howard Jablon, *David M. Shoup* (Lanham, MD: Rowman & Littlefield, 2005), p. 46.
38. George Chilcoat, *The Children of Topaz* (New York City: Holiday House, 1996), p. 45.
39. Masayo Umezawa, *Unlikely Liberators: the Men of the 110th & 442nd* (Toyko: Bungeishunjusha, 1983), pp. 207–208.
40. *Ibid.*, p. 208.
41. Oregon State Archives, a division of the Secretary of State's Office, Salem, OR.
42. Manzanar National Historic Site exhibit, National Park Service.
43. White House Office of the Press Secretary, June 21, 2000.
44. Joe Marquez, interview with the author, February 24, 2005.
45. *Ibid.*
46. *Ibid.*
47. *Ibid.*
48. *Ibid.*
49. Joe Marquez interview, February 2005.
50. *Ibid.*
51. *Ibid.*

52. *Ibid.*

53. *Ibid.*

54. Richard Newcomb, *Iwo Jima* (New York City: Macmillan, 2002), p. 33.

55. Gary Toyn, "The Quiet Hero: The Untold Medal of Honor Story of George E. Wahlen," (Clearfield, UT: American Legacy Media, 2006), p. 218.

56. "Jack Williams, An Unlikely Hero," Historical summary prepared by the Boone County Historical & Railroad Society in Harrison, Arkansas, p. 4.

57. Captain William Silliphant, USN, "Under the Japs in Bilibid," Prisoner-of-war diary, 1941–1945, p. 85.

58. *Ibid.*, p. 35.

59. A. B. Feuer, *FDR's Prisoner Spy, The POW Diary of CDR Thomas Hayes, USN* (Pacifica, CA: Pacifica Press, 1987), p. 6.

60. *Ibid.*, p. 55.

61. Captain William Silliphant, USN, "Under the Japs in Bilibid," p. 127.

62. Joe Keenan, letter to his family, March 1953.

63. *Ibid.*

64. Everett C. Jones, letter to Mike Keenan, March 10, 1992.

65. Mark. T. Hacala, USNR, "Commandant Awards Navy Cross for Heroism in a Forgotten War," *Navy Medicine* (July–August 1992), p. 10.

66. *Ibid.*

67. Keenan Family Archives.

68. *Ibid.*

69. *Ibid.*

70. *Ibid.*

71. *Ibid.*

72. Transcript of Joseph Keenan Award Ceremony, May 12, 1999.

73. *Ibid.*

74. *Ibid.*

75. Ed Blecksmith, Larry Nunez, interviews with the author, January 2005.

76. Nory Trevino, interview with the author, January 2005.

77. Craig Sullivan, interview with the author, January 2005.

78. *Ibid.*

79. *Ibid.*

80. Nunez interview, January 2005.

81. Ray Harton, interview with the author, February 2005.

82. Fr. Daniel L. Mode, *The Grunt Padre* (Oak Lawn, IL: CMJ Marian Publishers, 2000), p. 132.

83. Vincent Capodanno Medal of Honor Recommendation to Submission to the Secretary of the Navy, including signed statement by Frederick W. Tancke, October 9, 1967, p. 6.

84. Blecksmith interview, January 2005.

85. Harton interview, February 2005.

86. Zulema Leal, interview with the author, January 2005.

87. Dr. Gary Kirchner, interview with the author, September 2006.

88. Dr. Samuel Mowad, interview with the author, January 2007.

89. Kirchner interview, September 2006.

90. Gregory Freeman, *Sailors to the End* (New York City: HarperCollins, 2004), p.222.

91. Rory Quinn, interview with the author, January 2007.

92. Lance Corporal Ben Eberle, "Hospital Corpsman Receives Bronze Star," *Marine Corps News* (April 13, 2006).

93. Brad Watson, interview with the author, January 2007.

94. Rory Quinn, January 2007.

95. Neil Frustaglio, interview with the author, February 2007.

96. *Ibid.*

97. Kurtis Bellmont, interview with the author, February 2007.

98. Brad Watson, January 2007.

99. *Ibid.*

100. Transcript of Leoncio award ceremony, April 6, 2006.

101. Allen Breed, "Soldier in Famous Photo Never Defeated 'Demons'," *Associated Press*, July 20, 2008.

102. Brett T. Litz and William E. Schlenger, "PTSD in Service Members and New Veterans of the Iraq and Afghanistan Wars," *PTSD Research Quarterly*, Vol. 20, No. 1, Winter 2009.

103. Paul Baviello presentation. Used with permission.

Index

●●●●●●●

265

INDEX

INDEX